Elijah Time III

Is There a Final Fulfillment of Prophecy Yet to Come?

(Second Edition)

By John Bartels

TEACH Services, Inc.
PUBLISHING
www.TEACHServices.com • (800) 367-1844

World rights reserved. This book or any portion thereof may not be copied or reproduced in any form or manner whatever, except as provided by law, without the written permission of the publisher, except by a reviewer who may quote brief passages in a review.

The author assumes full responsibility for the accuracy of all facts and quotations as cited in this book. The opinions expressed in this book are the author's personal views and interpretations, and do not necessarily reflect those of the publisher.

This book is provided with the understanding that the publisher is not engaged in giving spiritual, legal, medical, or other professional advice. If authoritative advice is needed, the reader should seek the counsel of a competent professional.

Copyright© 2024 John Bartels

Copyright© 2024 TEACH Services, Inc.

ISBN-13: 978-1-4796-1675-6 (Paperback)

ISBN-13: 978-1-4796-1676-3 (ePub)

ISBN-13: 978-1-4796-1771-5 (Spiral)

Library of Congress Control Number: 2024903628

All scripture quotations, unless otherwise indicated, are taken from King James Version. Public domain.

Scripture quotations marked NKJV are taken from the New King James Version®. Copyright © 1982 by Thomas Nelson. Used by permission. All rights reserved.

Abbreviations

1T, 2T, 4T, 5T, 6T, 7T, 8T, 9T - *Testimonies for the Church*, vols. 1, 2, 4, 5, 6, 7, 8, 9

1SAT - *Sermons and Talks*, vol. 1

2SM, 3SM - *Selected Messages*, vols. 2 and 3

4SP - *The Spirit of Prophecy*, vol. 4

7aBC - *Seventh-day Adventist Bible Commentary*, vol. 7a

AA - *The Acts of the Apostles*

CCh - *Counsels for the Church*

ChS - *Christian Service*

COL - *Christ's Object Lessons*

Con - *Confrontation*

CSW - *Counsels on Sabbath School Work*

CTr - *Christ Triumphant*

CW - *Counsels to Writers and Editors*

DA - *The Desire of Ages*

Ev - *Evangelism*

EW - *Early Writings*

ExV - *A Sketch of the Christian Experience and Views of Ellen G. White*

FE - *Fundamentals of Christian Education*

GC - *The Great Controversy*

GW - *Gospel Workers*

LDE - *Last Day Events*

LHU - *Lift Him Up*

Mar - *Maranatha*

MH - *The Ministry of Healing*

OHC - *Our High Calling*

PP - *Patriarchs and Prophets*

PK - *Prophets and Kings*

RH - *Review and Herald*

SL - *The Sanctified Life*

SpM - *Spalding and Magan Collection*

ST - *The Signs of the Times*

TM - *Testimonies to Ministers*

TMK - *That I May Know Him*

YRP - *Ye Shall Receive Power*

The page numbering of quotations in this book is based on the decimal numbering system of the Ellen G. White database rather than on the physical paging of each book. For example, a statement that spans pages 36 and 37 of *Testimonies for the Church*, volume 8, is designated 8T 36.3 because the paragraph begins on page 36 and is the third full paragraph on that page.

Italics and boldfacing have been added to numerous quotations throughout this book, but it has been left unnoted in the reference for simplicity.

Table of Contents

Preface 13

    We Have an Elijah Message to Give and Elijah is a Key Example 13

Introduction 16

    Prophecies of the First Advent Misunderstood 18

    Critical, Thought-Provoking Quotations 21

Part 1: Future Context of Many Ellen G. White Quotations 22

    Ellen G. White's Writings 23

    Evidence of Final Fulfillment 26

        Increased light 26

        Matthew 24 28

        Daniel 8 to 12 29

        Habakkuk 2 32

        Revelation Chapters 1 Through 18 33

    Unique New Light to Shine on Us 47

    Warning Messages 48

    The Message to Present 50

    Landmarks Defined 50

Truths Realized from Prophetic Study 51

Part 2: A Case for 3½ Years 54

What Is the Context of Matthew 24? 54

What Is the Context of Daniel 12 and Its Three Time
Prophecies? 58

Daniel 12 with Explanations 64

Should We Apply the Time Periods of Daniel 12 to the
Prophetic Periods of the Past? 65

What Does the Word "Days" Mean in This Context? 70

Does the Spirit of Prophecy Agree with a Future Context
of Daniel 12? 71

So How Do the Daniel 12 Prophecies Fit Together? 74

What Is the "Daily"? 77

Signs Leading to the Removal of the "Daily" 79

The Second Rise of the Papacy—Seven Heads
(Rev. 17:10) 79

The Second Rise of the Papacy —"the Eighth"
(Rev. 17:11) 80

The Second Rise of the Papacy —the Ten Horns or Kings
(Rev. 17:12, 13) 80

Why Is Knowing All This Important? 84

Part 3: No Prophetic Time After 1844? 86

Doesn't Ellen G. White Say There Are No Time Prophecies after 1844? 87

Progressive Revelation of Ellen G. White's Teachings and Our Prophetic Understanding 91

Comparing Quotation with Quotation—End of the "Prophetic Periods" 94

Evaluation of Difficult Ellen White Quotations about "No More Test of Time" 97

Supporting Thoughts and Questions 105

Be Careful Not to Attack the Messenger of New Light 107

Part 4: Additional Prophecies with a Future Context 109

The Tarrying Time of Habakkuk 2:2, 3 109

The Days of Noah 110

Isaiah 58 111

Joel 112

Part 5: Key Points of Daniel and Revelation 114

Key Points of Daniel 8 through 12 115

Key Points of Revelation 1 through 18 140

Sequence of Final Events 228

Delineation of the Seven Thunders 227

Part 6: Outline of the Three Angels' Messages: Our Elijah Message 229

The Three Angels' Messages—a Call to the
Word of God 229

More Three Angels Concepts 230

Angel One—Revelation 14:6, 7 231

Angel Two—Revelation 14:8 233

Angel Three—Revelation 14:9–12 235

Another Angel—Revelation 18 239

Closing Thoughts from the Pen of Inspiration 241

What Characterizes the Final Time of Witnessing? 242

Part 7: The Most Important Questions 243

Quotations to Contemplate 243

Addendum 245

More Thought-Provoking Ellen G. White Quotations 245

Dedication

To my children, Steven and Sarah,

who listened to my excitement as I shared what I was learning and who helped me when I wrestled with new, forward-thinking, prophetic concepts.

To my close friends,
who shared and studied these concepts with me.

To my Bible study group, friends, and my mom,
who helped to refine the contents of this book.

I thank you all.

John Bartels

Special Acknowledgments to

My friend and mentor Franklin Fowler, who shared fundamental end-time prophetic concepts with me, which have become part of this book, and who helped me to edit the first edition.

My Lord Jesus Christ, who wakes me early,
morning by morning (Isa. 50:4),
teaching me one amazing new thing after another
from His Word (John 16:13),
encouraging me to be a good Berean (Acts 17:11)
and to share the things I have learned (Matt. 28:19, 20).

Author's Note

The study of end-time prophecies is an amazingly inspiring and exciting study that results in an "entirely different religious experience" (TM 114.3) for those who diligently study the divine messages that we have been given. The content of the prophecies is highly interrelated, and, for that reason, most will likely need to study the material contained in this book more than once in order to clearly see how all the prophetic pieces fit together. I can attest to the fact that the effort will be richly rewarded! "It shall be in thy mouth sweet as honey" (Rev. 10:9).

This book has been written with the idea that it would be a study guide, giving just enough information to provide a solid foundation from which to keep digging deeper and deeper. There is so much more we can learn from the depths of God's prophetic Word! It is my prayer that God will bless you exceedingly abundantly above all you ask or imagine as you study and that He will prepare you to stand for Jesus, proclaiming the three angels' messages to the world.

I look forward to meeting you in heaven!

Sincerely,
John

Preface

We Have an Elijah Message to Give and Elijah is a Key Example

The word of the Lord came to Elijah; he did not seek to be the Lord's messenger, but the word came to him. *God always has men to whom he intrusts his message. His Spirit moves upon their hearts, and constrains them to speak. Stimulated by holy zeal, and with the divine impulse strong upon them, they enter upon the performance of their duty without coldly calculating the consequences of speaking to the people the word which the Lord has given them.* But the servant of God is soon made aware that he has risked something. He finds himself and his message made the subject of criticism. His manners, his life, his property are all inspected and commented upon. His message is picked to pieces and rejected in the most illiberal and unsanctified spirit, as men in their finite judgment see fit. Has that message done the work God designed it should accomplish? No; it has signally failed, because the hearts of the hearers were unsanctified.

If the minister's face is not *flint*, if he has not *indomitable faith and courage*, if his heart is not made strong by *constant communion with God*, he will begin to shape his testimony to please the unsanctified ears and hearts of those whom he is addressing. In endeavoring to avoid the criticism to which he is exposed, he separates from God, and loses the sense of the divine favor, and his testimony becomes tame and lifeless. He finds that his courage and faith are gone, and his labors are powerless. The world is full of flatterers and dissemblers who have yielded to the desire to please; but the *faithful men, who do not study self-interest, but love their brethren too well to suffer sin upon them, are few indeed.* (RH, April 7, 1885)

God would have His honor exalted before men as supreme, and His counsels confirmed in the eyes of the people. The witness of the prophet Elijah on Mount Carmel gives the *example of one who stood wholly for God and His work in the earth*. The prophet calls the Lord by His name, Jehovah God, which He Himself had given to denote His condescension and compassion. Elijah calls Him the God of Abraham and Isaac and Israel. He does this that He may excite in the hearts of His backslidden people humble remembrance of the Lord, and assure them of His rich, free grace. Elijah prays, Be it known this day that thou art the God of Israel. The honor of God is to be exalted as supreme, but the prophet asks further that his mission also may be confirmed. "Let it be known this day that thou art God in Israel," he prays, "and that I am thy servant, and that I have done all these things at thy word. Hear me, O Lord," he pleads, "hear me."

His zeal for God's glory and his deep love for the house of Israel present lessons for the instruction of all who stand today as representatives of God's work in the earth. (Letter 22, 1911)

He "said to his servant, Go up now, look toward the sea. And he went up, and looked, and said, There is nothing. And he said, Go again seven times." The servant watched while Elijah prayed. Six times he returned from the watch, saying, There is nothing, no cloud, no sign of rain. *But the prophet did not give up in discouragement. He kept reviewing his life, to see where he had failed to honor God, he confessed his sins, and thus continued to afflict his soul before God*, while watching for a token that his prayer was answered. As he searched his heart, he seemed to be less and less, both in his own estimation and in the sight of God. It seemed to him that he was nothing, and that God was everything; and *when he reached the point of renouncing self, while he clung to the Saviour as his only strength and righteousness, the answer came*. The servant appeared, and said, "Behold, there ariseth a little cloud out of the sea, like a man's hand." (RH, May 26, 1891)

However courageous and successful a man may be in the performance of a special work, *unless he looks constantly to God* when circumstances arise to test his faith he will lose his courage. Even after God has given him marked tokens of his power, after he has been strengthened to do God's work, he will fail *unless he trusts implicitly in Omnipotence*. (RH, Oct. 16, 1913)

The success of the ministry of Elijah was not due to any inherited qualities he possessed, *but to the submission of himself to the Holy Spirit, which was given to him as it will be given to all who exercise living faith in God*. In his imperfection man has the privilege of linking himself up with God through Jesus Christ. (Ms. 148, 1899)

In this age, just prior to the second coming of Christ in the clouds of heaven, God calls for men who will prepare a people to stand in the great day of the Lord.... The Lord is giving messages to his people, through the instruments he has chosen, and he would have all heed the admonitions and warnings he sends.... Our message is not to be one of peace and safety. As a people who believe in Christ's soon appearing, we have a definite message to bear,—"Prepare to meet thy God." ...With the earnestness that characterized Elijah the prophet and John the Baptist, we are to strive to prepare the way for Christ's second advent. (SW March 21, 1905)

Introduction

The Desire of Ages is an amazing book giving us many insights into the life of Jesus. In the Bible, as well as in *The Desire of Ages*, it is made clear that the Pharisees, who were blinded by Satan, misunderstood the prophets and the prophecies relating to the advent of the Messiah.

> When God's written word was given, Satan studied the prophecies of the Saviour's advent. From generation to generation *he worked to blind the people to these prophecies*, that they might reject Christ at His coming. (DA 115.1)

> During the weeks that followed, John with new interest studied the prophecies and the teaching of the sacrificial service. He did not distinguish clearly the two phases of Christ's work,—as a suffering sacrifice and a conquering king,—but *he saw that His coming had a deeper significance than priests or people had discerned.* (DA 136.4)

When Jesus the Messiah appeared on the scene for three and a half years, He taught the religious leaders and the people the truth about the prophecies through His life and teachings. The people were left with a decision to make: Believe in Jesus, their Messiah, or hang onto the teachings of their revered leaders.

> Nathanael had withdrawn to a quiet grove to meditate upon the announcement of John and the prophecies concerning the Messiah. He prayed that if the one announced by John was the deliverer, it might be made known to him, and the *Holy Spirit rested upon him with assurance* that God had visited His people and raised up a horn of salvation for them. (DA 140.1)

The hope of national greatness was dwelt upon with kindling enthusiasm. Jesus knew that this hope was to be disappointed, for it was founded on a *misinterpretation of the Scriptures*. With deep earnestness He explained the prophecies, and tried to arouse the people to a closer study of God's word. (DA 154.2)

Since hearing Jesus, Nicodemus had anxiously studied the prophecies relating to the Messiah; and *the more he searched, the stronger was his conviction* that this was the One who was to come. (DA 168.1)

> *Jesus knew that this hope was to be disappointed, for it was founded on a misinterpretation of the Scriptures.*

The burden of Christ's preaching was, "The time is fulfilled, and the kingdom of God is at hand; repent ye, and believe the gospel." *Thus the gospel message, as given by the Saviour Himself, was based on the prophecies.* (DA 233.1)

The time of Christ's coming, His anointing by the Holy Spirit, His death, and the giving of the gospel to the Gentiles, were definitely pointed out. *It was the privilege of the Jewish people to understand these prophecies*, and to recognize their fulfillment in the mission of Jesus. *Christ urged upon His disciples the importance of prophetic study.* Referring to the prophecy given to Daniel *in regard to their time*, He said, "Whoso readeth, let him understand." Matthew 24:15. (DA 234.1)

He who had Himself given these prophecies now for the last time repeated the warning. In fulfillment of prophecy the people had proclaimed Jesus king of Israel. He had received their homage, and accepted the office of king. In this character He must act. *He knew that His efforts to reform a corrupt priesthood would be in vain; nevertheless His work must be done*; to an unbelieving people the evidence of His divine mission must be given. (DA 590.3)

Christ was the cornerstone of the Jewish economy, and of the whole plan of salvation. This foundation stone the Jewish builders, the priests and rulers of Israel, were now rejecting. *The Saviour called their attention to the prophecies that would show them their danger.* By every means in His power He sought to make plain to them the nature of the deed they were about to do. (DA 597.2)

Many even of the priests were convicted of the true character of Jesus. *Their searching of the prophecies had not been in vain*, and after His resurrection they acknowledged Him as the Son of God. (DA 775.1)

For three years and a half the disciples were under the instruction of *the greatest Teacher the world has ever known.* (AA 17.2)

Prophecies of the First Advent Misunderstood

Blinded by pride and selfishness, the Pharisees would not accept the truth for their day—their "present truth"—and they continued to promote the confusion that they believed in. They focused on aspects of the prophecies that fit their understanding as well as their selfish desires while overlooking aspects of the prophecies that they didn't understand. They taught these things, with their incorrect understandings, to the Jewish people.

Ultimately, this resulted in the destruction of Jerusalem and the loss of millions of souls that might have learned what is truth.

The people, in their darkness and oppression, and the rulers, thirsting for power, longed for the coming of One who would vanquish their enemies and restore the kingdom to Israel. *They had studied the prophecies, but without spiritual insight.* Thus they *overlooked those scriptures* that point to the humiliation of Christ's first advent, and *misapplied those* that speak of the glory of His second coming. *Pride obscured their vision.* They interpreted prophecy in accordance with their selfish desires. (DA 30.2)

> **they overlooked those scriptures that point to the humiliation of Christ's first advent, and misapplied those that speak of the glory of His second coming.**

In one of the earliest prophecies of Christ it is written, "The scepter shall not depart from Judah, nor a lawgiver from between his feet, until Shiloh come; and unto Him shall the gathering of the people be." Genesis 49:10. The people were gathering to Christ. The sympathetic hearts of the multitude accepted lessons of love and benevolence in preference to the rigid ceremonies required by the priests. *If the priests and rabbis had not interposed, His teaching would have wrought such a reformation as this world has never witnessed.* But *in order to maintain their own power*, these leaders determined to break down the influence of Jesus. (DA 205.1)

Caiaphas had studied the prophecies, and although ignorant of their true meaning, he spoke with great authority and assurance: "Ye know nothing at all, nor consider that it is expedient for us, that one man should die for the people, and that the whole nation perish not." (DA 539.3)

The world could not bear Him. Just three years and a half of public ministry and then *they got rid of Him*. (Ms. 12, 1894)

… reports of His mock trial, and of the inhumanity of the priests and rulers, were circulated everywhere. By men of intellect these *priests and rulers were called upon to explain the prophecies of the Old Testament concerning the Messiah*, and while trying to *frame some falsehood* in reply, they became like men insane. The prophecies that pointed to Christ's sufferings and death they could not explain, and many inquirers were convinced that the Scriptures had been fulfilled. (DA 776.4)

Satan is working that the history of the Jewish nation may be repeated in the experience *of those who claim to believe present truth*. (2SM 111.1)

Are we any different today? Did our Pioneers correctly understand *all* the prophecies about the second advent of Jesus, our Messiah? Have we continued to teach almost all the same things they taught in the 1840s? Have we overlooked aspects of the prophecies that don't fit our understanding? Have we misunderstood what is present truth for our day? Our modern-day prophet has told us that we have many things to learn and many, many things to unlearn (TM 30.3)! Have we misunderstood some of the things she attempted to explain to us? She has told us that heaven has glorious new truths for all who will listen and that new light will shine on all the grand truths of prophecy (8T 322.3; 3SM 390.4). Have we listened to her? Are we fasting, praying, and searching for the new light from heaven that we need in order to be prepared to give the present truth—*our present truth*—of the three angels' messages to the world?

This book seeks to bring understanding to some of these issues.

As the message of Christ's first advent announced the kingdom of His grace, *so the message of His second advent announces the kingdom of His glory*. And the second message, like the first, *is based on the prophecies*. The words of the angel to Daniel relating to the *last days* were to be understood in the **time of the end**. At that time, "many shall run to and fro, and knowledge shall be increased." (DA 234.4)

As the disciples searched the prophecies that testified of Christ, they were brought into fellowship with the Deity, and learned of Him who had ascended to heaven to complete the work He had begun on earth. (DA 507.1)

Study Revelation in connection with Daniel, for **history will be repeated ...** We, with all our religious advantages, ought to know far more today than we do know. (TM 116.3)

Great truths that have lain unheeded and unseen since the day of Pentecost, *are to shine from God's word* in their native purity. To those who truly love God the Holy Spirit will reveal truths that have faded from the mind, *and will also reveal truths that are entirely new*. Those who eat the flesh and drink the blood of the Son of God will bring from the books of *Daniel and Revelation* truth that is inspired by the Holy Spirit. (FE 473.2)

Those who eat the flesh and drink the blood of the Son of God will bring from the books of Daniel and Revelation truth that is inspired by the Holy Spirit.

Critical, Thought-Provoking Quotations

The **prophetic periods** of Daniel, extending to the *very eve of the great consummation,* throw a flood of light upon events **then** to transpire. (RH, Sept. 25, 1883)

The *truth is an advancing truth*, and we must walk in the *increasing light*.... We must have living faith in our hearts, and reach out for larger knowledge and more **advanced light**. (RH, March 25, 1890)

Daniel, God's prophet, stands in his place. John stands in his place. In the Revelation the Lion of the tribe of Judah has opened to the students of prophecy the book of Daniel, and thus is Daniel standing in his place. He bears his testimony, that which the Lord revealed to him in vision of the great and solemn events which *we must know* as we stand on the very threshold of their fulfillment. (Ms. 32, 1896)

The unsealing of the little book was the *message* in *relation to* **time**. (Ms. 59, 1900)

Increased light will shine upon **all** *the grand truths of prophecy,* and they will be seen in freshness and brilliancy because the bright beams of the Sun of Righteousness will illuminate the *whole*. (Ms. 18, 1888)

By the increase of knowledge a people is to be prepared to stand in the latter days. (2 SM 105.1)

A great work will be done in a short time. **A message** will soon be given by God's appointment that will swell into a **loud cry**. **Then** Daniel will stand in his lot, to give his testimony. (Letter 54, 1906)

Part 1: Future Context of Many Ellen G. White Quotations

As Seventh-day Adventists, we often look to Ellen G. White for the "answers," knowing that she is God's messenger to us. Is this how Ellen G. White encouraged us to study? Didn't she direct us to prove all our points from the Bible? (Ev 256.2). And didn't she say that her writings were for the purpose of leading us back to the Bible? (3SM 29.1–32.4). Yet, we as Adventists often look to her for the answers instead of studying the Bible diligently and then looking *afterward* to Ellen G. White's writings to fill in the holes. *This causes problems when it comes to understanding the final fulfillment of prophecy for these last days.* Why? Let's explore some answers to this question.

> Let all prove their positions *from the Scriptures* and substantiate every point they claim as truth from the revealed Word of God. (Ev 256.2; Letter 12, 1890)

> Endeavoring to lay aside all preconceived opinions, and dispensing with commentaries, he [William Miller] *compared scripture with scripture* by the aid of the *marginal references* and the *concordance.* He pursued his study in a regular and methodical manner; beginning with Genesis, and reading verse by verse, he proceeded no faster than the meaning of the several passages so unfolded as to leave him free from all embarrassment. When he found anything obscure, it was his custom to *compare it with every other text* which seemed to have any reference to the matter under consideration. Every word was permitted to have its proper bearing upon the subject of the text, and if his view of it *harmonized* with every collateral passage, it ceased to be a difficulty. Thus whenever he

met with a passage hard to be understood, he found an explanation in some other portion of the Scriptures. As he studied with *earnest prayer for divine enlightenment*, that which had before appeared dark to his understanding was made clear. He experienced the truth of the psalmist's words, "The entrance of thy words giveth light; it giveth understanding unto the simple." [Psalm 119:130.] (4SP 204.2)

Again and again did Wm. Miller urge that if his doctrine were false, he should be shown his error *from the Scriptures*....

At a later date he stated: "I have candidly weighed the objections advanced against these views; but I have seen no arguments that were sustained by the Scriptures that, in my opinion, invalidated my position. I cannot, therefore, *conscientiously* refrain from looking for my Lord, or from exhorting my fellow-men, as I have opportunity, to be in readiness for that event." (4SP 217.1, 2)

Ellen G. White's Writings

Ellen White wrote incredible materials concerning many different subjects including the events surrounding 1844 and the prophetic understanding of our pioneers. As she wrote about the events that took place during the Millerite movement and in the years that followed, she, to a large extent, *reported* what was being taught concerning the prophecies. The sequence of events leading up to and beyond 1844 was described according to the experience of our pioneers including their understanding of the prophecies. It is important to keep in mind that our pioneers believed all the prophecies were completed and came to an end in 1844! This of course was a mistake that adversely affected their understanding of prophetic events. So, when Ellen White writes about prophetic history, it is critical to understand the *context* of her thoughts! Is she writing about what our pioneers taught? Or is she adding information that God gave her to reveal to us?

> *As she wrote about the events that took place during the Millerite movement and in the years that followed, she, to a large extent, reported what was being taught concerning the prophecies.*

The testimony of the prophecies which **seemed** *to point to the coming of Christ in the spring of 1844* took deep hold of the minds of the people. As the message went from state to state, there was everywhere awakened widespread interest. Many were convinced that the arguments from the prophetic periods were correct, and, sacrificing their pride of opinion, they joyfully received the truth. (GC 368.2)

The proclamation of a **definite time** *for Christ's coming* called forth great opposition from many of all classes …. (GC 370.1)

Notice the following phrases as you continue to read on pages 398 to 400 of *The Great Controversy*: "formerly believed," "it was believed," "was regarded," and "the conclusion seemed irresistible." In these instances, and many others, she is *reporting* on our pioneers' discoveries and beliefs. *She is not prophesying.* Yet we as Adventists read what she wrote, we overlook the statements that indicate she was *reporting*, and take what we read as Gospel over the clear context of the Bible even though we know that our pioneers made errors *that God allowed for His purposes*. And when we study the Bible, we read it in the light of our understanding of Ellen G. White's comments, skipping over things in the Bible we don't understand because they don't fit with what we incorrectly believe Ellen G. White said. This is possibly the biggest reason she said to prove our points from the Bible. We read what she wrote in the context of our pioneer's understanding and use it as truth for our day instead of realizing that their context and their understanding is not our context. Their "present truth" was different from what our "present truth" is to be.

We have *many lessons to learn*, and *many, many to unlearn.* (TM 30.2)

Is it not time that **fresh light** should come to the people of God, to awaken them to greater earnestness and zeal? (RH, April 1, 1890)

Ellen White wrote a lot of letters and articles encouraging, instructing, and correcting people and our church. She wrote those letters and articles in the context of the time and issues she was dealing with. In relation to the prophecies, their context was different from our context as the last generation that will live on the earth. The last generation will need extra insight in order to be prepared to stand during earth's final crisis and still reflect the character of Jesus perfectly. What she said to people in the late 1800s was in an entirely different context compared to those living over 120 years (three biblical generations) later, faced with the greatest trial this earth has ever seen.

> By the increase of knowledge a people is to be prepared to stand in the latter days (2SM 105.1).

> "And this is life eternal, that they might know thee, the only true God, and Jesus Christ whom thou hast sent." The truth and light given to us of God is as a priceless treasure hid in a field. We are to buy the field and work every foot of it. The more we look at *the promises of the Word of God*, the brighter they grow. The more we *practice the principles of God's word*, the deeper will be our understanding of them. Our position and *faith is in the Bible*. And *never do we want any soul to bring in the testimonies ahead of the Bible.* (Ms. 7, 1894)

Ellen G. White often makes statements that indicate that she acknowledged the *partial fulfillments of prophecy in the past*. She doesn't always give a complete answer that includes its *complete fulfillment,* which was still future from her time. If you compare her statements with statements in other places in her writings, like we compare scripture with scripture, you realize that she understood both the *partial* past application and the *complete* and *final* future application. Again, unless one is incredibly well versed in *all* that Ellen G. White wrote on a subject, it would be very easy to not understand her complete thoughts on that subject and end up off course. We must *prove our points from the Bible* and look to Ellen G. White for *confirmation*. Then we can be assured that we have the correct understanding.

> Christ, upon the Mount of Olives, rehearsed the fearful judgments that were to precede His second coming: …While these prophecies received a *partial fulfillment* at the destruction of Jerusalem, *they have a more direct application* **to the last days**. (5T 753.1)

> *Then will take place the **final fulfilment** of the Revelator's prophecy.* [Rev. 13:4–18 quoted.] (Ms. 153, 1902)

> And they worshipped the dragon which gave power unto the beast: and they worshipped the beast, saying, Who is like unto the beast? Who is able to make war with him? And there was given unto him a mouth speaking great things and blasphemies; and *power was given unto him to continue forty and two months.* (Rev. 13:4, 5)

We preach about the importance of studying the context of a passage, but have we done a good job of actually following that advice? Now is the time to get back to the Bible and really understand it in all its details. When we do, we will gain a much deeper understanding of all it has to offer us so that we can make a proper preparation for the final days. When we understand the biblical context of the prophetic passages—especially in Daniel 8 to 12 and in Revelation—we will also correctly understand the added insight that Ellen G. White encouraged us to seek for in its proper context.

Evidence of Final Fulfillment

The remainder of Part 1 of this book is focused on simply listing Ellen G. White statements, separated by the topic or biblical passage they deal with, giving evidence of a future fulfillment of the prophecies.

Carefully study the context of each statement and notice the tense given *from the time she wrote it*. Is it past, present, or future? As you do this, prepare to see amazing new things that Ellen White wrote about the final fulfillment of these prophecies!

Increased Light

> *Increased light **will shine** upon all the grand truths of **prophecy**, and they **will be seen** in freshness and brilliancy because the bright beams of the Sun of Righteousness **will illuminate the whole**.* (Ms. 18, 1888)

> *By the increase of knowledge a people **is to be prepared** to stand in the latter days.* (Ms. 32, 1896)

> The *truth is an **advancing truth***, and we must walk in the ***increasing light***. … We must have living faith in our hearts, and reach out for *larger knowledge* and more ***advanced light***. (RH, March 25, 1890)

> Daniel, God's prophet, stands in his place. John stands in his place. In the Revelation the Lion of the tribe of Judah has opened to the students of prophecy the book of Daniel, and thus is Daniel standing in his place. He bears his testimony, that which the Lord revealed to him in vision of the great and solemn events which *we **must know*** as we stand on the *very threshold of their fulfillments*. (Ms. 32, 1896)

> The ***time*** for the *unfolding of **special truth*** in relation to the ***closing scenes** of this earth's history* is during the last generations that ***shall live*** upon the earth. (2T 692.2)

> Blow the trumpet in Zion; sound an alarm in the holy mountain. Gather the host of the Lord, with sanctified hearts, to hear what

the Lord will say unto His people; for *He has **increased light** for all who **will** hear*. Let them be armed and equipped, and come up to the battle—to the help of the Lord against the mighty. (TM 410.1)

As we near the closing scenes of this earth's history still more wonderful representations *will be made*. We need to study the Scriptures with humble, contrite hearts. Those who will devote their powers to the study of God's Word, and ***especially the prophecies referring to these*** **last days**, *will be rewarded by the* **discovery of important truths**. (Ms. 75, 1899)

Is it not time that ***fresh light*** should come to the people of God, to awaken them to greater earnestness and zeal? (RH, April 1, 1890)

There are *glorious truths* ***to come*** before the people of God. (8T 322.3)

Although we have in trust the grandest and most important truth ever presented to the world, *we are only **babes**, as far as understanding truth* in all its bearings is concerned. (CW 29.2; Letter 97, 1902)

There is need of a *much closer study* of the word of God; *especially should **Daniel and the Revelation** have attention **as never before*** in the history of our work. (TM 112.1)

We have **many lessons to learn**, and **many, many to unlearn**. (TM 30.2)

To those who truly love God the Holy Spirit will reveal truths that have faded from the mind, and will also reveal truths that are ***entirely new***. (FE 473.2)

God intends that, even in this life, *truth shall be **ever unfolding*** to His people. (5T 703.2)

Each period of the fulfillment of *prophetic history* is a *preparation* for the **advanced light** which **will** succeed each period. *As the prophecy comes to the end, there is to be a **perfect whole**.* (Letter 18, 1895)

> *To those who truly love God the Holy Spirit will reveal truths that faded from the mind, and will also reveal truths that are **entirely new**.*

A wonderful connection is seen between the universe of heaven and this world. The things revealed to Daniel were afterward *complemented* by the revelation made to John on the Isle of Patmos. *These two books should be carefully studied. Twice Daniel inquired,* **How long shall it be to the end of time?** ... The book of Daniel is unsealed in the revelation to John, and *carries us forward* to the *last scenes* of this earth's history.... **Teach** *these things*. (TM 114.6; 115.3, 5)

Behold, I will send you **Elijah the prophet** before the coming of the great and dreadful day of the LORD. (Mal. 4:5)

Matthew 24

For nearly **forty years** after the doom of Jerusalem had been pronounced by Christ Himself, the Lord delayed His judgments upon the city and the nation. Wonderful was the long-suffering of God toward the rejectors of His gospel and the murderers of His Son. (GC 27.3)

Christ, upon the Mount of Olives, rehearsed the fearful judgments that were to precede His second coming: ... While these prophecies received a **partial fulfillment** at the destruction of Jerusalem, they have a more direct application to the **last days**. (5T 753)

In his answer, Jesus did not take up separately the destruction of Jerusalem and the last great day of his coming. He *mingled* the description of these two events. When he spoke of the destruction of Jerusalem, his words referred also to the final destruction that will take place when the Lord rises out of his place to punish the world for its iniquity. The **entire chapter** *in which are recorded Christ's words regarding this, is a* **warning** *to all who* **shall live** *during the* **last scenes** *of this earth's history*. (RH, Dec. 13, 1898)

The Saviour's prophecy concerning the visitation of judgments upon Jerusalem is to have **another fulfillment**, of which that terrible desolation was but a *faint shadow*. In the fate of the chosen city we may behold the **doom of a world** that has rejected God's mercy and trampled upon His law. (GC 36.2)

The time is not far distant, when, like the early disciples, we *shall be forced* to seek a refuge in desolate and solitary places. As the siege of Jerusalem by the Roman armies was the signal for flight to the Judean Christians, so the assumption of power on the part

Part 1: Future Context of Many Ellen G. White Quotations   29

of our nation [the United States] in the *decree enforcing* the papal sabbath **will** be a **warning** to us. (Mar 180.2)

The *first day of the week* **is to be exalted** and presented to all for observance. Shall we be partakers of this *cup of* **abomination?** Shall we bow to the authorities of earth and despise God? The powers of darkness have been gathering their forces to bring this crisis about in the world, so that the man of sin may exalt himself above God. (RH, April 15, 1890; ST, March 3, 1890)

Daniel 8 to 12

The light that Daniel received from God was given especially for **these last days**. The visions he saw by the banks of the **Ulai** and the **Hiddekel**, the great rivers of Shinar, are now in the process of fulfillment, *and* **all** *the events foretold will* **soon** *come to pass.* (Letter 57, 1896)

Note: The Ulai and the Hiddekel visions encompass the visions of Daniel 8 through 12. (See Dan. 8:2 and 10:4.)

The **book that was sealed** was not the book of Revelation, but *that* **portion** *of the prophecy of Daniel which related to the* **last days**. (2SM 105.1)

Let us read and study the *twelfth chapter of Daniel.* It is a **warning** that we **shall** all need to understand **before** *the time of the end.* (Letter 161, 1903; LDE 15.4)

> *The visions he saw by the banks of the Ulai and the Hiddekel, the great rivers of Shinar, are now in the process of fulfillment, and all the events foretold will soon come to pass.*

The words of the angel to Daniel relating to the **last days were to be understood in the time of the end**. Dan. 12:4, 10. (DA 234.4)

The **prophetic periods** of Daniel, **extending** to the **very eve of the great consummation**, throw a flood of light upon events **then** to transpire. (RH, Sept. 25, 1883)

Daniel shall stand in his lot *at the end of the days.* **John sees the little book unsealed. Then** Daniel's prophecies have their proper place in the *first, second, and third angels' messages* **to be given** to

the *world. The unsealing of the little book was the message in **relation to time**.* (Ms. 59, 1900)

> **Daniel shall stand in his lot at the end of the days.**

*Present the eternal principles of truth. Show what the Word of God declares **is to take place** on this earth.* The God who gave Daniel instruction regarding the **closing scenes** of this earth's history will certainly confirm the testimony of His servants as at the **appointed time** they give the **loud cry** ... And there should be no delay in *repeating the message*, for the signs of the times are fulfilling; the closing work must be done. A great work *will be done* in a short time. *A message will **soon** be given by God's appointment that **will swell into a loud cry**. Then Daniel will stand in his lot, to give his **testimony**.* (Letter 54, 1906)

[Daniel] bears his **testimony**, that which the Lord revealed to him in vision of the great and solemn events **which we must know as we stand on the very threshold of their fulfillment.** (Ms. 32, 1896)

Twice Daniel inquired, How long shall it be to the end of time? (CTr 334.4; TM 114.6; Letter 59, 1896)

Daniel has been standing in his lot since the *seal* was removed and the *light of truth* has been shining upon his visions. He *stands in his lot*, bearing the **testimony** which was to be **understood at the end of the days.** (Ms. 50, 1893)

As Daniel's prayer is going forth [*in Daniel 9*], the angel Gabriel comes sweeping down from the heavenly courts to tell him that his petitions are heard and answered. This mighty angel has been commissioned to give him *skill and understanding*—to open before him *the mysteries of future ages*. Thus, while earnestly seeking to know and understand the truth, Daniel was brought into communion with Heaven's delegated messenger. (CCh 54.1)

In answer to his petition [*in Daniel 9*], Daniel received not only the light and truth which he and his people most needed, but *a view of the **great events** of the **future**, even to the **advent of the world's Redeemer**.* (SL 48.2 [1881])

*By the increase of knowledge a people is to be **prepared to stand in the latter days**.* (2SM 105.1; Ms. 32, 1896)

Part 1: Future Context of Many Ellen G. White Quotations

A wonderful connection is seen between the universe of heaven and this world. The things revealed to Daniel were afterward complemented by the revelation made to John on the Isle of Patmos. *These two books should be carefully studied. Twice Daniel inquired,* **How long shall it be to the end of time?** *... The book of Daniel is unsealed in the revelation to John, and carries us forward to the* **last scenes of this earth's history** *... Teach these things.* (TM 114.6; 115.3)

We have no time to lose. Troublous times are before us. The world is stirred with the spirit of war. Soon the scenes of trouble spoken of in the prophecies will take place. *The prophecy in the eleventh of Daniel has nearly reached its complete fulfilment. Much of the history that has taken place in fulfillment of this prophecy will be* **repeated**. In the thirtieth verse a power is spoken of that "shall be grieved, and return, and have indignation against the holy covenant: so shall he do; he shall even return, and have intelligence with them that forsake the holy covenant." [Verses 31–36, quoted.] Scenes similar to those described in these words *will take place*. We see evidence that Satan is fast obtaining the control of human minds, who have not the fear of God before them. **Let all read and understand** *the prophecies of this book, for we are now entering upon the time of trouble spoken of.* [Daniel 12:1–4, quoted.] (Letter 103, 1904)

> *The prophecy in the eleventh of Daniel has nearly reached its complete fulfilment.*

As the message of Christ's first advent announced the kingdom of His grace, so the message of His second advent announces the kingdom of His glory. And the *second message, like the first, is* **based on the prophecies**. *The words of the angel to Daniel relating to the* **last days were to be understood in the time of the end**. At that time, "many shall run to and fro, and *knowledge shall be increased.*" "The wicked shall do wickedly: and none of the wicked shall understand; but *the wise shall understand.*" Daniel 12:4, 10. (DA 234.4)

The **book that was sealed** was not the book of Revelation, but *that* **portion** *of the prophecy of Daniel which related to the* **last days**. (Ms. 32, 1896)

Prophecy has been fulfilling, line upon line. The more firmly we stand under the banner of **the third angel's message**, *the more clearly shall we understand the prophecy of Daniel*, for the **Revelation is the supplement of Daniel**. (Ms. 32, 1896)

The study of the Revelation directs the mind to the prophecies of Daniel, and **both** present *most important instruction*, given of God to men, concerning *events to take place* **at the close** of this world's history. (GC 341.3)

The judgments of God are in the land. The wars and rumors of wars, the destruction by fire and flood, say clearly that the time of trouble, which is to increase until the end, is very near at hand.

We have no time to lose. The world is stirred with the spirit of war. *The prophecies of the eleventh of Daniel have almost reached their final fulfillment* ... (Mar 25.5)

Habakkuk 2

We are not impatient. If the *vision* tarry, wait for it, for it will surely come, it will not tarry. *Although disappointed*, our *faith has not failed*, and we have not drawn back to perdition. The **apparent tarrying** is **not so** in reality, for at the **appointed time** our Lord will come, and we will, if faithful, exclaim, "Lo, *this is our God*; we have *waited for Him*, and *He will save us*" [Isaiah 25:9]. (Letter 38, 1888)

We must *cherish* and *cultivate the faith* of which prophets and apostles have testified—the *faith that lays hold on the promises of God* and *waits for* **deliverance** in His appointed time and way. The *sure word of prophecy will* meet its **final fulfillment** in the glorious advent of our Lord and Saviour Jesus Christ, as King of kings and Lord of lords. *The time of waiting may seem long*, the soul may be oppressed by discouraging circumstances ... *Let us ever hold in remembrance the cheering message,* "The **vision** is *yet* for an **appointed time**, but **at the end** it shall speak, and not lie: though it tarry, wait for it; because **it will surely come**, it will not tarry ... The just shall live by his *faith*." Habakkuk 2:3, 4. (PK 387.2)

The return of Christ to our world *will* **not be long** *delayed*. Let this be the keynote of every message. (6T 406.1)

The time of tarrying is almost ended. The pilgrims and strangers who have so long been seeking a better country are almost home. I feel as if I must cry aloud, Homeward bound! ... "Wherefore, beloved, seeing that ye look for such things, *be diligent that ye may be found of him in peace, without spot, and blameless."* 2 Peter 3:14. (OHC 367.6)

Revelation Chapters 1 Through 18

Revelation chapter 1

Christ came to John exiled on the Isle of Patmos to give him the truth for **these last days**, to show him that which must **shortly come to pass**. Jesus Christ is the great trustee of divine revelation. It is through Him that we have a knowledge of *what we are to look for in the **closing scenes*** of this earth's history. (Ms. 129, 1905)

The instruction to be communicated to John was **so important** that **Christ** *came from heaven to give it to His servant*, telling him to send it to the churches. (Ms. 129, 1905)

God and Christ and the heavenly host were John's companions on the isle of Patmos. From them he received instruction which he imparted to those separated with him from the world. There he wrote out the visions and revelations he received from God, *telling of the things which would take place in the **closing period*** *of this earth's history.* (Ms. 150, 1899)

The book of *Revelation* is to be understood because it is a revelation of the things *which shall be* in the **last days**. The *future* is large with importance to all who act a part in the **closing scenes** *of this earth's history,* **when** only two parties **will be** recognized, the lowly who keep the commandments of God, and the disloyal, who refuse allegiance, and trample on the fourth commandment and every other law that stands in the way of their interests. (Ms. 150, 1899)

Revelation chapter 2

Upon the heads of the overcomers, Jesus with His own right hand places the crown of glory. For each there is a crown, bearing his own "*new name*" (Revelation 2:17), and the inscription, "Holiness to the Lord." In every hand are placed the victor's palm and the shining harp. ***Then***, as the commanding angels strike the note, every hand sweeps the harp strings with skillful touch, awaking sweet music in rich, melodious strains. Rapture unutterable thrills every heart, and each voice is raised in grateful praise: "Unto Him that loved us, and washed us from our sins in His own blood, and hath made us kings and priests unto God and His Father; to Him be glory and dominion for ever and ever." Revelation 1:5, 6. (GC 645.3)

Revelation chapter 3

In the message to the church at *Sardis two parties* are presented—those who have a name to live, but are dead; and those who are *striving to overcome.* **Study** *this message, found in the third chapter of Revelation....*

To the church of the present day this message is sent. I *call upon our church members to read the* **whole** *of the* **third chapter of Revelation***, and to make an application of it.* The message to the church of the Laodiceans applies especially to the people of God today. It is a message to professing Christians who have become so much like the world that no difference can be seen. (RH, Aug. 20, 1903)

I was shown that the commandments of God and the testimony of Jesus Christ relating to the shut door could not be separated, and that the time for the commandments of God to shine out with all their importance, and for God's people to be tried on the Sabbath truth, was when the door was opened in the most holy place in the heavenly sanctuary, where the ark is, in which are contained the ten commandments. *This door was not opened* **until** *the mediation of Jesus was finished in the holy place of the sanctuary in 1844.* **Then** Jesus rose up and shut the door of the holy place, and opened the door into the most holy, and passed within the second veil, where He now stands by the ark, and where the faith of Israel now reaches.

I saw that Jesus had shut the door of the holy place, and no man can open it; and that He had opened the door into the most holy, and no man can shut it (Revelation 3:7, 8); and that *since Jesus has opened the door into the most holy place*, which contains the ark, the commandments have been shining out to God's people, and *they are being tested on the Sabbath question.* (EW 42.1, 2)

Revelation chapters 4 and 5

As the bow in the cloud is formed by the union of the sunlight and the shower, so *the rainbow encircling the throne* represents the *combined power of* **mercy** *and* **justice**. (RH, Dec. 13, 1892)

The *fifth chapter of Revelation* needs to be *closely studied*. It is of great importance to those *who shall act* a part in the work of God for these last days. (9T 267.1)

Thus the Jewish leaders made their choice. *Their decision was registered in the book which John saw in the hand of Him that sat upon the throne, the book which no man could open.* In all its vindictiveness this decision will appear before them in the day *when this book* is *unsealed* by the Lion of the tribe of Judah. (COL 294.1)

This roll was written within and without. John says: "I wept much, because no man was found worthy to open and to read the book, neither to look thereon" [verse 4]. The vision as presented to John made its impression upon his mind. *The destiny of every nation was contained in that book.* John was distressed at the utter inability of any human being or angelic intelligence to read the words, or even to look thereon. His soul was wrought up to such a point of agony and suspense that one of the strong angels had compassion on him, and laying his hand on him assuringly, said, "Weep not: behold, the *Lion of the tribe of Judah*, the Root of David, hath *prevailed to open the book*, and to *loose the seven seals thereof.*" (Letter 65, 1898)

The Saviour is presented before John under the symbols of "the Lion of the tribe of Judah" and of "a Lamb as it had been slain." Revelation 5:5, 6. *These symbols represent the union of omnipotent power and self-sacrificing love.* The Lion of Judah, so terrible to the rejectors of His grace, **will be** the Lamb of God to the obedient and faithful. (AA 589.2)

Christ is our Mediator and officiating High Priest in the presence of the Father. He was *shown to John as a Lamb that had been slain, as in the very act of pouring out His blood in the sinner's behalf.* When the law of God is set before the sinner, showing him the depth of his sins, he should then be pointed to the Lamb of God, that taketh away the sin of the world. *He should be taught repentance toward God and faith toward our Lord Jesus Christ.* Thus will the labor of Christ's representative be in harmony with His work in the heavenly sanctuary. (4T 395.2)

The Lamb of God is represented before us as "in the midst of the throne" of God. *He is the great ordinance by which man and God are united and commune together.* Thus men are represented as sitting in heavenly places in Christ Jesus. This is the appointed place of meeting between God and humanity.... Christ brought human nature into a personal relation with His own divinity. *Thus He has given a center for the faith of the universe to fasten upon.* (TM 124.2)

Revelation chapter 6

Here were scenes presented to John that were not in reality but that which *would be* in a ***period of time in the future****.* [Revelation 6:1-4 quoted.] (Letter 65, 1898)

The same spirit is seen today that is represented in Revelation 6:6–8. *History is to be repeated. That which has been* **will be again**. (Letter 65, 1898)

When the *defiance of God's law is* ***almost universal***, ***when*** his people are pressed in affliction by their fellow men, *God will interpose.* ***Then*** will the voice be heard from the graves of martyrs, ***represented*** *by the souls that John saw slain for the Word of God, and for the testimony of Jesus Christ*, which they held—***then*** the prayer will ascend from every true child of God: "It is time for thee, Lord, to work: for they have made void thy law." *The fervent prayers of his people will be answered*; for **God** *loves to have his people seek him with all the heart, and depend upon him as their deliverer.* He will be sought unto to do these things for His people, and *he* **will** *arise as their* ***protector and avenger****.* "Shall not God avenge his own elect, which cry day and night unto him?" (RH, Dec. 21, 1897)

When *the fifth seal was opened*, John the Revelator in vision saw beneath the altar the company that were slain for the Word of God and the testimony of Jesus Christ. ***After this*** *came the scenes described in* ***the eighteenth of Revelation***, *when those who are faithful and true are called out from Babylon.* [Revelation 18:1-5 quoted.] (Ms. 39, 1906)

The cries of the faithful, persecuted ones ascend to heaven. And *as the* **blood of Abel** *cried from the ground, there are voices also crying to God from martyrs' graves*, from the sepulchers of the sea, from mountain caverns, from convent vaults: "*How long, O Lord, holy and true, dost Thou not judge and avenge our blood on them that dwell on the earth?*" The Lord is doing His work. All heaven is astir. *The Judge of all the earth is* **soon** *to arise and* **vindicate His insulted authority**. The mark of deliverance will be set upon the men who keep God's commandments, who revere His law, and who refuse the mark of the beast or of his image. *God has revealed what is to take place in the last days, that His people may be prepared to stand* against the tempest of opposition and wrath. (5T 451.2–452.1)

In view of the infinite price paid for man's redemption, how dare any professing the name of Christ treat with indifference one of *His little ones*? How carefully should brethren and sisters in the church guard every word and action *lest they hurt the oil and the wine!* (5T 614.2)

Let everyone who loves God consider that now while it is day is the time to work, not among the sheep already in the fold, but to go out in search of the lost and perishing ones. These need to have special help to bring them back to the fold. Now is the time for the careless to arouse from their slumber. Now is the time to entreat that souls shall not only hear the word of God, but without delay secure oil in their vessels with their lamps. *That oil is the righteousness of Christ. It represents* **character**, and character is not transferable. No man can secure it for another. Each must obtain for himself a character purified from every stain of sin. (TM 233.2)

Revelation chapter 7

Already kingdom is rising against kingdom. There is *not now* a determined engagement. As yet *the four winds are held* **until** *the servants of God shall be sealed in their foreheads.* **Then** the Powers of earth will marshal their forces *for the last great battle. How carefully* we should improve the little remaining period of our probation! *How earnestly we should examine ourselves!* We should eat the flesh and drink the blood of the Son of God; *that is, carefully study the Word, eat it, digest it, make it a part of our being.* We are to live the Word, not keep it apart from our lives. The character of Christ is to be our character. We are to be *transformed* by the renewing of our hearts. Here is our **only safety**. Nothing can separate a living Christian from God. (RH, Nov. 27, 1900)

About four months since, I had a vision of events, **all in the future**. And I saw the time of trouble, such as never was,—Jesus told me it was the time of Jacob's trouble, and that we should be delivered out of it by the voice of God. **Just before** we entered it, we all received the seal of the living God. **Then** I saw the *four Angels cease to hold the four winds.* And I saw famine, pestilence and sword, nation rose against nation, and the whole world was in confusion. (*The Day Star*, March 14, 1846)

Revelation chapters 8 and 9

Solemn events before us are **yet to transpire. Trumpet after trumpet is to be sounded,** *vial after vial poured out* one after another upon the inhabitants of the earth. *Scenes of stupendous interest are* **right upon us** ... (Letter 112, 1890)

A world is represented in the destruction of Jerusalem, and *the* **warning** *given then comes sounding down along the line* **to our time**: "And there shall be signs in the sun, and in the moon, and in the stars; and upon the earth distress of nations, with perplexity; the sea and the waves roaring." Yes, *the sea* **shall** *pass its borders,* and destruction will be in its track. *It* **will** *engulf the ships that sail upon its broad waters*; and with the burden of their living freight, these will be hurled into eternity. (RH, Dec. 7, 1890)

The tempest is coming, and we must get ready for its fury by having repentance toward God and faith toward our Lord Jesus Christ. *The Lord* **will arise** *to shake terribly the earth.* We shall see troubles on all sides. *Thousands of ships* **will** *be hurled into the depths of the sea.* Navies will go down, and *human lives* **will** *be sacrificed by millions.* (Mar 37.4)

Probationary time will not continue much longer. Now **God is withdrawing His restraining hand** from the earth. Long has He been speaking to men and women through the agency of His Holy Spirit; but they have not heeded the call. Now He is speaking to His people, and to the world, by His judgments. *The time of these judgments is a time of mercy for those who have not yet had opportunity to learn what is truth.* Tenderly will the Lord look upon them. His heart of mercy is touched; His hand is still stretched out to save. *Large numbers* will be admitted to the fold of safety *who in these* **last days will** *hear the truth for the first time.* (YRP 159.2)

The ***time*** of God's *destructive judgments* is the *time of mercy* for those who have no opportunity to learn what is truth. Tenderly *will* the Lord look upon them. His heart of mercy is touched; his hand is still stretched out to save, *while the door is closed to those who would not enter*. Large numbers *will be admitted* who in these **last days** hear the truth for the first time. (RH, July 5, 1906)

> *The time of these judgments is a time of mercy for those who have not yet had opportunity to learn what is truth.*

Long had God delayed His judgments, but now He would visit His displeasure upon them as *a **last effort** to check* them in their evil course. (PK 425.2)

God has a storehouse of *retributive judgments*, which he permits to fall upon those who have continued in sin in the face of great light. (3SM 418.3)

The ***time*** is right upon us when there will be sorrow in the world that no human balm can heal. The flattering monuments of men's greatness will be crumbled in the dust, even **before** the *last great destruction comes upon the world* [in the seven vial plagues]... (3SM 418.4)

Four mighty angels are *still holding* the four winds of the earth. Terrible destruction is forbidden to come **in full**. The accidents by land and by sea; the loss of life, steadily increasing, by storm, by tempest, by railroad disaster, by conflagration; the terrible floods, the earthquakes, and the winds will be the stirring up of the nations to one deadly combat, while the angels hold the four winds, forbidding the terrible power of Satan to be exercised in its fury **until** the *servants of God are sealed in their foreheads. Get ready, get ready, I beseech you, get ready before it shall be forever too late!* The ministers of vengeance will pour all the terrible judgments upon a God-forsaken people. (RH, June 7, 1887)

While He does not delight in vengeance, He will execute judgment upon the transgressors of His law. *He is forced to do this,* **to preserve the inhabitants of the earth from utter depravity and ruin.** *In order to save some He must cut off those who have become hardened* *in sin.... By terrible things in righteousness He will vindicate the authority of His downtrodden law.* (PP 628.1)

As Jesus moved out of the most holy place, I heard the tinkling of the bells upon His garment; and as He left, a cloud of darkness covered the inhabitants of the earth. There was then no mediator between guilty man and an offended God. ***While Jesus had been standing between God and guilty man, a restraint was upon the people***; but when He stepped out from between man and the Father, *the restraint was removed and Satan had entire control of the finally impenitent.* (EW 280.2)

The wrath of Satan increases as his time grows short, and *his work of **deceit** and **destruction** reaches its culmination **in the time of trouble***. God's long-suffering has ended. The world has rejected His mercy, despised His love, and trampled upon His law. The wicked have passed the boundary of their probation, and *the Lord withdraws His protection*, and *leaves them to the **mercy of the leader they have chosen***. Satan will have power over those who have yielded themselves to his control, and *he will plunge the inhabitants of the earth into one great, final trouble.* As the angels of God cease to hold in check the fierce winds of human passion, all the elements of strife will be let loose. *The **whole world** will be involved in ruin more terrible than that which came upon Jerusalem of old.* (Mar 275.3)

Revelation chapter 10

"The angel ... sware by him that liveth for ever ... that there should be time no longer." Revelation 10:5, 6.

The message of **Revelation 14**, proclaiming that *the hour of **God's judgment** is come*, is given **in the time of the end**; and the angel of **Revelation 10** is represented as having one foot on the sea and one foot on the land, **showing** that *the message* **will be carried** to distant lands, the ocean **will be crossed**, and the islands of the sea **will hear** the **proclamation** of the **last message of warning**....

"And the angel which I saw stand upon the sea and upon the earth lifted up his hand to heaven, and sware by him that liveth for ever and ever, who created heaven, and the things that therein are, and the earth, and the things that therein are, and the sea, and the things which are therein, *that there should be time no longer*" (Revelation

10:5, 6). *This message announces the end of the prophetic periods [to be proclaimed—future context].* (Mar 18.1-3)

After these seven thunders uttered their voices, the injunction comes to John, as to Daniel, *in regard to the little book*: "Seal up those things which the seven thunders uttered." These [thunders] relate to **future events** which **will be disclosed in their order**. Daniel shall *stand in his lot at* **the end of the days**. John sees the little book unsealed. **Then** *Daniel's prophecies have their proper place* in the **first, second, and third angels' messages to be given** to the world. The unsealing of the little book was *the message in relation to* **time**....

John heard the mysteries which the thunders uttered, but he was commanded not to write them. The **special light** given to John which was expressed in the **seven thunders** was a *delineation of events* **which would transpire** *under the first and second angels' messages.* **It was not best for the people to know these things**, for *their faith must necessarily be* **tested**. (Ms. 59, 1900)

It was the Lion of the tribe of Judah who unsealed the book and gave to John the revelation *of what should be in these last days*. Daniel stood in his lot to bear his testimony, which was sealed *until the time of the end*, when the first angel's message should be proclaimed to our world. *These matters are of* **infinite importance** *in these last days*.... The book of Daniel is unsealed in the revelation to John, and it carries us forward to the *last scenes* of this earth's history. (CTr 334.5)

The *prophetic periods of Daniel, extending to the very eve of the great consummation*, throw a flood of light upon events **then to** *transpire*. (RH, Sept. 25, 1883)

The unsealing of the little book was the *message* in *relation to* **time**. (Ms. 59, 1900)

A great work will be done in a short time. *A message* will **soon** be given by God's appointment that will swell into a *loud cry.* **Then** *Daniel will stand in his lot, to give his testimony.* (Letter 54, 1906)

> *The unsealing of the little book was the message in relation to* **time**.

Revelation chapter 11

The time has come when everything is to be shaken that can be shaken, that those things which cannot be shaken may remain. *Every case is coming in review* before God; He is *measuring the temple and the **worshipers therein**.* (7T 219.2)

But here is the work going on, measuring the temple and its worshipers *to see **who will stand in the last day**.* (Ms. 4, 1888)

When *God's temple in heaven is opened*, what a triumphant time that will be for all who have been faithful and true! In the temple will be seen the ark of the testament in which were placed the two tables of stone, on which are written God's law. These tables of stone **will be brought forth** from their hiding place, and on them will be seen the ten commandments engraved by the finger of God. These tables of stone now lying in the ark of the testament *will be* a convincing testimony to the truth and binding claims of God's law. (Letter 47, 1902)

We may have long followed the narrow path, but it is not safe to take this as proof that we shall follow it to the end. If we have walked with God in fellowship of the Spirit, it is because we have sought Him daily by faith. *From the two olive trees the golden oil flowing through the golden pipes* has been communicated to us. But those who do not cultivate the spirit and habit of prayer cannot expect to receive the *golden oil of goodness, patience, long-suffering, gentleness, love.* (TM 511.1)

The Lord calls for His people to locate away from the cities.... Let all who would understand the meaning of these things *read the eleventh chapter of Revelation*. Read every verse, and *learn the things that are **yet to take place*** in the cities. Read also the scenes portrayed in the eighteenth chapter of the same book. (Letter 158, 1906)

The substitution of the false for the true is the last act in the drama. **When** *this substitution becomes universal*, God will reveal himself. When the laws of men are exalted above the laws of God, when the powers of this earth try to force men to keep the first day of the week, know that the time has come for God to work. *He will arise in His majesty, and will **shake terribly the earth**. He will come out of His place to punish the inhabitants of the world for their iniquity.*

The earth shall disclose her blood, and shall no more cover her slain. (RH, April 23, 1901, Art. A)

Revelation chapter 12

Under the symbols of a great red dragon, a leopard-like beast, and a beast with lamblike horns, the *earthly governments* which would especially engage in *trampling upon God's law and persecuting His people*, were presented to John. *The war is carried on till the **close of time**.* The people of God, symbolized by a holy woman *and her children*, were represented as greatly in the minority. **In the last days** only a remnant still existed. Of these John speaks as they "which keep the commandments of God, and have the testimony of Jesus Christ." (ST, Nov. 1, 1899)

There are only two parties upon this earth—those who stand under the bloodstained banner of Jesus Christ and those who stand under the black banner of rebellion. In the twelfth chapter of Revelation is represented *the great conflict* between the obedient and the disobedient. [Rev. 12:17; 13:11–17 quoted.] (Ms. 16, 1900)

Revelation chapter 13

The ***prophecy of Revelation 13*** declares that the power represented by the beast with lamblike horns shall cause "the earth and them which dwell therein" to worship the papacy—there symbolized by the beast "like unto a leopard." ... **this prophecy** will be fulfilled **when** the United States shall enforce Sunday observance, which Rome claims as the special acknowledgment of her supremacy. (GC 578.3)

"He that leadeth into captivity shall go into captivity: he that killeth with the sword must be killed with the sword. Here is the patience and the faith of the saints." [Rev. 13:10.] This **entire chapter** is a revelation of what **will** surely take place. [Rev. 13:11, 15–17, quoted.] (Ms. 88, 1897)

The Sabbath question will be the issue in the great conflict in which all the world will act a part. [Revelation 13:4–8, 10 quoted.] This **entire chapter** is a revelation of what **will** surely take place. [Verses 11, 15–17 quoted.] (Ms. 88, 1897)

In the **last days** Satan will appear as an angel of light, with great power and heavenly glory, and claim to be the Lord of the whole earth. He will declare that the Sabbath has been changed from the seventh to the first day of the week; and as lord of the first day of the week he will present this spurious sabbath as a test of loyalty to him. ***Then*** *will take place the **final fulfillment*** of the Revelator's prophecy. "They worshiped the dragon which gave power unto the beast: and they worshiped the beast, saying, Who is like unto the beast? who is able to make war with him? And there was given unto him a mouth speaking great things and blasphemies; and power was given unto him to *continue **forty and two months**....*" (Revelation 13:4, 5). [Rev. 13:6–8 quoted.] (Ms. 153, 1902)

Revelation chapter 14

The fourteenth chapter of Revelation is a chapter of the deepest interest. This scripture ***will soon be understood in all its*** *bearings,* and the messages given to John the revelator will be repeated with distinct utterance. (RH, Oct. 13, 1904)

The *third angel's message **is to be given*** with power. The power of the proclamation of the first and second messages is to be *intensified in the third*. In the Revelation John says of the heavenly messenger who unites with the third angel: "I saw another angel come down from heaven, having great power; and the earth was lightened with his glory. And he cried mightily with a strong voice." Revelation 18:1, 2. (6T 60.1)

"She made all nations drink of the wine of the wrath of her fornication" (Revelation 14:6–8). How is this done? By forcing men to accept a spurious sabbath. (8T 94 (1904); LDE 198.2)

Not yet, however, can it be said that ... "she made all nations drink of the wine of the wrath of her fornication." *She has not yet made all nations do this....* (LDE 198.3)

Not until this condition shall be reached, and the union of the church with the world shall be fully accomplished throughout Christendom, will the fall of Babylon be complete. The change is a progressive one, and **the perfect fulfillment of Revelation 14:8 is yet future**. (GC 389.3; LDE 198.4)

When do her sins reach unto heaven? [Rev. 18:2–5.] When the law of God is finally made void by legislation. (ST, June 12, 1893, par. 13; LDE 198.5)

The "mark of the beast" still *remains to be defined*. (GC 445.2)

Revelation chapters 15 and 16

The nations are now getting angry, but **when** our High Priest has finished his work in the Sanctuary, he will *stand up*, put on the garments of vengeance, and **then** *the seven last plagues will be poured out*. I saw that the four angels would *hold the four winds* **until** Jesus' work was done in the Sanctuary, and **then** will come the seven last plagues. (ExV 19.1 [1851])

Men are prone to abuse the long-suffering of God, and to presume on His forbearance. But there is a point in human iniquity when it is time for God to interfere; and terrible are the issues. "The Lord is slow to anger, and great in power, and will not at all acquit the wicked" (Nahum 1:3). The long-suffering of God is wonderful, because He puts constraint on His own attributes; but punishment is nonetheless certain. Every century of profligacy has treasured up wrath against the day of wrath; ***and when the time comes, and the iniquity is full, then God will do His strange work. It will be found a terrible thing to have worn out the divine patience; for the wrath of God will fall so signally and strongly that it is presented as being unmixed with mercy;*** and the very earth will be desolated. (2SM 372.3)

Little by little he has prepared the way for his masterpiece of deception in the development of spiritualism. He has not yet reached the full accomplishment of his designs; but *it* **will** *be reached in the last remnant of time*. Says the prophet: "I saw three unclean spirits like frogs; … they are the spirits of devils, working miracles, which go forth unto the kings of the earth and of the whole world, to gather them to the battle of that great day of God Almighty." , 14. Except those who are kept by the power of God, through faith in His word, *the whole world* **will** *be swept into the ranks of this delusion*. The people are fast being lulled to a fatal security, to be awakened only by the outpouring of the wrath of God. (GC 561.2)

The wrath of Satan increases as his time grows short, and his work of deceit and destruction reaches its culmination in the ***time of*** *trouble*. God's long-suffering has ended. The world has rejected His mercy, despised His love, and trampled upon His law. The wicked have *passed the **boundary of their probation***, and the Lord *withdraws His protection*, and leaves them to the mercy of the leader they have chosen. Satan will have power over those who have yielded themselves to his control, and *he will plunge the inhabitants of the earth into one great, final trouble*. **As the angels of God cease to hold in check** the fierce winds of human passion, all the elements of strife will be let loose. The *whole world* will be involved in ruin more terrible than that which came upon Jerusalem of old. (Mar 275.3)

Revelation chapter 17

In the seventeenth of *Revelation* is **foretold** the *destruction of all the churches* who corrupt themselves by idolatrous devotion to the service of the papacy, those who have drunk of the wine of the wrath of her fornication. [Revelation 17:1–4 quoted.]

Thus is represented the *papal power*, which with all deceivableness of unrighteousness, by outside attraction and gorgeous display, *deceives **all nations***; promising them, as did Satan our first parents, all good to those who receive its mark, and all harm to those who oppose its fallacies. The power which has the deepest inward corruption will make the greatest display, and will clothe itself with the most elaborate signs of power. The Bible plainly declares that this covers a corrupt and deceiving wickedness. "Upon her forehead was a name written, Mystery, Babylon the Great, The Mother of Harlots and Abominations of the Earth."

What is it that gives its kingdom to this power? **Protestantism**, a power which, while professing to have the temper and spirit of a lamb and to be allied to Heaven, *speaks with **the voice of a dragon***. It is moved by a power from beneath. (Letter 232, 1899)

(Revelation 17:13, 14 quoted). "These have one mind." ***There will be a universal bond of union, one great harmony, a confederacy of Satan's forces.*** "And shall give their power and strength unto the beast." Thus is manifested the same arbitrary, oppressive power against religious liberty, freedom to worship God according to the dictates of conscience, as was manifested by the papacy, *when in the past* it persecuted those who dared to refuse to conform with the religious rites and ceremonies of Romanism.

In the warfare *to be waged* **in the last days** *there will be* **united**, in opposition to God's people, **all** *the corrupt powers* that have apostatized from allegiance to the law of Jehovah. In this warfare the Sabbath of the fourth commandment will be the great point at issue, for in the Sabbath commandment the great Law-giver identifies Himself as the Creator of the heavens and the earth. (Ms. 24, 1891)

Revelation chapter 18

The prophecies in the eighteenth of Revelation will **soon be fulfilled**. *During* the proclamation of the *third angel's message*, "another angel" is to "come down from heaven, having great power," and the earth is to be "lighted with his glory." The Spirit of the Lord will so graciously bless consecrated human instrumentalities that men, women, and children will open their lips in praise and thanksgiving, filling the earth with the knowledge of God, and with his unsurpassed glory, as the waters cover the sea.

Those who have held the beginning of their confidence firm unto the end **will be** *wide-awake during the time that the third angel's message is proclaimed with great power*. During the *loud cry*, the church, aided by the providential interpositions of her exalted Lord, will diffuse the knowledge of salvation so abundantly that light will be communicated to every city and town. *The earth* **will be** *filled with the knowledge of salvation*. So abundantly will the renewing Spirit of God have crowned with success the intensely active agencies, that the light of present truth **will be seen** flashing everywhere. (RH, Oct. 13, 1904)

Unique New Light to Shine on Us

There are *glorious truths* **to come** before the people of God. (8T 322.3)

Although we have in trust the grandest and most important truth ever presented to the world, *we are only babes,* **as far as understanding truth** in all its bearings is concerned. (CW 29.2)

We have **many lessons to learn**, and *many, many to* **unlearn**. (TM 30.2)

We have only the glimmerings of the rays of the light that is **yet to come** *to us*. (RH, June 3, 1890)

The time for the **unfolding of special truth** in relation to the **closing scenes** of this earth's history is during the last generations that **shall live** upon the earth. (2T 692.2)

The *prophecies of Daniel and of John* are to be understood. They interpret each other. They give to the world truths which *every one should understand. **These prophecies are to be witnesses in the world.*** (Ms. 10, 1900)

The study of the Revelation directs the mind to the prophecies of Daniel, and **both** *present most important instruction, given of* God *to men, concerning events to take place at the **close of this world's history***. (GC 341.3)

> *The study of the Revelation directs the mind to the prophecies of Daniel, and both present most important instruction, given of God to men, concerning events to take place at the close of this world's history.*

There is need of a much closer study of the word of God: *especially should Daniel and the Revelation have attention as never before* in the history of our work. (TM 112.1)

The solemn messages that have been given in their order in the *Revelation* are to *occupy the first place* in the minds of God's people. **Nothing else is to be allowed to engross our attention.** (8T 302.1)

When the books of Daniel and Revelation are better understood, believers will have **an entirely different religious experience**. *They will be given such glimpses of the open gates of heaven that heart and mind will be impressed with* **the character that all must develop** *in order to realize the blessedness which is to be the reward of the pure in heart.* (TM 114.3)

Warning Messages

Every **new truth** has made its way against hatred and **opposition**. (GC 609.1)

Those who turn away from the light which God has given, or who neglect to seek it when it is within their reach, are **left in darkness**. (GC 312.3)

> *When the books of Daniel and Revelation are better understood, believers will have an entirely different religious experience.*

When a doctrine is presented that does not meet our minds, we should go to the word of God, seek the Lord in prayer, and *give no place for the enemy to come in with suspicion and prejudice*. We should never permit the spirit to be manifested that arraigned the priests and rulers against the Redeemer of the world. They complained that He disturbed the people, and they wished He would let them alone; for He caused perplexity and dissension. *The Lord sends light to us to prove what manner of spirit we are of.* We are not to deceive ourselves.

… If we but knew *the evil of the spirit of intolerance,* how carefully would we shun it! (GW 301.3; 302.1)

I saw Satan would work more powerfully now than ever he has before. He knows that his time is short and that the sealing of the saints will place them beyond his power, and he will now work in every way that he can and will try his every insinuation to get the saints off from their guard and get them **asleep** on the **present truth** or **doubting it**, so as to **prevent their being sealed** with the seal of the living God. (Ms 7, 1850, "A Vision God Gave Me at Brother Harris," Aug. 24, 1850)

If light come, and that light is **set aside or rejected***, then comes* **condemnation and the frown of God***.* (1T 116.1)

There is no excuse for any one in taking the position *that there is no more truth to be revealed, and that all our expositions of Scripture are without an* **error***.* (RH, Dec. 20, 1892)

The prophecies which the great I AM has given in His word, uniting link after link in the chain of events, from eternity in the past to eternity in the future, tell us where we are today in the procession of the ages, and what may be expected in the time to come. All that prophecy has foretold as coming to pass, until the present time, has been traced on the pages of history, and **we may be assured that all which is yet to come will be fulfilled in its order***.* (Mar 68.2)

The Message to Present

Our lesson for the present time is, *How may we most clearly comprehend and present the gospel that Christ came in person to present to John on the Isle of Patmos,—the gospel that is termed "the revelation of Jesus Christ"?* We are to present to our people a clear explanation of Revelation. We are to give them the word of God just as it is, with as few of our own explanations as possible. No one mind can do this work alone. Although we have in trust the grandest and most important truth ever presented to the world, we are only babes, as far as understanding truth in all its bearings is concerned. Christ is the great teacher, and *that which He revealed to John, we are to tax our minds to understand and clearly to define.* We are facing the most important issues that men have ever been called upon to meet. (CW 29.2)

The theme of *greatest importance* is the third angel's message, embracing the messages of the first and second angels. All should understand the truths contained in these messages and demonstrate them in daily life, for this is *essential to salvation.* We shall have to study earnestly, prayerfully, in order to understand these grand truths. Letter 97, 1902. (CW 29.3)

Landmarks Defined

In Minneapolis God gave precious gems of truth to His people in new settings. *This light from heaven* by some *was rejected* with all the stubbornness the Jews manifested in rejecting Christ, and there was much talk about standing by the old landmarks. But there was evidence they knew not what the old landmarks were. There was evidence and there was reasoning from the word that commended itself to the conscience; *but the minds of men were fixed, sealed against the entrance of light,* because they had decided it was a dangerous error removing the "old landmarks" when it was not moving a peg of the old landmarks, but they had perverted ideas of what constituted the old landmarks. (Ms. 13, 1889; CW 30.1)

The passing of the time in 1844 was a period of great events, opening to our astonished eyes the cleansing of the sanctuary transpiring in heaven, and having decided relation to God's people upon the earth, [also] the first and second angels' messages and the third, unfurling the banner on which was inscribed, *"The commandments of God and the faith of Jesus."* One of the **landmarks** under this message was the *temple of God*, seen by His truth-loving people in heaven, *and the ark containing the law of God.* The *light of the Sabbath of the fourth commandment* flashed its strong rays in the pathway of the transgressors of God's law. The *nonimmortality of the wicked* is an old landmark. I can call to mind nothing more that can come under the head of the old landmarks. All this cry about changing the old landmarks is all imaginary. (CW 30.2)

Now at the present time *God designs a new and fresh impetus shall be given to His work.* Satan sees this, and he is determined it shall be *hindered*. He knows that if he can deceive the people who claim to believe present truth, [and make them believe that] the work the Lord designs to do for His people is a removing of the old landmarks, something which they should, with most determined zeal, resist, then he exults over the deception he has led them to believe. The work for this time has certainly been a surprising work of various hindrances, owing to the false setting of matters before the minds of many of our people. *That which is food to the churches is regarded as dangerous*, and should not be given them. And this slight difference of ideas is allowed to unsettle the faith, to cause apostasy, to break up unity, to sow discord, all because they do not know what they are striving about themselves. Brethren, is it not best to be sensible?

Heaven is looking upon us all, and what can they think of recent developments? While in this condition of things, building up barriers, **we not only deprive ourselves of great light and** *precious advantages, but just now, when we so much need it,* **we place ourselves where light cannot be communicated from heaven that we ought to communicate to others.** (Ms. 13, 1889; CW 31.1)

Truths Realized from Prophetic Study

One thing will certainly be understood from the study of Revelation—that the connection between God and His people is *close and decided.* (TM 114.5)

A wonderful connection is seen between the universe of heaven and this world. The things revealed to Daniel were afterward complemented by the revelation made to John on the Isle of Patmos.

These two books *should be carefully studied. Twice Daniel inquired, How long shall it be to the end of time?* (TM 114.6)

Daniel stood in his lot to bear his testimony which was sealed *until the time of the end, when the first angel's message should be proclaimed to our world.* These matters are of **infinite importance** in these last days; but while "many shall be purified, and made white, and tried," "the wicked shall do wickedly: and none of the wicked shall understand." How true this is! Sin is the transgression of the law of God; and those who will not accept the light in regard to the law of God will not understand the proclamation of the first, second, and third angel's messages.

The book of Daniel is unsealed in the revelation to John, and **carries us forward** *to the last scenes of this earth's history.* (TM 115.3)

Will our brethren bear in mind that we are living amid the perils of the last days? Read Revelation in connection with Daniel. *Teach these things.* (TM 337.2)

Study Revelation in connection with Daniel, for **history will be repeated....** We, with all our religious advantages, ought to know far more today than we do know. (TM 116.3)

A message that will arouse the churches *is to be proclaimed.* Every effort is to be made to give the light, not only to our people, but to the world. I have been instructed that *the prophecies of Daniel and the Revelation should be printed in small books, with the necessary explanations, and should be sent all over the world.* **Our own people** need to have the light placed before them in clearer lines. (TM 117.3)

"Nevertheless, if thou warn the wicked of his way to turn from it, ... thou hast delivered thy soul." Ezekiel 33:7-9.

The words of the prophet declare the solemn responsibility of those who are appointed as guardians of the church of God, stewards of the mysteries of God. *They are to stand as* **watchmen on the walls of Zion**, to sound the note of alarm at the approach of the enemy. Souls are in danger of falling under temptation, and they will perish unless God's ministers are faithful to their trust. If for any reason their spiritual senses become so benumbed that they are unable to discern danger, and through their failure to give warning the people perish, God will require at their hands the blood of those who are lost.

*It is the **privilege** of the **watchmen on the walls** of Zion to live so near to God, and to be susceptible to the impressions of His Spirit, that He can work through them to tell men and women of their peril and point them to the place of safety. Faithfully are they to warn them of the sure result of transgression, and faithfully are they to safeguard the interests of the church. At no time may they relax their vigilance. Theirs is a work requiring the exercise of every faculty of the being. In trumpet tones their voices are to be lifted, and never are they to sound one wavering, uncertain note. Not for wages are they to labor, but because they cannot do otherwise, because they realize that there is a woe upon them if they fail to preach the gospel. Chosen of God, sealed with the blood of consecration, they are to rescue men and women from impending destruction. (AA 360.4–361.2)*

Part 2: A Case for 3½ Years

What evidence do we have for the context of Matthew 24? Does Matthew 24 point us back in history or does it point us forward to the future? Perhaps it is both.

What Is the Context of Matthew 24?

There are three main pieces of evidence that guide our understanding of the context of Matthew 24 and the parallel passages in Mark 13 and Luke 21. The *first* piece of evidence is given when Jesus prophesied of the destruction of the temple in response to His disciples asking Him key questions.

> And Jesus said unto them, See ye not all these things? verily I say unto you, There shall not be left here one stone upon another, that shall not be thrown down. And as he sat upon the mount of Olives, the disciples came unto him privately, saying, Tell us, **when** shall *these things be?* ***And*** *what shall be* the *sign of thy coming*, and of the *end of the world*? And Jesus answered and said unto them ... (Matt. 24:2–4)

The chapter starts with two contextual questions, "**When** shall these things *be?*" and "***what*** *shall be the sign of thy coming, and of the end of the world?*" Although the disciples didn't understand it, they were asking two *questions of timing*: (1) When would the fall of Jerusalem occur? and (2) When will Jesus return?

Along with these two *timing questions*, they also asked Him *what signs* would accompany those events. Jesus intermingled His answers to these questions throughout the rest of the chapter. Therefore, the context of this chapter has to do with the *timing* concerning the destruction of Jerusalem and the *timing* concerning the destruction of the entire world at Jesus' second coming. Any application of the events in this chapter to other periods of time can only be a partial or parallel application. The fulfillment of this prophecy is limited to the two points of time in question: the fall of Jerusalem and the return of Jesus.

The *second* piece of evidence is given in Matthew 24:34. In this verse, Jesus further restricts the timing of this passage to a very short time—that of one generation.

> Verily I say unto you, **This generation** shall not pass, till all **these things** be fulfilled. (Matt. 24:34)

Jesus is telling us that the generation that is living *when* "all these things" happen will not pass away until all the events foretold take place. "All these things" include the wars, natural disasters, persecution, false prophets, abomination, desolation, signs in the sun, moon, stars, and final deliverance as listed in this chapter.

The word "generation" gives us important timing information for the passage. A generation in the Bible is a 40-year period of time. (See Num. 32:13; Deut. 1:35; Ps. 95:10.) Therefore, Matthew 24:34 tells us that *all the events* foretold in this chapter must happen within a 40-year window of time. The destruction of Jerusalem took place within forty years from the time Jesus spoke these words (AD 31 to AD 70). All the final events listed in Matthew 24, leading to the destruction of the world just prior to the second coming, will take place within a 40-year period of time as well.

Jesus, in AD 31, gave the information in Matthew 24 while conversing with His disciples on the mount of Olives. Thirty-nine years later, in AD 70, Jerusalem was destroyed (within one generation). Rapidly increasing disasters are strong evidence indicating that we are currently within that final end-time window of forty years. See the following graph, found at https://1ref.us/jbet1.

> *Matthew 24:34 tells us that* all the events foretold in this chapter must happen within a 40-year window of time.

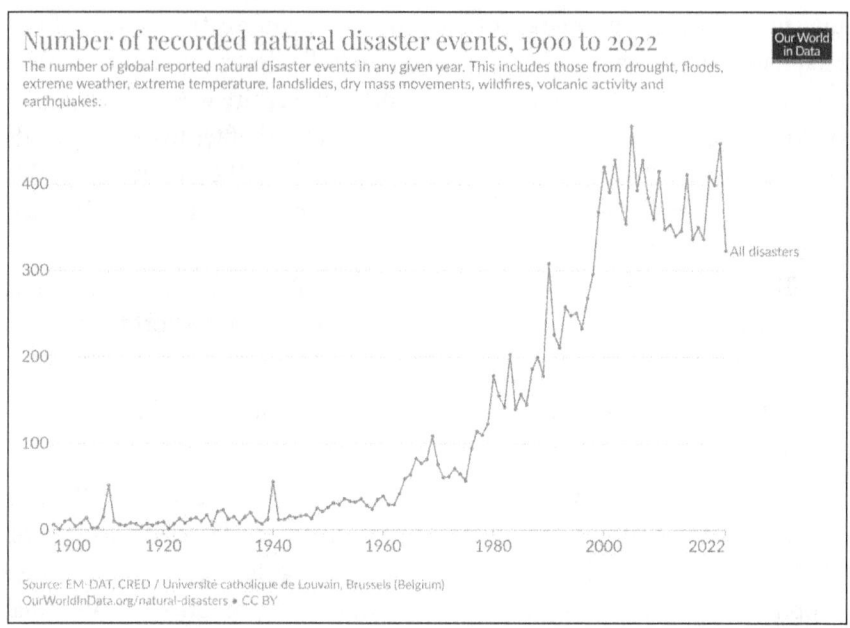

Notice that the chart begins going exponential in the late 1970s. Also note that Pope John Paul II came to power in 1978 (45 years ago). No other Pope has rallied the troops of Rome and pushed the idolatrous standard of Sunday like he did. When does the 40-year period of time begin? We are not told. But the evidence strongly suggests that we are within that 40-year window and that the end is very near!

The *third* piece of evidence is given in verse 15. In the same end-time context, Jesus states that there will be an "abomination," or idolatrous transgression, that results in "desolation."

> When ye therefore shall see the **abomination** of **desolation**, spoken of by Daniel the prophet, stand in the holy place, (whoso readeth, let him understand:). (Matt. 24:15)

> And when ye shall see Jerusalem **compassed with armies**, then know that the **desolation** thereof is nigh. (Luke 21:20)

> But when ye shall see the **abomination** of **desolation**, spoken of by Daniel the prophet, standing where it ought not, (let him that readeth understand,) then let them that be in Judaea flee to the mountains: (Mark 13:14)

These verses contain information that warned God's people in Jerusalem of the coming Roman army with its idolatrous standards (abomination) resulting in the "desolation" (destruction) of Jerusalem within a generation. Within the context of these verses is also contained a warning of the coming idolatrous and false day of worship (abomination) and the "desolation" (destruction) of the entire world in our generation. Desolation took place in Jerusalem, and desolation of the entire world is soon to come.

Let me restate this point: The *first abomination* that resulted in desolation was the Roman armies with their idolatrous standards who encircled the Jewish people and destroyed those who were not faithful to God. God's faithful people fled before Jerusalem was destroyed. The *second abomination,* which will result in the destruction of the world, will again be by the "armies of Rome," who will encircle God's people with the idolatrous standard of a false day of worship. Accepting (or rejecting) a false day of worship, which the Bible never directs, will be the final test of loyalty to God. When enforcement of that false day of worship appears on the scene, it will be God's final warning to flee from the cities to safe homes in the country and, ultimately, to desolate and solitary places among the mountains.

Note that Matthew 24 gives three pieces of evidence that establish the context of the chapter:

1. *Destruction* is prophesied twice. First, the time of Jerusalem's destruction is prophesied. Second, the end-time destruction of the world, prior to Jesus' second coming, is prophesied.

2. The *signs* foretold for each event will take place within one generation, or forty years.

3. The *"abomination"* that results in *"desolation"* takes place at two different points in time within a forty-year time period each. One time period led up to the destruction of Jerusalem, and the other period will be just before Jesus' second coming.

> It will then be time to leave the large cities, preparatory to leaving the smaller ones for retired homes in secluded places among the mountains. (5T 464.3)

If these biblical evidences and conclusions are correct, the Spirit of Prophecy, God's delegated messenger Ellen White, must affirm these thoughts. What are we told?

> For nearly **forty years** after the doom of Jerusalem had been pronounced by Christ Himself, the Lord delayed His judgments upon the city and the nation. Wonderful was the long-suffering of God toward the rejectors of His gospel and the murderers of His Son. (GC 27.3)

Christ, upon the Mount of Olives, rehearsed the fearful judgments that were to precede His second coming: ... While these prophecies received a *partial fulfillment* at the destruction of Jerusalem, they have a more direct application to the **last days**. (5T 753.1)

In his answer, Jesus did not take up separately the destruction of Jerusalem and the last great day of his coming. He *mingled* the description of these two events. When he spoke of the destruction of Jerusalem, his words referred also to the final destruction that will take place when the Lord rises out of his place to punish the world for its iniquity. *The* **entire chapter** *in which are recorded Christ's words regarding this, is a* **warning** *to all who* **shall live** *during the* **last scenes** *of this earth's history.* (RH, Dec. 13, 1898)

The Saviour's prophecy concerning the visitation of judgments upon Jerusalem is to have *another fulfillment*, of which that terrible desolation was but a *faint shadow*. In the fate of the chosen city we may behold the ***doom of a world*** that has rejected God's mercy and trampled upon His law. (GC 36.2)

As the siege of Jerusalem by the Roman armies was the signal for flight to the Judean Christians, so the assumption of power on the part of our nation [the United States] in the decree *enforcing the* **papal sabbath** *will be a* **warning** *to us.* (5T 464.3)

The *first day of the week* is to be exalted and presented to all for observance. Shall we be partakers of this *cup of* **abomination**? Shall we bow to the authorities of earth and despise God? The powers of darkness have been gathering their forces to bring this crisis about in the world, so that the man of sin may exalt himself above God. (RH, April 15, 1890)

The context given by both Jesus' words and the Spirit of Prophecy state that all the signs and events listed are for the "last days." From the context of those passages, the events listed still have a ***complete fulfillment*** in the ***future*** extremity of time.

What Is the Context of Daniel 12 and Its Three Time Prophecies?

There are three main pieces of evidence that guide our understanding of the context of Daniel 12.

Read Daniel 12 and notice all of the events listed. As you read, determine which ones are past, present, or future *based on the context of the chapter*. Notice that all of the events listed are given in an end-time context:

- Michael stands up (v. 1).
- There is a time of trouble such as never was (v. 1).
- God delivers His people (v. 1).
- A special resurrection takes place (v. 2).
- The book is sealed until the time of the end (vss. 4, 9).
- Many are running to and fro, and knowledge is increased (v. 4).
- Twice Daniel asks how long it will be to the end of time (vss. 6, 8).
- Jesus answers Daniel's timing questions with three timing prophecies (vss. 7, 11, 12).
- There is an abomination that leads to *desolation* (v. 11).
- Many are purified who then convert many others, but the wicked do not understand (v. 10).
- Daniel will "stand in his lot" *at the end* (v. 13).

Everything listed in this chapter is either happening now (like the purification of a holy people in this final generation), or it is still to come. With the exception of the abomination of desolation as applied to ancient Jerusalem, none of the events listed in this chapter have happened in the past. However, the abomination of desolation is given here in a chapter focused completely on end-time events.

Evidence number one for this is that the entire chapter is written in an end-time context.

Evidence number two is given in verse 11. Here, Jesus tells us of the abomination of desolation followed by a very important time prophecy.

And *from* the time *that* the daily sacrifice shall be taken away, and the **abomination that maketh desolate set up**, *there shall be a thousand two hundred and ninety days.* (Dan. 12:11)

Please don't miss this! Jesus told us of the abomination of desolation (the Sunday law that will lead to destruction) in a very end-time context in Matthew 24:15. In that verse, and in that end-time context, He sends readers back to the book of Daniel. Therefore, whenever Daniel speaks of the abomination (or transgression) of desolation, *we must understand these events in the same end-time context that Jesus gave them in.*

So, in verse 11, we have the "abomination that maketh desolate set up," and following that event (which is the coming Sunday law) there is a *1290-day time period given*. The coming Sunday law is a **timing marker** for the **beginning** of a 1290-day time period.

> *The coming Sunday law is a **timing marker** for the beginning of a 1290-day time period.*

In addition to the end-time context of Matthew 24, remember that the entire context of Daniel 12 is also end-time (that is, future), including: the time of trouble (v. 1), the deliverance of God's people (v. 1), the special resurrection (v. 2), the purification of God's people (v. 10), the Sunday Law (v. 11), and many references to the "end" of time (verses 4, 6, 7, 8, 9, and 13). We cannot take timing information and rip it out of an end-time context and place it somewhere else back in history! It must be understood in the context in which it was given.

Evidence number two tells us of a Sunday law, and a specific time period that follows it. Jesus made it clear in Matthew 24—and the context of Daniel 12 makes it clear—that this is still a future prophecy.

Daniel's questions give us **evidence number three**. Twice Daniel asks how long it will be to "the end." The first time he asks this question is in verse 6: "How long shall it be to the **end** of these wonders?"

> And at that time shall Michael stand up, the great prince which standeth for the children of thy people: and there shall be a **time of trouble, such as never was** since there was a nation *even* to that same time: and at that time **thy people shall be delivered**, every one that shall be found written in the book. And many of them that sleep in the dust of the earth **shall awake**, some to everlasting life, and some to shame *and* everlasting contempt ... And *one* said to the man clothed in linen, which *was* upon the waters of the river, How long *shall it be* **to the end** of these **wonders**? (Dan. 12:1, 2, 6)

What *wonders* are these? The Hebrew word for "wonders" actually means *miracles* (see *Strong's Exhaustive Concordance*, H8540). What wonders, or miracles, are these? What two miraculous events directly precede the question in the text? The two miraculous events given are the *deliverance of God's people* (v. 1) and the *special resurrection* (v. 2).

When do these miracles take place? The deliverance of God's people and the special resurrection take place immediately before Jesus returns. The question is: *How long until the final miracles that immediately precede Jesus' return?* In answer to this question in verse 6, Jesus gives a timing prophecy in verse 7:

> … *it shall be* for a **time, times, and an half** [time = one year, times = two years, half = half a year]; and when he shall have accomplished to scatter the power of the holy people, all these *things* shall be *finished*. (Dan. 12:7)

Jesus tells us that a time period equaling 1260 days or 3½ years ("time, times and an half") will be accomplished right up to "the *end* of *these wonders*." The *context* is unmistakable. A direct question of how much time until the *end* is immediately followed by an answer from Jesus with a specific *time* prophecy until "all these things shall be *finished*." Until *what* things shall be *finished?* What was the question that Jesus was answering? The **time** until the **deliverance of God's people** and the **special resurrection**.

Notice also that Jesus used the word "*scatter*." The scattering of God's people is the result of persecution that will begin after the enforcement of an idolatrous day of worship. God's persecuted people, aided by the power of the Holy Spirit, will be scattered around the globe, effectively spreading the three angel's messages of Jesus' love and soon return wherever they go. An example of this, in the time of the apostles, is given in Acts 8:

> And Saul was consenting unto his death. And at that time there was a *great persecution* against the church which was at Jerusalem; and they were all **scattered** abroad throughout the regions of Judaea and Samaria, except the apostles. (Acts 8:1)

The deliverance of God's people and the special resurrection are timing markers that identify the end of the 1260-day time period of persecution. *Does that mean that there is another 1260 years of persecution coming?* That is out of context of what the Bible is describing (see Matt. 24:34 and 1 Thess. 5:1–3). The *context* is 1260 days, or three and a half years. (See the discussion in the section, "What does the word 'days' mean in this context?" in Part 2 of this book for more information on the year/day concept. Pg. 70)

A *second time* Daniel asks, "How long to the end?" Verse 8 says:

> And I heard, but I understood not: then said I, O my Lord, what *shall be* the end of these *things?* (Dan. 12:8)

Jesus' answer to Daniel's question includes a timing prophecy, and, in this case, two timing prophecies are given:

And from the time *that* the daily ~~sacrifice~~ shall be taken away, and the abomination that maketh desolate set up, *there shall be* a thousand two hundred and ninety days. Blessed *is* he that waiteth, and cometh to the thousand three hundred and five and thirty days. (Dan. 12:11, 12)

In this case, the coming abomination that "maketh desolate" (the Sunday law) is the timing marker for the 1290 days that follow. Can the 1290 days be in the past? No, they can't. The question was asked, How long to the *end*? The *context* of the chapter is *end-time*, and the Sunday law is still future, as Jesus said in the Olivet Discourse while referring His readers back to Daniel. Notice also what *Strong's Exhaustive Concordance* says about the words "the end." It defines "the end" as "*extremity*" and "*border*." Therefore, these events must take place at the **extremity of time** of this world and the **border of eternity**.

The two questions asking how long to "the end" (extremity of time) make it clear that the context is still future. The Bible's three evidences are solid:

1. Daniel 12 is written in an end-time context.
2. The future abomination of desolation which Jesus and Daniel warned us about in an end-time context is a timing marker for the beginning of a 1290-day time prophecy.
3. Twice Daniel asks how long to "the end," and twice we are given end-time timing prophecies in response.

If these conclusions are correct, the Spirit of Prophecy must affirm these thoughts. Notice this statement written in 1903:

Let us read and study the twelfth chapter of Daniel. It is a **warning** that we **shall all need** to understand *before* the *time of the end*. (Letter 161, 1903; LDE 15)

Notice that she is tying the gospel chapters of Matthew 24, Mark 13, and Luke 21 together with Daniel 12 as last-day *warnings* that are critical to understand *before* the last scenes of this earth's history, or the "time of the end." She is stating them in a context future to her time, in 1903, and she is implying that we don't understand the twelfth chapter of Daniel at present. Therefore, we need to be searching for new truths!

The following statement is referring to the warning given in Matthew 24. Both Matthew 24 and Daniel 12 are *warnings* for us to study.

The time is not far distant, when, like the early disciples, we shall be *forced* to seek a refuge in desolate and solitary places. As the siege of Jerusalem by the Roman armies was the signal for flight to the Judean Christians, so the assumption of power on the part of our nation [the United States] in the *decree enforcing the papal sabbath* will be a **warning** to us. (Mar 180.2)

Notice that, in this statement, the warning is specifically tied to the passing of the Sunday law. This is definitely something that must be understood before the event happens so that we will be prepared and act accordingly. It also directly ties to her statements in the Olivet Discourse and Daniel 12 on the subject of the coming Sunday law and the events that will then transpire.

> *As the siege of Jerusalem by the Roman armies was the signal for flight to the Judean Christians, so the assumption of power on the part of our nation [the United States] in the decree enforcing the papal sabbath will be a **warning** to us.*

Daniel asks how long to the end of time (verses 6 and 8), and twice Jesus gives answers with time prophecies. The Spirit of Prophecy affirms Daniel's questions:

Twice Daniel inquired, How long shall it be to the end of time? (CTr 334.4; TM 114.6; Letter 59, 1896)

Therefore, Daniel 12 and the Spirit of Prophecy make it clear that there is a final three-and-a-half-year period of time (time, times, and a half) that are still to be fulfilled *at the extremity of time and the border of eternity.*

- "... *it shall be* for a *time, times, and an half*; and when he shall have accomplished to scatter the power of the holy people, *all these things* shall be *finished*" (Dan. 12:7).

- "The **prophetic periods** of Daniel, extending to the *very eve of the great consummation*, throw a flood of light upon events **then** to transpire" (RH, Sept. 25, 1883).

- "But ye, brethren, are not in darkness, that that day should overtake you as a thief. Ye are all the children of light, and the children of the day: we are not of the night, nor of darkness" (1 Thess. 5:4, 5).

Daniel 12 with Explanations

1. And at that *time* shall Michael [*Jesus*] stand up, the great prince which standeth for the children of thy people: and there shall be a *time* of trouble, such as never was since there was a nation *even* to that *same time*: and at *that time* thy people shall be *delivered*, every one that shall be found written in the book.

2. And many of them that sleep in the dust of the earth shall *awake*, some to everlasting *life*, and some to shame *and* everlasting *contempt*.

3. And they that *be wise* [*God's 144,000*] shall shine as the brightness of the firmament [*like Jesus*]; and they that turn many to righteousness [*under the "latter rain" and "loud cry"*] as the stars for ever and ever.

4. But thou, O Daniel, shut up the words [*close them so no one is able to understand*], and seal [*lock*] the book, *even* to the *time of the end* [*the extremity of time, the very last days*]: many shall run to and fro, and knowledge [*of the end-time time prophecies*] shall be increased.

5. Then I Daniel looked, and, behold, there stood other two [*two witnesses to what Jesus is about to say*], the one on this side of the bank of the river, and the other on that side of the bank of the river.

6. And *one* [*Daniel*] said to the man clothed in linen [*Jesus our High Priest*], which *was* upon the waters of the river, How long *shall it be to* the end of these wonders [*miracles—deliverance and special resurrection*]?

7. And I heard the man clothed in linen [*Jesus*], which *was* upon the waters of the river, when he held up his right hand and his left hand [*both hands held up means an oath with His life and blood*] unto heaven, and sware by him that liveth for ever that *it shall be* for a time, times, and an half [*3½ years, or 1260 days*]; and when he shall have accomplished to scatter [*the results of persecution*] the power of the holy people, all these *things* shall be finished [*completed with deliverance, a special resurrection, persecution, etc.*].

8. And I [*Daniel*] heard, but I understood not: then said I, O my Lord, what *shall be* the end of these *things* [*how long till the end of time*]?

9. And he said, Go thy way, Daniel: for the words *are* closed up and sealed [*locked*] till the time of the end [*the extremity of time*].

10. Many shall be purified, and made white, and tried; but the wicked

shall do wickedly: and none of the wicked shall understand; but the wise shall understand [*the end-time prophecies and the final messages to be given to the world*].

11. And from the time *that* the daily [*Jesus' ministry in the sanctuary, which is linked to the Sabbath*] ~~sacrifice~~ shall be taken away [*obscured by papal tradition and the Sunday law*], and the abomination [*transgression by way of the Sunday law*] that maketh desolate [*that leads to destruction*] set up, there shall be a thousand two hundred and ninety days [*literal 1290 days*].

12. Blessed *is* he that waiteth, and cometh to the thousand three hundred and five and thirty days [*a literal 1,335 days*].

13. But go thou thy way till the end [*the extremity of time*] be: for thou shalt rest, and stand in thy lot [*proclaim these timing messages*] at the end of the days [*during the 3½ years*].

Should We Apply the Time Periods of Daniel 12 to the Prophetic Periods of the Past?

There is no biblical authority to take the timing prophecies of Daniel 12 out of an end-time context and apply them to the past. Additionally, the time prophecies of Daniel 12 do not fit mathematically when applied to events of the past. For example, beginning with the antitypical Day of Atonement, which began in October of 1844, and using the 1335-day time period of Daniel 12:12, many try to tie 1844 to the year 508 AD when the first Arian king was overthrown by the papal power (using a day for a year). 1844 AD minus 1335 equals 509 AD. The math doesn't work out and, therefore, this cannot be a correct interpretation.

Jesus spoke of the abomination of desolation in the context of both the destruction of Jerusalem and the end-time destruction of the world. Daniel presents the abomination of desolation several times in Daniel 8 through 12, including Daniel 12:11, which we have seen is in an end-time context. Since the context of Jesus' words in Matthew 24 and the same abomination of desolation context of Daniel 12:11 must be in harmony, the time periods of Daniel 12 must be end-time.

Applying the time periods of Daniel 12 to events of the past is out of context and doesn't fit. The only interpretation that fits the context of the Bible and the Spirit of Prophecy is a future one.

But didn't our advent pioneers teach that the 1290 and 1335 days took place in the past? Yes, they did. But remember, they believed that Daniel's time prophecies came to an end in 1844, and they interpreted the prophecies to fit this understanding. This, of course, was incorrect, and so was their understanding of a number of the end-time prophecies. The new chart created in 1850 **excluded** the 1335-day prophecy!

Why was the 1335-day time prophecy, along with the year "1843" that had been in the 1843 chart, removed from the 1850 chart? John Fry warned that the year 1843, as proposed in the chart, was wrong (*Prophetic Faith of our Fathers*, vol. 3, p. 494). It is

> *they believed that Daniel's time prophecies came to an end in 1844, and they interpreted the prophecies to fit this understanding.*

important to understand that light increases as time moves on. We must not accept their mistakes once more as truth for today, but we must learn from the subsequent truths discovered. Consider the quotations below and notice how they fit with the idea of increasing light, as time goes on.

> The Lord showed me that the 1843 chart was directed by his hand, and that no part of it should be altered; that the figures were as he wanted them. That his hand was over and hid a **mistake** in **some of the figures**, so that none could see it, *until his hand was removed*. (*The Present Truth*, Nov. 1, 1850; see the 1843 chart in "Part 2: A Case for 3½ Years")

> *His hand covered a **mistake** in the reckoning of the **prophetic periods**.* (EW 235.5; 4SP 228.1; GC 373.2)

> God told Ellen G. White that a new chart was needed.
> God shewed me the necessity of getting out a chart. I saw it was needed and that the truth made plain upon tables would effect much and would cause souls to come to the knowledge of the truth. (Letter 26, 1850, Nov. 1; see the 1850 chart in "Part 2: A Case for 3½ Years")

> I saw that the *old chart* was directed by the Lord, and that not a figure of it should be altered except by inspiration. I saw that the figures of the chart were as God would have them, and that His hand was over and hid a **mistake** in **some of the figures**, so that none should see it **till** His hand was removed. (SpM 1.3, March 18, 1852)

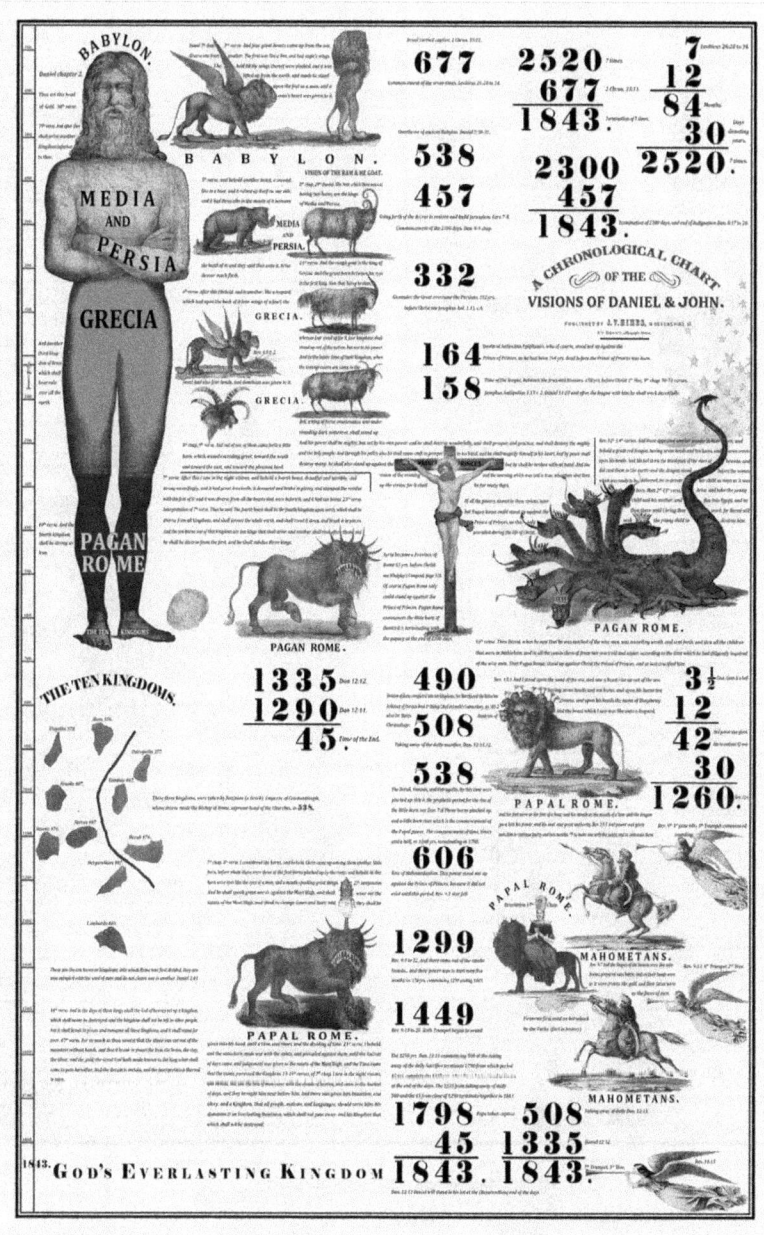

Joshua V. Himes 1843 prophecy chart

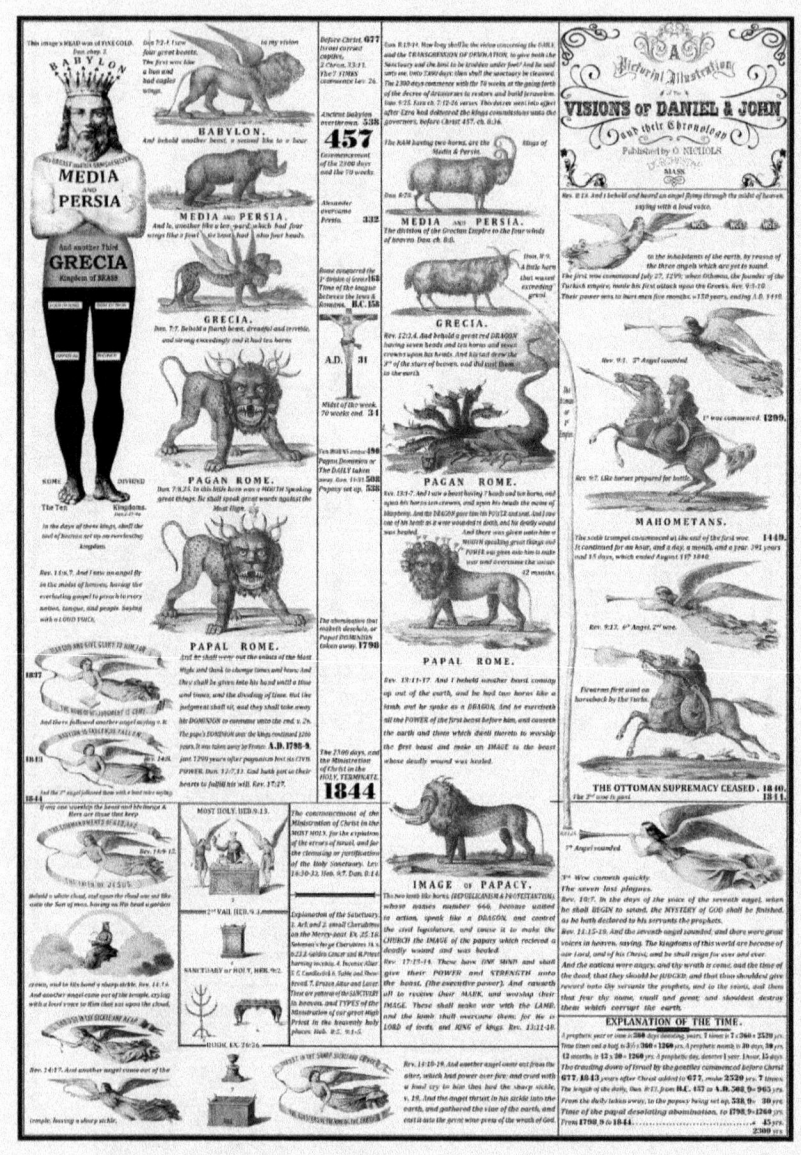

Otis Nichols' 1850 prophecy chart

God has removed His hand, and our understanding of Daniel's prophecies is increasing!

Blessed are the eyes which saw the things that were seen in 1843 and 1844. The message was given. And there should be no delay in *repeating the message*, for the signs of the times are fulfilling; the closing work must be done. A great work will be done in a short time. A *message* will **soon be given** by God's appointment that will swell into a *loud cry*. *Then* Daniel will **stand in his lot, to give his testimony**. (Letter 54, 1906)

Daniel shall stand in his lot *at the end of the days*. John sees the little book unsealed. ***Then* Daniel's prophecies have their proper place in the first, second, and third angels' messages *to be given to the world*.** The unsealing of the little book was the *message* in relation *to time*. (Ms. 59, 1900)

Notice the future tense of the last two statements above. Daniel's timing *messages* given in chapter 12 (where he is told he will "stand in thy lot at the end of the days," v. 13) *will soon be given to the world as part of the loud cry.*

Wasn't the book of Daniel unsealed in 1798? Yes, it was.

Since 1798 the book of Daniel has been unsealed. (GC 356.2)

Notice the following sequence of events that show the progression of our understanding:

- 1798 - Daniel is unsealed.

- 1843/1844 - God covered a mistake in their understanding.

- A new chart was created in 1850 that excluded a Daniel 12 timing mistake that was on the 1843 chart (the 1335 days). Daniel 12 still was not understood at that point in time.

- God is now bringing an increased understanding to His people regarding the timing of the final prophecies and the events that are just before us.

- *The Ellen G. White statements declare that a message relating to Daniel standing in his lot at the extremity of time will soon be given to the world.*

Daniel has been standing in his lot since the ***seal*** was removed and the *light of truth* has been shining upon his visions. He stands in his lot, bearing the testimony which was to be **understood at the end of the days**. (1SAT 225.5 [1893])

The seal was removed, and light has been shining on the prophecies. However, *understanding comes progressively* "at the *end* of the days" (the very extremity of time, *Strong's Exhaustive Concordance*).

By the increase of knowledge a people is to be prepared to stand in the latter days. (2SM 105.1)

What Does the Word "Days" Mean in This Context?

The word "day" can be used in many different ways. Daniel 12:11, 12, uses the Hebrew word "day" (*yôm*) that literally means "day," and the passage fits with a short three-and-one-half year end-time context. We are told that the final events will be "rapid ones," and literal days fit with that understanding.

Non-literal meanings of the Hebrew word *yôm* (day) in the Old Testament are "always found in connection with prepositions, prepositional phrases with a verb, compound constructions, formulas, technical expressions, genitive combinations, construct phrases, and the like. In other words, extended, non-literal meanings of this Hebrew term have special linguistic and contextual connections which indicate clearly that a non-literal meaning is intended. If such special linguistic connections are absent, the term *yôm* does not have an extended, non-literal meaning; it has its normal meaning of a **literal** day of 24 hours. When the word *yôm*, 'day' is employed together with a numeral, which occurs 150 times in the Old Testament, it refers in the Old Testament invariably to a literal day of 24 hours" (Gerard F. Hasel, "The 'Days' of Creation in Genesis 1: Literal 'days' or figurative 'Periods/Epochs' of time?" at https://1ref.us/jbet5).

Here are some examples of passages using a literal day with a numerical qualifier:

And the waters prevailed upon the earth an hundred and fifty *days*. (Gen. 7:24)

Prove thy servants, I beseech thee, ten *days*; and let them give us pulse to eat, and water to drink. (Dan. 1:12)

But the prince of the kingdom of Persia withstood me one and twenty *days*: but, lo, Michael, one of the chief princes, came to help me; and I remained there with the kings of Persia. (Dan. 10:13)

The word "day" (*yôm*), when used with a number in the form of a simple noun without some additional literary construct, means a literal 24-hour day. Yet, many have said that anytime you see the word "day" in prophecy, it **always** means a year. Is there any place in the Bible that gives a definition of a day for a year or a clear mandate to always use a day for a year in prophecy?

There is no text in the Bible regarding a comparison of a day for a year or some other time period except 2 Peter 3:8 which says, "But, beloved, be not ignorant of this one thing, that one day *is* with the Lord as a thousand years, and a thousand years as one day." Here the Bible equates a day with one thousand years. There is no similar definition in the Bible mandating a "day for a year" in prophecy.

Many people hang onto the two examples in Numbers 14:34 and Ezekiel 4:6. These are very clear examples of where the *context* gives clear direction to use a day for a year (or a year for a day). But there is no hint of biblical evidence that these passages say that we must *always* use a day for a year. There are examples where the context tells us that a day for a year is the correct way to interpret a passage. But there are also examples where the context tells us to interpret a day as a literal day. *There is no direct biblical mandate to assume a day means a year **every time** we see the word "day" in prophecy.*

The context of the Daniel 12 timing prophecies makes it clear that the "days" foretold must be interpreted as literal days. Are there any additional examples of literal prophetic days in the Bible that are readily accepted? There are. Consider Jonah 3:4.

> And Jonah began to enter into the city a day's journey, and he cried, and said, Yet *forty days*, and Nineveh shall be overthrown (Jonah 3:4).

This is a clear example of a time prophecy using literal days. In Jonah 4:5, we are told that Jonah went out of the city to see what would become of the city. He certainly didn't sit there for forty years! The Bible is clear. The context of a passage must determine how we interpret timing prophecies.

Does the Spirit of Prophecy Agree with a Future Context of Daniel 12?

If these conclusions regarding the *future* application of Daniel 12 are correct, the Spirit of Prophecy must affirm these thoughts. What are we told?

> The light that Daniel received from God was given especially for *these last days*. The visions he saw by the banks of the Ulai and the Hiddekel, the great rivers of Shinar, are now in the process of fulfillment, *and all the events foretold will **soon** come to pass.* (Letter 57, 1896)

The Ulai and Hiddekel visions encompass the visions of Daniel 8 to 12 (see Dan. 8:2; 10:4). When Ellen White wrote this, she said they would *soon come to pass. This is written in future context from her time*, and it was written in 1896, long after the great disappointment of October 22, 1844.

As Daniel's prayer is going forth [*in Daniel, chapter 9*], the angel Gabriel comes sweeping down from the heavenly courts to tell him that his petitions are heard and answered. This mighty angel has been commissioned to give him skill and understanding—to open before him the mysteries of future ages. Thus, while earnestly seeking to know and understand the truth, Daniel was brought into communion with Heaven's delegated messenger.

> In answer to his petition, Daniel received not only the light and truth which he and his people most needed, but *a view of* the **great events** of the **future**, even to the **advent of the world's Redeemer**. (SL 48.1, 2)

Again, she is using *future* context *from her time*, and she applies Daniel's prophecies **even to the advent of Jesus**. Additionally, this statement specifically reveals that **parts of the Daniel 9 prophecy** extend to the Second Advent!

> A wonderful connection is here seen between the universe of heaven and this world. The things revealed to Daniel were afterward complemented by the revelation made to John on the Isle of Patmos. These two books should be carefully studied. *Twice Daniel inquired,* **How long shall it be to the end of time?** ... The book of Daniel is unsealed in the revelation to John, and carries us forward to the **last scenes of this earth's history** ... *Teach these things.* (*Testimonies to Ministers*, pp. 114, 115, written in 1896)

Twice the question is asked (in Daniel 12:6, 8), "How long shall it be to the end of time?" Daniel's prophecies carry "us forward to the *last scenes* of this earth's history."

> The **prophetic periods** of Daniel, *extending* to the **very eve of the great consummation** [the second coming of Jesus], throw a flood of light upon events **then** to transpire. (RH, Sept. 25, 1883)

This verbiage is unmistakably clear. The *prophetic periods* (time prophecies) of Daniel extend to the "very eve" of the great consummation. They "throw a flood of light upon events **then** to transpire." *This is written in the context of the future from 1883.*

Daniel shall *stand* [future tense] *in his lot at the end of the days.* John sees the little book unsealed. *Then* Daniel's

> *The prophetic periods of Daniel, **extending** to the **very eve of the great consummation** throw a flood of light upon events **then** to transpire.*

prophecies have their proper place in the first, second, and third angels' messages to be given [future] to the world. (Ms. 59, 1900)

Ellen White is using language found only in Daniel 12. She links these words of Christ Himself (the man above the waters, clothed in linen, Daniel 12:7-13) to the three angels' messages that will go to the world in the future after 1900. To make sure there are no misunderstandings as to when these things apply, God instructed her to emphasize the Daniel 12 end-time theme in 1906 in the quotation below:

> A great work will be done in a short time. *A message* will soon be given by God's appointment that will swell into a loud cry. (Letter 54, 1906)

> ***Then*** Daniel will stand in his lot, *to give his testimony.* (Letter 54, 1906)

A "message" regarding 3½ years (that she did not clearly define) will swell into the loud cry. "***Then*** Daniel will stand in his lot" (Dan. 12:13). This was written in context that was to take place after the time of writing—*1906*.

> As the message of Christ's first advent announced the kingdom of His grace, so the message of His second advent announces the kingdom of His glory. And the second message, *like the first, is based on the prophecies. The words of the angel to Daniel relating to the* **last days were to be understood in the time of the end**. At that time, "many shall run to and fro, and knowledge shall be increased." "The wicked shall do wickedly: and none of the wicked shall understand; but the wise shall understand." Daniel 12:4, 10. (DA 234.4)

Ellen G. White teaches that the knowledge of God's prophecies will increase. *The context is the understanding of the wise compared to the lack of understanding of the wicked.* God's people (the wise) *will* understand.

She emphasizes this with the following statement: "… 'many shall run to and fro' (a Hebrew expression for observing and thinking upon the time), 'and *knowledge*' (regarding that time) 'shall be increased.' … Wolff, *Researches and Missionary Labors*, pages 404, 405" (GC 359.2). "The **book that was sealed** was not the book of Revelation, but *that* **portion** *of the prophecy of Daniel which related to the* **last days**" (2SM 105.1).

Note that the word "vision" is used in two different ways in Daniel 8 through 12. One Hebrew word for vision is *chazôn*, which refers to the final battle between good and evil in the last days (the future) and is the portion that was sealed (Dan. 8:26; 12:4, 9, 13). The other Hebrew word for vision is *mareh*, and it refers to the perfection of a covenant-keeping people in the last days. In Daniel 10:1, we are told that Daniel understands the *mareh* portion of the vision (2300 Days). The *chazôn* vision remained sealed.

> Daniel shall stand in his lot *at the end of the days*. **John sees the little book unsealed.** Then Daniel's prophecies have their proper place in the first, second, and third angels' messages **to be given** to the world. *The unsealing of the little book was the message in relation to time.* (Ms. 59, 1900)

"To be given to the world" is future context! **The sealed portion of the message was the *message* relative to *time*!** Daniel 8 to 12 deals with the appointed time that is still to be fulfilled in the future. (See Daniel 8:17, 19.)

So How Do the Daniel 12 Prophecies Fit Together?

Daniel 12:7 says,

> ... that it shall be for a time, times, and an half; and when he shall have accomplished to scatter the power of the holy people, all these things shall be finished.

Here we have a 1260-day time prophecy ("time, times, and an half") with information concerning an *ending* ("all these things shall be finished") but no information about a beginning. Events at the end of the time period include the deliverance of God's people and the special resurrection (verses 1, 2, and 6).

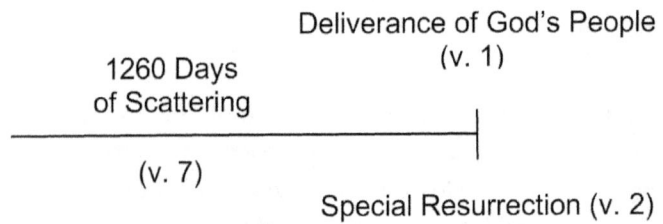

In Daniel 12:8–10, Daniel doesn't understand, and he asks for the second time how long it shall be to the "end of these things." Jesus responds saying that it was "sealed till the time of the end" (v. 9) when there would be two classes of people living in the world. There will be those who are purified, wise, and who have understanding, and there will be those who are wicked and do not understand (v. 10). Then, as Jesus' answer continues in verse eleven, He gives a second timing prophecy:

And from the time that the daily *sacrifice* shall be taken away, and the abomination that maketh desolate set up, *there shall be* a thousand two hundred and ninety days. (Dan. 12:11; "sacrifice" is stricken through because it does not occur in the original language)

Jesus is now explaining the 1260-day prophecy further by introducing a second time prophecy with additional information to add to our understanding of the events that will take place. The words "from the time" mean we have information about a *beginning*, but, in this instance, we have no information about the ending of the time prophecy. The events marking the beginning are the removing of the daily and the setting up of the abomination of desolation (v. 11).

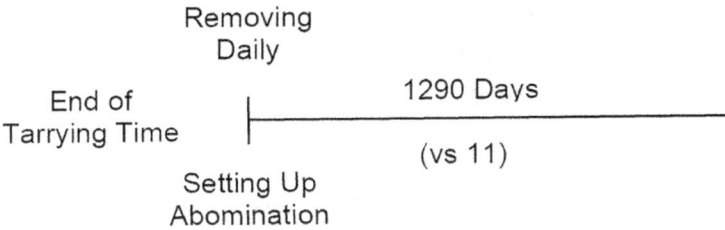

The Hebrew word used for "abomination" is *shigguwts*. This noun is always used to refer to idols that are abhorrent and detestable to God. Several texts declare: Idols are an abomination (Jer. 16:18; Ezek. 5:11; 7:20; 2 Chron. 15:8). The "daily" (*tamiyd*) is taken away by an idolatrous standard (a false day of worship) that is set up by the papacy (see discussion in the next section on the "daily" p. 77). When this happens, the 1290 days will *begin*. This idolatrous standard can be none other than the false sabbath. The promotion of Sunday worship is an attempted change of the Ten Commandments, which reflect God's character, law, authority, and the keys to His everlasting covenant.

At this point, we have a beginning for the 1290 days and an ending for the 1260 days. Through verse 11, other than the lengths of time, it is unknown how far apart or close together these periods are.

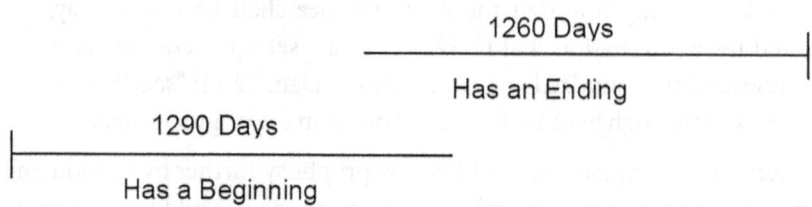

The 1290 days begin with the Sunday laws. The 1260 days ends with the deliverance of God's people and the special resurrection. Therefore, the 1290-day prophecy must begin before the 1260-day prophecy, but we need more information to understand the timing between them.

Jesus now "fills in the gap." Verse 12 is a beatitude with promise. However, the blessing is tied to a time period that has neither a beginning nor an ending. Those who wait for all these events and remain faithful through them, covering *1335 days*, will be blessed. Tying the 1260 days (which have an ending) to the *end* of the 1335 days and tying the 1290 days (which has a beginning) to the *beginning* of the 1335 days solves the puzzle. No other combination makes sense with the evidence we are given. The *beginning* of the 1290 days and the *ending* of the 1260 days are *1335 days apart*.

Why is this the only way that makes sense of these time periods? Because there must be a Sunday law (removal of the "daily") before persecution (the scattering) can result from the Sunday law. The Sunday law and its 1290-day time period must begin before we have the scattering and persecution of the 1260 days.

Why do the 1335 days carry a blessing? Isn't that a time of terrible persecution? Yes, it is. But it is also the time when God's people will perfectly reflect God's character, and their connection with Jesus during that time will be a perfect moment-by-moment connection that cannot be broken. It will be like a honeymoon with Jesus. It will be the most intimate connection with Jesus we have ever had.

> It is impossible to give any idea of the experience of the people of God who shall be alive upon the earth when celestial glory and a repetition of the persecutions of the past are blended. They will walk in the light proceeding from the throne of God. By means of the angels there will be constant communication between heaven and earth. (9T 16.1)

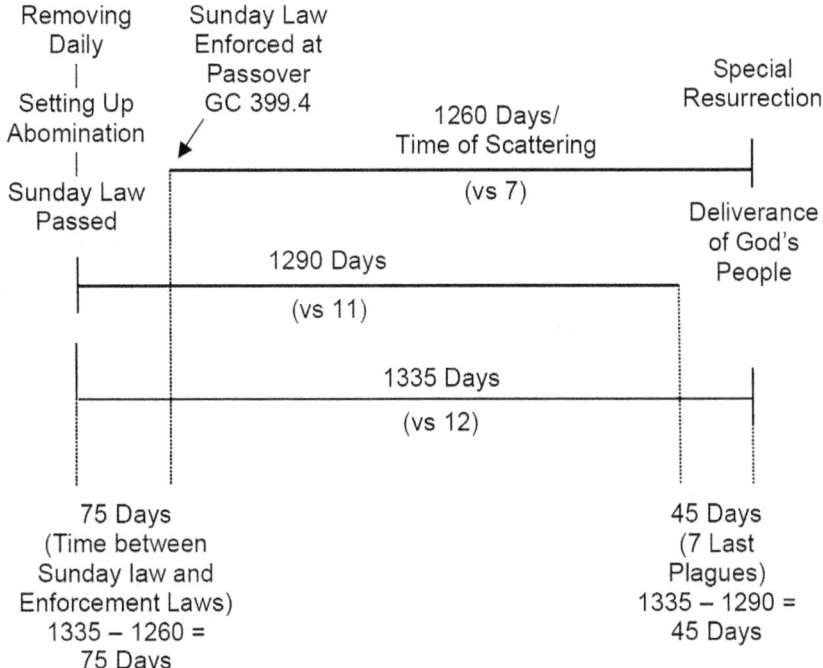

Please note that a date for the return of Christ has not been set by this prophecy but only the time of deliverance for God's people. No man knows the day or the hour of Christ's return. However, from *Early Writings*, pp. 14, 15, we do know that the day and the hour will be announced!

> Soon we heard the voice of God like many waters, which gave us the day and hour of Jesus' coming. (EW 14.1)

> *No man knows the day or the hour of Christ's return.*

What Is the "Daily"?

And from the time *that* the ***daily sacrifice*** shall be taken away, and the abomination that maketh desolate set up, *there shall be* a thousand two hundred and ninety days. (Dan. 12:11)

The Hebrew word *tamiyd*, translated "daily," means "continual" or "perpetual." In most of the Old Testament, this word is used as a descriptive adjective, referring to the morning and evening burnt offering. But here it is used as a noun, which is something that is "taken away" and replaced by something evil (see also Daniel 8:11 and 11:31). The word "sacrifice" was added to the verse and only adds confusion in understanding the message, as Ellen White observed.

Then I saw in relation to the "daily" (Daniel 8:12) that the word "sacrifice" was supplied by man's wisdom, and does not belong to the text. (EW 74.2)

The Hebrew word *tamiyd* is used in a variety of ways:

- *Tamiyd* is used for the showbread of continuity, or continual presence of God (Exod. 25:30; Lev. 24:8; 2 Chron. 2:4; Num. 4:7). The showbread symbolizes God's presence on His throne. This symbolizes God's presence that was renewed each Sabbath.

- *Tamiyd* is used to indicate the perpetual light from the golden candlesticks (Lev. 24:3, 4; Exod. 27:20, 21). This symbolizes God's perpetual presence through His Holy Spirit.

- *Tamiyd* is used to represent the continual burning of incense at the altar of incense (Exod. 30:7, 8). This symbolizes Jesus' mediatorial work and His atoning blood ever pleading for man.

- *Tamiyd* is associated with the continual presence of God in the cloud and fire above the tabernacle (Num. 9:16).

What does the "little horn," or the "king of the north," do to take away, or remove, the heavenly presence from the tabernacle? (See 2 Thess. 2:3–8.)

- He opposeth and exalteth himself above all that is called God.
- He is as God.
- He functions as if he were sitting in the temple of God.
- He has deceivableness of unrighteousness.
- His followers don't receive the love of the truth.
- He and the wicked will be revealed.
- The mystery of iniquity will be taken out of the way.
- Then Jesus will come.

God's work of providing light, intercession, and life *is taken away*. Jesus' work on man's behalf, His righteousness in the incense, and His cleansing blood are *blocked* from working on men's hearts. The "little horn," which is the "king of the north" and the papacy, *blocks God's law* from being written in the heart (Jer. 31:33; Heb. 8:10).

In place of the lifesaving presence of God, man's presence and power are appealed to through *artificial standards* and *claims*. The papacy's (the "little horn's") agents *try* to forgive sins, crucify Jesus over and over in the eucharist, claim salvation through an earthly organization, and attempt to exchange God's Sabbath day of worship for a *false day of worship*. The *papacy* (the "little horn," or the "king of the north") has changed so many of God's laws and biblical principles by *tradition* (with much of that tradition coming from pagan roots) that God can no longer dwell in the sanctuary (meaning the church and the heart) (see *Strong's Exhaustive Concordance* on the word "sanctuary" in Daniel 8:13).

By contrast, the shewbread was refreshed every Sabbath morning, representing the renewal of God's presence and provision. The twelve loaves, representing each of the twelve tribes, symbolized God's continual relationship and presence among them. The Sabbath became a symbol of the day His presence was refreshed among His people.

What is man's continual reminder of God's promise to restore man?

> Wherefore the children of Israel shall keep the sabbath, to observe the sabbath throughout their generations, *for* a perpetual covenant. (Exod. 31:16, emphasis original)

The "daily," in the Daniel 12 context, refers specifically to the Sabbath as God's perpetual refreshing presence (which has been replaced by an abomination). The Sabbath is a continual reminder of God's power and promise to complete the everlasting, or perpetual, covenant with us—God's spiritual Israel (see Exod. 31:13, 16, 17; Lev. 24:8; Ezek. 20:12).

Signs Leading to the Removal of the "Daily"

How close are we to the removal of the daily? When will the abomination that leads to desolation of the world be instituted? When will the Sunday law be enforced? These are all the same question, and there are a number of signs that make it clear that this event is just around the corner. Each of these signs, or events, can be studied in detail. The signs described briefly below deserve deep and prayerful study so that we are not caught unawares.

The Second Rise of the Papacy—Seven Heads (Rev. 17:10)

> And there are seven kings: five are fallen, and one is, *and* the other is not yet come; and when he cometh, he must continue a short space. (Rev. 17:10)

As most students of prophecy know, the papacy received a "deadly wound" in 1798 when General Berthier took Pope Pius VI captive. Many students of prophecy do not realize, however, that new popes were elected and the papacy lived on. The *completion of the deadly wound* didn't occur until 1870 when the Italian army under General Cadorna captured Rome on September 20, 1870. The Papal States were confiscated, and the Catholic Church was reduced to an ecclesiastical body. *Its civil power was broken.*

On February 11, 1929, Benito Mussolini, Prime Minister of Italy, on behalf of King Victor Emmanuel III and Cardinal Pietro Gasparri, Secretary of State for Pope Pius XI, signed three Lateran Accords. This restored the Church-State union. *The Vatican City State was formed, and its civil power was restored.*

From 1929 to February 28, 2013, there were seven popes (symbolized by heads that represented kings). The sixth "king" that "is" was Pope John Paul II, and the seventh "king" that reigned for a short time was Pope Benedict XVI.

The Second Rise of the Papacy—"the Eighth" (Rev. 17:11)

And the *beast* that was, and is not, even he is the eighth, and is of the seven, and goeth into perdition. (Rev. 17:11)

The symbol of the eighth is tied to the **beast** power **and** its rise during the time of the **seven kings**. This eighth power therefore represents the Holy See, which is a combination of both the papal power **and** the pope(s) that lead the church after Pope Benedict XVI.

The Holy See is the eighth and final power presented before it goes into perdition (Rev. 19:20; 20:10). There are no more powers after this eighth power. We are living in the extreme time of the end.

Key Point: The "eighth" is not identified as a "head" but as "the beast"! We are living in the time of the beast!

The Second Rise of the Papacy—the Ten Horns or Kings (Rev. 17:12, 13)

And the ten horns which thou sawest are ten kings, which have received no kingdom as yet; but receive power as kings one hour with the beast. These have one mind, and shall give their power and strength unto the beast. (Rev. 17:12, 13)

Horns usually represent kings, or kingdoms, who give their authority, or power, to the beast they are on (see Dan. 7:24). They can also represent groups of people (see Dan 8:8).

The picture described in Revelation 17:12, 13 takes place before the horns have received their crowns, or power. Revelation 13:1 shows the ten horns when they have received crowns (that is, the power to rule) and what happens in our world at that point in time.

"Ten" represents fullness or completion. These ten powers shall give their support and power to the beast. The "Club of Rome" and the United Nations have divided the world into ten divisions:

This map shows the divisions as proposed by the "Club of Rome," reported in "Regionalized and Adaptive Model of the Global World System," September 17, 1973, at https://1ref.us/jbet2.

United Nations Millennium Development Goals Report 2009 10 Regional Groups

- Developed regions
- Countries of the Commonwealth of Independent States (CIS)
- Northern Africa
- Sub-Saharan Africa
- South-Eastern Asia
- Oceania
- Eastern Asia
- Southern Asia
- Western Asia
- Latin America & the Caribbean

This report presents data on progress towards the Millennium Development Goals for the world as a whole and for various country groupings. A complete list of countries included in each region and subregion is available at https://1ref.us/jbet6.

This map shows the divisions as proposed by the United Nations, at https://1ref.us/jbet3.

See the link above for a full report on "The Millennium Development Goals Report 2009" by the United Nations. You will find this map on page 55 of that report. Notice in the referenced document above that 2015 was the target date for achieving their goals.

So, what does the final timeline of events look like?

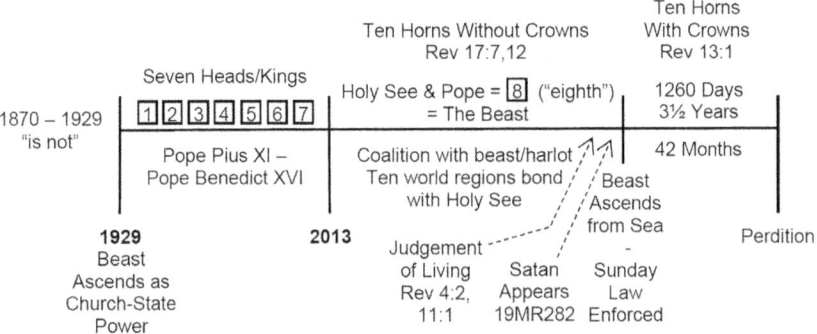

What other signs are there that show us that the removal of the "daily" and the beginning of the 1260 days are imminent?

- The preparation of the saints to announce Christ's coming to the sleeping virgins and the world (Matt. 25:6)
- The early rain experience of the 144,000 before the Sunday laws preparing them to give the final message (Rev. 10; 11; 6:1, 2)
- Growing opposition to Christians—restriction of religious liberty (2 Tim. 3:1–5)
- An outcry against the declining morals of society (GC 587.1)
- The world wondering after the beast (Rev. 17:8, 12, 13)
- Growing support for the Ten Commandments and religious laws (Matt. 24:15; Dan. 8, 9, 11, 12)
- Leaders pointing to calamities as judgments (Ms. 85, 1899)
- Economic problems (GC 590.1)
- A unified Protestant movement (GC 588.1)
- Division within the remnant church (LDE 172.3; 175.2)
- Satan appearing as an angel of light (Ms. 153, 1902)

Each of these signs is in the process of being fulfilled and can be fulfilled at any moment. We have no time to lose. Each of us must earnestly seek to prepare for the work we have to do so that we may stand during the time of trouble and be prepared to meet our God.

Why is knowing all this important?

God is love!
- God ***loves*** us so much that He wants us to *understand* all that is going to happen so that we have the opportunity to be prepared to *stand for Jesus* during earth's darkest hour. Once we understand the timing of the final events, we can *mentally* and *spiritually prepare* for the trials and the mission that is before us (2SM 105.2–106.2).

- He ***loves*** us and wants us to *prepare* so that He can work through us to *save* as many people as possible.

- He ***loves*** us and wants us to *understand* that Daniel 8 to 12 and Revelation contain the most *solemn warning* ever given to our world. It will be the *last chance* the world has to *accept Jesus* and spend eternity with Him.

In response to God's love for all of us and our love for Him and His people, God is pleading with us to—

- ***eat*** (study and understand) the little open book found in Daniel 8 to 12 (Rev. 10:9),

- ***prophesy again*** (teach Daniel and Revelation) to all peoples, nations, tongues, and kings (Rev. 10:11),

- ***proclaim*** that the judgment of the living has come and call for people to worship the true God. The choice that you make for or against the true God will determine your destiny! (Rev 11:1; 14:7),

- ***proclaim*** that "Babylon has fallen"! The Holy See has made all nations believe in her falsehoods (Rev. 14:8),

- ***warn*** the world that, if they worship the Holy See by keeping Sunday Holy and believe what the Holy See teaches or just go along with what the Holy See says, they will receive the "mark of the beast." Then they will suffer the seven last plagues and be eternally separated from God (Rev. 14:9–11),

- ***call*** everyone to "come out of her my people" (Rev. 18:4).

He loves you! He loves ALL people and doesn't want anyone to be lost. Therefore, we need to study and prepare like never before.

I saw that many were neglecting the preparation so needful and were looking to the time or "refreshing" and the "latter rain" to fit them to stand in the day of the Lord and to live in His sight. Oh, how many I saw in the time of trouble without a shelter! They had neglected the needful preparation; therefore they could not receive the refreshing that all must have to fit them to live in the sight of a holy God. (EW 71.2)

> *He loves you! He loves ALL people and doesn't want anyone to be lost. Therefore, we need to study and prepare like never before.*

We have no time for dwelling on matters that are of no importance. Our time should be given to proclaiming the last message of mercy to a guilty world. *Men are needed who move under the inspiration of the Spirit of God.* The sermons preached by some of our ministers will have to be much more powerful than they are now, or many backsliders will carry a tame, pointless message, which lulls people to sleep. Every discourse should be given under a sense of the awful judgments *soon* to fall on the world. The *message of truth* is to be proclaimed by lips touched with a live coal from the divine altar. (8T 36.3)

Part 3: No Prophetic Time After 1844?

Many have said that there are no more time prophecies after 1844. Are we sure this is correct? Consider the future time elements in the following:

And he laid hold on the dragon, that old serpent, which is the Devil, and Satan, and bound him a *thousand years*, and cast him into the bottomless pit, and shut him up, and set a seal upon him, that he should deceive the nations no more, till the *thousand years* should be *fulfilled*: and after that he must be loosed a little season. (Rev. 20:2, 3)

Then will take place the *final fulfillment* of the Revelator's prophecy. [Revelation 13:4–18, quoted.] (Ms. 153, 1902)

The *prophetic periods* of Daniel, extending to the *very eve of the great consummation* … (RH, Sept. 25, 1883)

There is no excuse for any one in taking the position that there is no more truth to be revealed, and that all our expositions of Scripture are without an *error*. (RH, Dec. 20, 1892)

Let all prove their positions from the Scriptures and substantiate every point they claim as truth from the revealed Word of God. (Letter 12, 1890)

Doesn't Ellen G. White Say There Are No Time Prophecies after 1844?

Time has not been a *test* since 1844, and it will never again be a *test*. The Lord has shown me that the message of the third angel must go, and be proclaimed to the scattered children of the Lord, but it must not be hung on time. *I saw that some were getting a false excitement, arising from preaching time*; but the third angel's message is stronger than time can be. I saw that this message can stand on its own foundation and needs not time to strengthen it; and that it will go in mighty power, and do its work, and will be cut short in righteousness. (EW 75.1)

At first glance, it appears that those who have contested the times of Daniel 12 in a future application are correct. But ask yourself some questions: What is the context of what Ellen White was writing? What type of test is she referring to? What was happening at the time of her writing that led to such statements?

To understand the answers to these questions, we must study the context of this statement and others like it. Begin by studying the first three paragraphs of the chapter entitled, "The Gathering Time," on page 74 and 75 of *Early Writings*, and then read "William Miller's Dream," on pages 81 to 83.

Before 1844, there was great unity among God's people. Following the Great Disappointment there was "darkness and confusion," and God's people were scattered. A variety of errors sprang up involving issues like the daily and spiritualism. Additionally, new dates for the coming of Jesus were set. Time and time again Ellen G. White had to explain why a date for Christ's return was allowed to be preached and that *never again would a date or time for Jesus' return be set* in the future of prophecy *for the purpose of testing His people*. She explained that the continued preaching of the 3rd angel based on a "time" of Jesus' return was causing a "false excitement" *(see quote above)*, and she wrote against this practice on many occasions in an effort to prevent further harm to the cause of God. The context of the issue concerns the setting of a "*time*" for the *return of Jesus*.

Study the explanations given regarding "*time*" in the following quotations for a clearer understanding:

Yet God accomplished His own beneficent purpose in permitting the warning of the judgment to be given just as it was [regarding Jesus coming in 1844]. The great day was at hand, and in His providence the people were brought **to the test of a definite time**, in order to reveal to them what was in their hearts. The message was designed for the testing and purification of the church. They were to be led to see whether their affections were set upon this world or upon Christ and heaven. They professed to love the Saviour; now they were to prove their love. **Were** *they ready to renounce their worldly hopes and ambitions, and* welcome with joy the **advent of their Lord**? The message was designed to enable them to discern their true spiritual state; it was sent in mercy to arouse them to seek the Lord with *repentance* and *humiliation*. (GC 353.1)

When called to endure the scoffs and reproach of the world, and the **test of a delay** and disappointment, would they renounce the faith? Because they did not immediately understand the dealings of God with them, would they cast aside truths sustained by the clearest testimony of His word? (GC 353.2)

The proclamation of a **definite time for Christ's coming** called forth great opposition from many of all classes … (GC 370.1)

It had been God's purpose to conceal the future and to bring His people to a point of decision. Without the preaching of **definite time for the coming of Christ**, *the work designed of God would not have been accomplished*. Satan was leading very many to look far in the future for the great events connected with the judgment and the end of probation. It was necessary that the people be brought to seek earnestly for a present preparation. (EW 246.2)

The message that God sent for the **testing** and purification of the church revealed all too surely how great was the number who had set their affections *on this world* rather than upon **Christ**. (GC 380.1)

Again and again have I been warned in regard to time-setting. There will never again [after 1844] be a message for the people of God that will be based on time. *We are not to know the **definite time** either for the **outpouring of the Holy Spirit** or **for the coming of Christ***. (RH, March 22, 1892)

Notice her definition of *what type of time* she was referring to. She is referring to the *time* of the "outpouring of the Holy Spirit" and the *time* of "the coming of Christ." She was *not* saying that there would be no more prophetic time *for other events* in the future!

It is not in the providence of God that any finite man shall, by any device or reckoning that he may make of figures, or of symbols, or of types, know with any *definiteness* in regard to the very period of the **Lord's coming**. (Ms. 9, 1891)

No one has a true message *fixing the time when Christ is to come* or not to come. Be assured that God gives no one authority to say that Christ delays His coming five years, ten years, or twenty years. "Be ye also ready: for in such an hour as ye think not the Son of man cometh" (Matthew 24:44). This is our message, the very message that the three angels flying in the midst of heaven are proclaiming. The work to be done now is that of sounding this last message of mercy to a fallen world. A new life is coming from heaven and taking possession of all God's people. But divisions will come in the church. Two parties will be developed. The wheat and tares grow up together for the harvest. (2SM 113.3)

The proclamation of Jesus' coming used the **time of Christ's return** as a test for the people of God in 1844! A major part of their focus and experience was *the time* of the return of Christ. Ellen G. White says a date for Jesus' return will *not* be a testing point ever again. But she does say what time of year the return of Christ will be.

These types were fulfilled [by the crucifixion and resurrection], not only as to the event, but as to the ***time***....

In like manner the types which relate to the second advent must be fulfilled at the ***time*** pointed out in the symbolic service. (GC 399.3, 4)

Ellen G. White is here pointing out that the return of Christ must be fulfilled at the ***time*** pointed out in the symbolic service. The great *Day of Atonement* occurs in the *fall* and that is the ***time*** of year that Jesus will return.

Soon we heard the voice of God like many waters, *which gave us* ***the day and hour of Jesus' coming***. (EW 14.1)

Isn't this a time prophecy of the day and the hour of Jesus' return? It certainly is! But it won't be a "test of time" for us at that point, and therefore it is in harmony with Ellen G. White statements. Yet it is an example of the fact that there are still timing prophecies to be fulfilled.

In *Early Writings* (as quoted above), we are told that God will tell us the day and hour of His coming, and that we will experience a time of deliverance when the wicked can no longer harm us. "***Soon***" after that *time* we will witness the return of Christ. There is no explanation of how much time we will have on this earth between our deliverance and Jesus' return. We will have to wait to find this out. A clearer example of time still to be fulfilled is Revelation 20:2–5. No one can deny that this is a time prophecy that is yet to be fulfilled!

More powerful than the words of God's servant are the words of God's Word. Study the underlying meanings of the words in Daniel 8:17 and Daniel 8:19 carefully. "… for at the *time of the end* shall be the vision" (v. 17) and "… I will make thee *know* what shall be in the last *end* of the indignation: for at the *time appointed* the *end* shall be" (v. 19). These verses clearly point to an **appointed time**, at the time of **indignation** (God's wrath, in the trumpets and plagues) at the **end** (H7093, defined in Strong's Concordance as "extremity of time"), right before Jesus' return. In addition, it says, "***I will make thee know* …**" We will know about this appointed time and what will happen then! As we will see later in this book, Daniel 8:17 and 8:19 directly relate to the time periods given in Daniel 12, and the context of Daniel 12 is clearly written in an "end-time" context, using a term that means the "extremity of time." Chapter 12 discusses the *final deliverance*, the *resurrection*, the *purification of God's people*, the *conversion of many*, *questions concerning time remaining*, and the *time of the end statements*, among other things. In addition, these verses, given in a very end-time context, contain timing prophecies. None of these prophecies pinpoint the timing for Jesus' return. Only God knows how long the delay will be between the end of these time frames and His coming. **There is no "definite time" or "test of time"** concerning a date for the return of Christ given in these passages.

> The words of the angel to Daniel relating to the **last days** were to be understood **in the time of the end.** At that time, "many shall run to and fro, and knowledge shall be increased." "The wicked shall do wickedly: and none of the wicked shall understand; but the wise shall understand." Daniel 12:4, 10. (DA 234.4)

> The message itself [Rev. 14:6, 7] sheds light as to the time when this movement is to take place. It is declared to be a part of the "everlasting gospel:" and it announces the opening of the judgment. The message of salvation has been preached in all ages; but this message is a part of the gospel which could be proclaimed only in the last days, for only then would it be true that the hour of judgment had come. The prophecies present a succession of events leading down to the opening of the judgment. This is especially true of the book of Daniel. **But that** part of his prophecy which related to the last days, **Daniel was bidden to close up and seal "to the time of the end."** (GC 355.3)

Note that in Daniel 8:17 and 12:9, *eth qets* is Hebrew for "extremity of time." We are now living at the time of the end, and the prophecies declare that understanding about the final events of Daniel and Revelation is being opened up to us. "… and knowledge shall be increased" (Dan. 12:4). God is faithful!

Progressive Revelation of Ellen G. White's Teachings and Our Prophetic Understanding

Everyone born on this planet grows in their understanding and wisdom as time marches on. This fact applied to Adam and Eve, Jesus Himself, our founders including Ellen White, and the Remnant church as a whole. We must never say that we understand everything perfectly.

> And Jesus increased in **wisdom** and stature, and in favour with God and man. (Luke 2:52)

> Each period of the fulfillment of prophetic history is a **preparation** for the **advanced light** which will succeed each period. As the prophecy comes to the end, there is to be a **perfect whole**. (Letter 8, 1895)

As we grow, we then discover that some of the things that we thought we understood were in reality off course or incomplete. When that discovery is made, then we need to "unlearn" those things that were off course or incomplete and follow that which is truth.

> We have many lessons to learn, and *many*, **many to unlearn**. (TM 30.2)

We need to "unlearn" those things that were off course or incomplete and follow that which is truth.

As our pioneers passed the evening of the Great Disappointment, it became apparent that a new understanding had to come to prophecy. The meaning of the 2300 years was soon opened to them. It would be several years before they would understand that the "time periods" of Daniel 12 had been misunderstood. At that time, in 1850, Ellen G. White commissioned the creation of a new prophetic chart to replace the 1843 chart.

> The Lord showed me that the 1843 chart was directed by his hand, and that no part of it should be altered; that the figures were as he wanted them. That his hand was over and hid a ***mistake in some of the figures***, so that none could see it, *until* his hand was removed. (*Present Truth*, Nov. 1, 1850)

*His hand covered a **mistake** in the reckoning of the **prophetic periods**.* (EW 235.3; 4SP 228.1; GC 373.2)

God shewed me the necessity of getting out a chart. I saw it was needed and that the truth made plain upon tables would effect much and would cause souls to come to the knowledge of the truth. (Letter 26, 1850, Nov. 1)

The new chart changed the year "1843," as the end of the 2300-day prophecy, to "1844," and it eliminated the 1335 days of Daniel 12. Why was the 1335 days excluded from the 1850 chart? I would suggest that it was because they didn't understand it, and God's people wouldn't understand it until many years after God revealed to Ellen White that we would have an increase in understanding of Daniel 12. In 1863, the General Conference voted to develop a new and improved prophetic chart. None of the Daniel 12 timing was included. (See the 1843 and 1850 charts in "Part 2: A Case for 3½ Years." p. 54)

After 1850, there was prophetic silence for many years. God had other truths to open to these new Advent believers. The Sabbath and church organization, among others, were areas to discover and learn about.

In 1883, there was an isolated message given to Ellen G. White that the "time periods of Daniel" (looking *beyond* 1883) would go right up to the "eve of the great consummation." She was referring to Daniel 12.

The **prophetic periods** of Daniel, extending to the **very eve of** the *great consummation*, throw a flood of light upon events **then** to transpire. (RH, Sept. 25, 1883)

Time passed until the 1888 message of "Righteousness by Faith" came into our church against great opposition. At about the same time, God began to reveal amazing new truths to Ellen G. White. Between this time and 1906 she received significant new light that is critical to, and affirming of, our understanding of end time prophecy. These are just a few examples:

Increased light **will shine** upon **all** the grand truths of **prophecy**, and they **will be seen** in freshness and brilliancy, because the bright beams of the Sun of Righteousness **will illuminate the whole**. (Ms. 18, 1888, in 3SM 390)

[There are] great and solemn events which *we must know* as we stand on the very threshold of their fulfillments. (Ms. 32, 1896)

Daniel shall stand in his lot *at the end of the days*. **John sees the little book unsealed**. Then Daniel's prophecies have their proper place in the first, second, and third angels' messages **to be given** to the world. *The unsealing of the little book was the message in **relation to time**.* (Ms. 59, 1900)

Let us read and study the *twelfth chapter of Daniel*. It is a **warning** that we **shall** all need to understand *before the time of the end*. (Letter 161, 1903; LDE 15)

A message will soon be given by God's appointment that will swell into the loud cry. **Then** Daniel will *stand in his lot*, to give his testimony. (Letter 54, 1906)

In relation to these messages, God led her to write a very firm and eye-opening warning in 1892:

> *Let us read and study the twelfth chapter of Daniel. It is a **warning** that we **shall** all need to understand before the time of the end.*

> **There is no excuse for any one in taking the position** that there is no more truth to be revealed, **and** that all our expositions of Scripture are **without an error.** The fact that certain doctrines have been held as truth for many years by our people, is **not a proof that our ideas are infallible.** Age will not make error into truth, and truth can afford to be fair. No true doctrine will lose anything by close investigation. (RH, Dec. 20, 1892)

> *Age will not make error into truth, and truth can afford to be fair. No true doctrine will lose anything by close investigation.*

Understanding the progressive revelation of prophetic information given to Ellen G. White helps in great measure to understand the truth God is revealing.

It also reveals a source of a lot of misunderstanding. Once this becomes clear, we can much more easily correct our path in these previously uncharted waters.

Because we are constantly learning and we have been directly told that we have things to unlearn, we must diligently search for those things that are incorrect, and we must correct our course where necessary.

A spirit of Phariseeism has been coming in upon the people who claim to believe the truth for these last days. They are self-satisfied. They have said, 'We have the truth. There is no more light for the people of God.' But *we are not safe when we take a position that we* *will not accept **anything else** than that upon which we have settled as truth. We should take the Bible, and investigate it closely for ourselves.* We should dig in the mine of God's word for truth. (RH, June 18, 1889)

Whenever the people of God are growing in grace, they will be **constantly** *obtaining a clearer understanding of His word.* ***They will discern new light and beauty in its sacred truths.*** This has been true in the history of the church in all ages, and thus it will continue to the end. But as real spiritual life declines, it has ever been the tendency to cease to advance in the knowledge of the truth. (GW 297.2)

New light means that it is new! Therefore, we must be looking for things that are in error, we must correct our course, *and* we must look for things that Ellen White did not already write about.

Increased light will shine upon all the grand truths of prophecy, and they will be seen in freshness and brilliancy because the bright beams of the Sun of Righteousness will illuminate the whole. (Ms. 18, 1888)

[Daniel 12:8, 9, 4, 10, 13 quoted.] The time has come for Daniel to *stand in his lot.* The time has come for the light given him to go to the world as never before. If those for whom the Lord has done so much will walk in the light, *their knowledge of Christ and the prophecies relating to Him will be **greatly increased*** as they near the *close* of this earth's history. (Ms. 176, 1899)

Comparing Quotation with Quotation—the End of the "Prophetic Periods"

We are encouraged, when studying our Bibles, to compare scripture with scripture to accurately understand the complete truth about what the Bible teaches on a given subject. The Bible itself tells us: "For precept *must be* upon precept, precept upon precept; line upon line, line upon line; here a little, *and* there a little" (Isa. 28:10). Furthermore, the Bible says, "To the law and to the testimony: if they speak not according to this word, *it is* because *there is* no light in them" (Isa. 8:20). As an example, we are told that, "When he [William Miller] found anything obscure, it was his custom to **compare it with every other text** which seemed to have any reference to the matter under consideration" (4SP 204.2). Do we still study this way?

When we study the writings of Ellen G. White, do we implement the same principles and compare quotation with quotation? If we did, there would likely be little or no difficulty in anyone's mind about the final fulfillment of prophecy in the future. Why? Let's look at a couple of examples.

Plugging the phrase "definite time" into an Ellen G. White search engine, we find that the phrase appears ninety-eight times. Reading each one reveals that the quote applies to three subjects. (1) In one instance, she encourages us to have a "definite time" for prayer. (2) In eight other instances, we are told that we are not to know the "definite time" for the outpouring of the Holy Spirit. (3) In every other case where the phrase "definite time" is used, it refers to a definite time (or date) *for the second coming of Jesus*. Notice the following example:

> Many who have called themselves Adventists have been time-setters. Time after time has been set for Christ to come, but repeated failures have been the result. *The **definite time** of our Lord's coming is declared to be beyond the ken of mortals.* Even the angels, who minister unto those who shall be heirs of salvation, know not the day nor the hour. "But of that day and hour knoweth no man, no, not the angels of heaven, but My Father only."—*Testimonies for the Church* 4:307 (1879). (LDE 32.3)

In another example, as we search for the phrase "time no longer" (which comes from Rev. 10:6), we discover that the phrase shows up *seven times* in the search results (besides its use as a title). Each time the phrase is mentioned in the text, we are told in the very next sentence, "This message announces the end of the prophetic periods." Many have used this to say that the "prophetic periods" ended in 1844 and that there are no more time prophecies after 1844. Are we sure that that is what she means? It is true that, of the 104 times the phrase "prophetic periods" shows up in a search, the vast majority of the instances relates to the 2300-day prophecy, which *did end* in 1844. Said in a different way, when we compare all the statements containing this phrase, the *context* is about the ending of the prophetic periods relating to Daniel 8:14, which pointed to the final phase of Jesus' ministry in the Most Holy Place, beginning in 1844. With only a few exceptions, that is the context. One fascinating exception is when the "prophetic periods" have to do with the fall of the Ottoman empire in August of 1840 (GC88 334.4). Another exception is in searching for the term "prophetic period" in the singular. The singular term pops up twenty-five times *and* refers to "a different portion of the same great prophetic period" (GC 351.1) of Daniel 8:14, pointing to the advent of our Messiah in the 70-week prophecy of Daniel 9 (DA 98.4). Are there any other "prophetic periods" mentioned? Are the three timing events we have mentioned *all* that Ellen G. White has said about "prophetic periods"? There is one other. Notice the future context of this passage as you read.

> In the Scriptures are presented truths that relate especially to our own time. To the *period just prior to the appearing of the Son of man*, the prophecies of Scripture point, and *here* their warnings and threatenings pre-eminently apply. The **prophetic periods** of Daniel, *extending to the very eve of the great consummation*, throw a flood of light upon events *then* to transpire. The book of Revelation is *also* replete with warning and instruction for the *last generation*. The beloved John, under the inspiration of the Holy Spirit, portrays the fearful and thrilling scenes connected with the *close of earth's history*, and presents the duties and dangers of God's people. None need remain in ignorance, none need be unprepared for the coming of the day of God. (RH, Sept. 25, 1883)

> *The prophetic periods of Daniel, extending to the very eve of the great consummation, throw a flood of light upon events then to transpire.*

In summary, when we compare statement with statement, the context of Ellen White's words becomes clear. The words "definite time" (and other similar phrases) show that the context of the passages is primarily about *not* setting a specific date for the return of Jesus. When we see the phrase "prophetic periods" or "prophetic period," the context relates to one of the following time frames:

- The end of the 2300 days, which point to the beginning of the final phase of Jesus' high priestly ministry in 1844
- The timing of the advent of our Messiah in the 70-week prophecy
- The fall of the Ottoman Empire in 1840
- The prophetic periods of Daniel that "relate especially to our own time" to "the period just prior to the appearing of the Son of man" (RH, Sept. 25, 1883).

We now know with certainty that the prophetic periods of Daniel 12, given in a future context, extend to the very eve of the great consummation. These timing messages and other related passages are the "end of the

Part 3: No Prophetic Time After 1844? 97

prophetic periods" that are to be proclaimed. "New light" is certainly shining on all the "grand truths of prophecy."

Evaluation of Difficult Ellen White Quotations about "No More Test of Time"

- **Quotation 1**

   I am compelled to state that I have not had the least faith in Mr. Garmire [James Monroe Garmire (1848–1931)] or his work. The pamphlet that was issued last fall at the time of our Jackson camp meeting had not the least sanction of our people. They were sent broadcast by stealing the RH list.

   The daughter of Mr. Garmire [18-year-old Anna Barbara Garmire (1870–1964)] claims, or he claims for her, to have visions; but they bear not the stamp of God. They are of the same character as many such things we have met in our experience—a delusion of Satan.

   I plainly stated at the Jackson camp meeting to these fanatical parties that they were doing the work of the adversary of souls; they were in darkness. They claimed to have great light that probation would close in October, 1884.

   I there stated in public that the Lord had been pleased to show me that there would be no definite time in the message given of God since 1844; and that I knew that this message, which four or five were engaged in advocating with great zeal, was heresy. The visions of this poor child were not of God. This light came not from heaven. Time was short; but the end was not yet. A great work was to be accomplished to prepare a people to be sealed with the seal of the living God. ("An Exposure of Fanaticism and Wickedness" [pamphlet], pp. 9, 10 [1885], in 2SM 72.3–73.3)

What did Ellen G. White mean by this statement? If she means that there are no further "timing messages," she would be contradicting her own "inspiration." In *The Great Controversy*, she says that the death of Christ was on the exact time—the exact day and hour—of the Passover Feast. *Then she clearly says that the fall feasts pointed to the time **when the end-time events would occur**.* We know exactly when the **time** of the fall feasts is. She specifically states that the final events must be *fulfilled* at the **time** pointed out in the symbolic service.

In like manner the types which relate to the second advent must be fulfilled at the *time* pointed out in the symbolic service. (GC 399.4)

Then, in *Review and Herald*, September 25, 1883, she says that the timing periods of Daniel go right up to the eve of the great consummation, the return of Jesus. Notice the future tense of her statements.

In the Scriptures are presented truths that relate especially to our own time. To the period *just prior* to the appearing of the Son of man, the prophecies of Scripture point, and here their *warnings* and *threatenings pre-eminently apply*. The **prophetic periods of Daniel**, extending to the *very eve of the great consummation*, throw a flood of light upon events **then** to transpire. The book of Revelation is also replete with *warning* and *instruction* for **the last generation**. The beloved John, under the inspiration of the Holy Spirit, portrays the fearful and thrilling scenes connected with the close of earth's history, and presents the duties and dangers of God's people. None need remain in ignorance, none need be unprepared for the coming of the day of God. (RH, Sept. 25, 1883)

The timing issue she refers to is directly related to Daniel 12. Notice the context of the paragraph. It is entirely related to the final events of prophecy that are just about to be fulfilled. She also notes, in Ms. 153, 1902, that when Satan appears as an angel of light, the "final fulfillment" of Revelation 13 would then take place. She then quotes a forty-two-month time prophecy.

In the last days Satan will appear as an angel of light, with great power and heavenly glory, and claim to be the Lord of the whole earth. He will declare that the Sabbath has been changed from the seventh to the first day of the week; and as lord of the first day of the week he will present this spurious sabbath as a test of loyalty to him. *Then* will take place the final fulfilment of the Revelator's prophecy. [Revelation 13:4–18 quoted.] (Ms. 153, 1902)

And there was given unto him a mouth speaking great things and blasphemies; and power was given unto him to continue forty *and* two months. (Rev. 13:5)

In her direct reference, in Quotation 1, to "time" future to 1885, what might she mean? We must be precise. As we saw earlier in this book, her use of the words, "definite time," referred to setting a specific date for the second coming of Jesus. That was the context of her statement. There is to be no "definite time" set for the second coming of Jesus after 1844.

- **Quotation 2**

  The world placed all time proclamation on the same level and called it a delusion, fanaticism, and heresy. Ever since 1844 I have borne my testimony that we were now in a period of time in which we are to take heed to ourselves lest our hearts be overcharged with surfeiting and drunkenness, and cares of this life, and so that day come upon us unawares. Our position has been one of waiting and watching, **with no time proclamation to intervene between the close of the prophetic periods in 1844 and the time of the Lord's coming**. We do not know the day nor the hour, or when the *definite time* is, and yet the prophetic reckoning shows us that Christ is at the door. (Letter 38, 1888)

The information needed to understand this statement is given in the context. This statement, by itself, could be interpreted several ways, proving different interpretations. But, did Ellen G. White give the context in the previous paragraph? Yes, she did. Let's read the two paragraphs together.

The **time-setters** have pronounced the curse of the Lord upon me as an unbeliever who said, My Lord delayeth **His** *coming [context issue]*. But I have told them that the books of heaven would not make my record thus, for the Lord knows that I loved and longed for the *appearing of Christ*. But their oft-repeated *message of definite time [regarding His coming]* was exactly **what the enemy wanted**, and it served his purpose well to unsettle the faith in the first proclamation of time, that was of heavenly origin.

The world placed all time proclamation on the same level and called it a delusion, fanaticism, and heresy. ***Ever since 1844*** I have borne my testimony that we were now in a period of time in which we are to ***take heed*** to ourselves lest our hearts be overcharged with surfeiting and drunkenness, and cares of this life, and so *that day [the Second Coming]* **come upon us unawares**. Our position has been one of waiting and watching, with **no time proclamation** to intervene between the close of the prophetic periods in 1844 and the **time of the** Lord's coming. *[Since 1844, when there was a time proclamation of "heavenly origin," there will not be another date set for His coming. That is the context.]* We do not know the **day nor the hour** *[of the second coming]*, or when the **definite time** is, and yet the *prophetic reckoning shows us* that *Christ is at the door*. (Letter 38, 1888)

When carefully analyzed, the context is clear. The whole message above relates to overzealous people who "*were*" setting dates for Jesus to come. She is simply stating that there was to be only *one* date set for the return of Christ (October 22, 1844), and that date "was of heavenly origin."

- **Quotation 3**

    This time, which the Angel declares with a solemn oath, is not the end of this world's history, neither of probationary time, but of prophetic time, which should precede the advent of our Lord.

    That is, the people will not have another message upon *definite time*. **After this period of time, reaching from 1842 to 1844, there can be no definite tracing of the prophetic time.** The longest reckoning reaches to the autumn of 1844. (7BC 971; Ms. 59, 1900)

At first glance, this statement appears to be pretty solidly against specific times after 1844, but let's take a closer look. First, notice that this is not an isolated statement. It comes from a larger thought concerning Revelation chapter 10. Let's look at the context as it appears in 7BC, page 971.

[Par. 3] The mighty Angel who instructed John was no less a personage than Jesus Christ. Setting His right foot on the sea, and His left upon the dry land, shows the part which He is acting in the *closing scenes* of the great controversy with Satan. This position denotes His supreme power and authority over the whole earth. The controversy had waxed stronger and more determined from age to age, and will continue to do so, to the ***concluding scenes when*** the masterly working of the powers of darkness shall reach their height. Satan, united with evil men, will deceive the *whole world **and*** the *churches* who receive not the love of the truth. But the mighty Angel demands attention. He cries with a loud voice. He is to show the power and authority of His voice to those who have united with Satan to oppose the truth.

[Par. 4] After these seven thunders uttered their voices, the injunction comes to John as to Daniel in regard to the little book: "**Seal up those things which the seven thunders uttered.**" These relate to future events which will be disclosed in their order. *Daniel shall stand in his lot at the **end of the days**.* John sees the little book unsealed. *Then Daniel's prophecies* have their proper place in the first, second, and third angels' messages to be given to the world. The unsealing of the little book was the *message* in relation to **time**.

[Par. 5] The books of Daniel and the Revelation are one. One is a prophecy, the other a revelation; one a book sealed, the other a book opened. John heard the mysteries which the thunders uttered, but he was commanded not to write them.

[Par. 6] The special light given to John which was expressed in the seven thunders was a delineation of events which would transpire under the first and second angels' messages. *It was **not best for the people to know these things, for their faith must** necessarily be tested. In the order of God most **wonderful and advanced truths would be proclaimed**.* The first and second angels' messages were to be proclaimed, *but **no further light*** was to be revealed ***before*** these messages had done their specific work. This is represented by the Angel standing with one foot on the sea, proclaiming with a most solemn oath that time should be no longer.

[Par. 7] This time, which the Angel declares with a solemn oath, is not the end of this world's history, neither of probationary time, but of ***prophetic time***, which should precede the advent of our Lord. "***That is, the people will not have another message upon definite time.***" After this period of time, reaching from 1842 to 1844, there can be no definite tracing of the prophetic time. The longest reckoning reaches to the autumn of 1844.

[Par. 8] The Angel's position, with one foot on the sea, the other on the land, signifies the ***wide extent*** of the proclamation of the message. ***It will*** cross the broad waters and be proclaimed in other countries, even to ***all the world***. The comprehension of truth, the glad reception of the message, is represented in the eating of the little book. The truth in regard to the ***time of the*** advent of our Lord was a precious message to our souls. (7BC 971; Ms. 59, 1900)

Notice the contextual timing words "closing scenes," "concluding scenes," "future events," "end of the days," "in the order of God," "all the world," etc. Also notice the timing clues, such as "when," "will," "then," and "before." This is an entirely end-time passage within a future context, written in 1900.

Let's unpack these statements paragraph by paragraph.

- **Paragraph 4**

    … The unsealing of the little book was the *message* in relation to *time*.

In addition to the future context of the passage, she says that the unsealing, or opening, of the little book corresponds to the "**message in relation to *time***"! Also, she says that the seven thunders are "*future* events which will be disclosed [unsealed] in their ***order***." In the same breath, she adds that Daniel will stand in his lot at the end of the days *and* that his prophecies will have their place in the Three Angels' Message. The implication is that the "order" or "timing" of the final events before the return of Christ will be understood! Daniel gives the timing of the final events in chapter 12, and these messages are to be proclaimed with the Three Angels' Message at the "end of the days." Amazing!

Remember: "The **prophetic periods** of Daniel, extending to the *very eve of the great consummation*, throw a flood of light upon events **then** to transpire" (RH, Sept. 25, 1883).

- **Paragraph 5**

    … John heard the mysteries which the thunders uttered, but he was commanded not to write them.

Notice that the seven thunders were effectively sealed just as the end-time portion of Daniel was sealed.

The **book that was sealed** was not the book of Revelation, but *that **portion** of the prophecy of Daniel which related to the **last days***. (Ms. 32, 1896)

- **Paragraph 6**

    … *It was not best for the people to know these things, for their faith must necessarily be tested. In the order of God most **wonderful and advanced truths would be proclaimed**.* …

Here she explains further that the details of Daniel's last-day timing prophecies were not to be understood so God's people in 1844 could be tested. If they had known their misinterpretation of the time prophecy, the Advent movement would *not* have started! But she goes on to say that, in the order of God, most wonderful and advanced truths *will be proclaimed!* She is saying that the things that were not understood will be understood and proclaimed to the world. This statement confirms her thoughts:

> It had been God's purpose to conceal the future and to bring His people to a point of decision. Without the preaching of **definite time** *for the coming of Christ*, the work designed of God would *not* have been accomplished. Satan was leading very many to look far in the future for the great events connected with the judgment and the end of probation. It was necessary that the people be brought to seek earnestly for a present preparation. (EW 246.2)

- **Paragraph 7** (*the quote in question*)

> This time, which the Angel declares with a solemn oath, is not the end of this world's history, neither of probationary time, but of **prophetic time**, which should precede the advent of our Lord. ***That is, the people will not have another message upon definite time.*** After this period of time, reaching from 1842 to 1844, there can be no definite tracing of the prophetic time. The longest reckoning reaches to the autumn of 1844.

In this paragraph, she says that the angel is proclaiming the end of "prophetic time." But in paragraph 4 she said, "Daniel *shall* stand in his lot," and, "The unsealing of the little book was the message in relation to *time*" (Ms. 59, 1900). Plus, she says that the prophetic periods of Daniel extend to the "eve of the great consummation." How do we reconcile the apparent contradiction?

Notice that she uses the words, "***That is,***" at the beginning of the second sentence. These words tell us that she is explaining what she just said in the first sentence! The rest of the sentence that follows "that is" defines the context of what she means by the words "***prophetic time***" in the first sentence. She defines her use of the words "prophetic time" as "***definite time.***" Note that Ellen G. White used "definite time" in a number of places to mean that there was to be no more preaching of a definite time for Jesus' return! She never intended to say that we would not understand the timing of events *prior* to His return.

> Yet God accomplished His own beneficent purpose in permitting the warning of the judgment to be given just as it was [that Jesus

was coming in 1844]. The great day was at hand, and in His providence the people were brought *to the test of a **definite time***, in order to reveal to them what was in their hearts. (GC 353.1)

The proclamation of a ***definite time** for Christ's coming* called forth great opposition from many of all classes … (GC 370.1)

These statements should make it plain that Ellen G. White is saying that there shall never again be a message setting a definite time, or date, for the return of Jesus. Yet, though we do not know a specific date for His return, we know that it is close!

We do not know the day nor the hour, or when the ***definite time*** is, and *yet the prophetic reckoning shows us that Christ is at the door.* (Letter 38, 1888)

Remember:

The **prophetic periods** of Daniel, extending to the *very eve of the great consummation*, throw a flood of light upon events **then** to transpire. (RH, Sept. 25, 1883)

How do we explain the remaining sentences in this paragraph? "After this period of time, reaching from 1842 to 1844, there can be no *definite* tracing of the prophetic *time*. The longest reckoning reaches to the autumn of 1844" (Ms. 59, 1900). Remember that different dates were set for the return of Jesus, and, as one date passed, their reckoning (calculation) of the time was extended to a new date. The "longest" reckoning extended to the "autumn of 1844" and the Karaite reckoning of the day of Atonement, which we know was October 22, 1844. After this longest date of reckoning, there can be no more "tracing," or calculation, of a "definite time" or date for the return of Jesus. This is the message she is trying to communicate. There must be no more calculation of a specific date for the return of Jesus.

- **Paragraph 8**

    Finally, in the last paragraph, we are told in a future context that the "message in relation to *time*," *will go* to "all the world"!

There are timing messages relating to the final events just prior to the return of Christ that will be preached to all the world. The timing messages of Daniel chapter 12 and Revelation chapter 13 make up a portion of this final message.

Supporting Thoughts and Questions

Greater light first and then a lesser light

The Bible points people to Jesus, the "Greater Light," and teaches us that all foundational doctrines must be derived and defended solely on the Word of God. As we have seen, some unknowingly base their beliefs entirely on Ellen G. White quotations that are *taken out of context*, when there are clear prophecies in the Bible about events still to take place in the future, which are specifically associated with *time*.

Very soon the loud cry message will go forth, and it must be founded solidly on the Bible. The people must hear, "Thus saith the Lord," not, "Thus saith Ellen White." The purpose of Ellen White's writings was to lead men and women back to Jesus and the Bible.

> *Little heed is given to the Bible, and the Lord has given a lesser light to lead men and women to the greater light.*

> Little heed is given to the Bible, and the Lord has given a lesser light to lead men and women to the greater light. (RH, Jan. 20, 1903, Art. B)

> He (John the Baptist) was the lesser light, which was to be followed by a greater. (DA 220.2)

> Christ makes no apology when He declares, "I am the light of the world." He was, in life and teaching, the gospel, the foundation of all pure doctrine. Just as the sun compares with the lesser lights in the heavens, so did Christ, the Source of light, compare with the teachers of His day. He was before them all, and shining with the brightness of the sun, He diffused His penetrating, gladdening rays throughout the world. (TMK 97.3)

> The testimonies of Sr. White should not be carried to the front. God's Word is the unerring standard. The Testimonies are not to take the place of the Word. Great care should be exercised by all believers to advance these questions carefully, and always stop when you have said enough. ***Let all prove their positions from the Scriptures and substantiate every point you claim as truth from the revealed Word of God.*** (Letter 12, 1890)

The more we look at the promises of the Word of God, the brighter they grow. The more we practice the principles of God's Word, the deeper will be our understanding of them. Our position and faith is in the Bible. And ***never do we want any soul to bring in the testimonies ahead of the Bible.*** (Ms. 7, 1894)

Their work is to catch the light *from the Word* and let it shine forth to the world in clear, steady rays. (PK 148.1, emphasis added)

Are all of our expositions of Scripture infallible?

Many have mentioned that our founding fathers wrote about and believed certain doctrines, and we must not cross those boundaries. Does Ellen G. White agree?

> *We must not think*, "Well, we have all the truth, we understand the main pillars of our faith, and we may rest on this knowledge." The *truth is an advancing truth*, and we must walk in the increasing light. (CW 33.2)

> **There is no excuse for any one in taking the position** that there is no more truth to be revealed, and **that all our expositions of Scripture are without an error. The fact that certain doctrines have been held as truth for many years by our people, is not a proof that our ideas are infallible.** *Age will not make error into truth*, and truth can afford to be fair. No true doctrine will lose anything by close investigation. We are living in perilous times, and it does not become us to accept everything claimed to be truth without examining it thoroughly; neither can we afford to reject anything that bears the fruits of the Spirit of God; but we should be teachable, meek and lowly of heart. *There are those who oppose everything that is not in accordance with their own ideas, and by so doing they endanger their eternal interest as verily as did the Jewish nation in their rejection of Christ.* (RH, Dec. 20, 1892)

If we are told that we have many lessons to *unlearn*, then we must be diligently searching for where we have been in *error* in the past! Where we have been wrong, we must learn what is true.

The straight testimony

Very soon a message of "straight testimony" will be preached to the people of God, and we are told that this message will cause a shaking among God's people. This message will be so controversial that many will reject the message that God is presenting, and it will be of such intensity that many will leave God's remnant church. Could it be that this new light of additional details concerning the prophecies just ahead will be a cause of this shaking?

> I asked the meaning of the shaking I had seen and was shown that it would be caused by the *straight testimony* called forth by the counsel of the True Witness *to the Laodiceans*. This will have its effect upon the heart of the receiver, and will lead him to exalt the standard and pour forth the **straight truth**. Some will not bear this straight testimony. They will *rise up against it*, and *this is what will cause a shaking* among God's people. (EW 270.2)

> In Minneapolis God gave precious gems of truth to His people in new settings. This light from heaven by some was rejected with all the stubbornness the Jews manifested in rejecting Christ, and there was much talk about standing by the old landmarks. But there was evidence they knew not what the old landmarks were. There was **evidence and there was reasoning from the Word** that commended itself to the conscience; but the minds of men were fixed, sealed against the entrance of light, because they had decided it was a dangerous error, removing the 'old landmarks'—**when it was not moving a peg of the old landmarks**, but they had perverted ideas of what constituted the old landmarks. (Ms. 13, 1889)

> Blow the trumpet in Zion; sound an alarm in the holy mountain. Gather the host of the Lord, with sanctified hearts, to hear what the Lord will say unto His people; for **He has increased light for all who will hear.** Let them be armed and equipped, and come up to the battle—to the help of the Lord against the mighty. (TM 410.1)

Be Careful Not to Attack the Messenger of New Light

Ellen G. White had *much* to say on this subject in the chapter, "Among Snares," in *The Desire of Ages*. In other places, she noted the following:

> **When** *new light* **is presented to the church, it is perilous to shut yourselves away from it.** Refusing to hear **because** you are **prejudiced against the message or the messenge**r will not make your case excusable before God. *To condemn that which* **you** *have not heard and* **do** *not understand* will not exalt your wisdom in the eyes of those **who are candid** in their investigations of truth. And

to speak with contempt of those whom *God has sent with a message of truth*, is folly and madness. (CSW 32.1)

But **the message seemed to them an idle tale**, and they believed it not. *Emboldened* in their wickedness **they mocked the messenger** of God, made light of his entreaties, and even accused him of presumption. (GC 337.3)

If he can **lead men to distrust the messenger**, or to attach **no sacredness to the message**, he knows that they will feel under *no obligation to heed the word of God* to them. And when *light is set aside as darkness*, Satan has things his own way. (LHU 361.2; RH, April 7, 1885)

In the days of Paul there was need of warning … If **the message or the messenger** *differed* in some little degree from their preconceived ideas, *they closed the door firmly* **against the light and the lightbearer.** (ST, May 15, 1893)

We must be careful!

I saw Satan would work more powerfully now than ever he has before. He knows that his time is short and that the sealing of the saints will place them beyond his power; he will now work in every way that he can and will try his every insinuation to get the saints off from their guard and get them **asleep** upon the *present truth* **or doubting it**, so as to **prevent their being sealed** with the seal of the living God. (Ms. 7, 1850, "A Vision the Lord Gave Me at Brother Harris', August 24, 1850")

And in response to his supplications, light from the heavenly courts was communicated for *those who should live in the latter days*. With what earnestness, then, should we seek God, that He may open our understanding to comprehend the truths brought to us from heaven. (SL 50.1; RH, Feb. 8, 1881)

We must seek with **all our heart** to understand these things.

How somber a thought it is that being asleep on "present truth" or doubting it will prevent us from being sealed! We must understand the final prophetic messages God gives us in His Word and be prepared to share these truths with the world.

Part 4: Additional Prophecies with a Future Context

Many passages of Scripture outside of Daniel and Revelation contain prophecies with a final fulfillment that is yet to come. Here are just a few passages to consider:

The Tarrying Time of Habakkuk 2:2, 3

And the LORD answered me, and said, Write the vision, and make *it* plain upon tables, that he may run that readeth it. For the vision *is* yet for an ***appointed time***, but at ***the end*** it shall speak, and not lie: though it tarry, wait for it; because it will surely come, *it will not tarry*. (Hab. 2:2, 3)

Notice the similarities to Daniel 8:17, 19 and Matthew 24.

- The same Hebrew word for vision (*chazôn*)
- The same "appointed time"
- The same context of "the end"
- The same destruction of Jerusalem and end-time parallel destruction of the world (Hab. 2:3, 8, 14; 3:6, 12)

Notice also that the Spirit of Prophecy gives an end-time context to these verses:

We must cherish and cultivate the faith of which prophets and apostles have testified—the faith that lays hold on the promises of God and *waits for deliverance* in *His appointed time and way*. The sure word of prophecy will meet its final fulfillment in the glorious advent of our Lord and Saviour Jesus Christ, as King of kings and Lord of lords. *The time of waiting may seem long*, the soul may be oppressed by discouraging circumstances ... *Let us ever hold in remembrance the cheering message,* "The vision is *yet* for an *appointed time*, but at *the end* it shall speak, and not lie: though it tarry, wait for it; because *it will surely come*, it will not tarry.... The just shall live by his faith." [Habakkuk 2:3, 4.] (PK 387.2)

The *chazôn* vision will come very soon.

We do not know the day nor the hour, or when the **definite time** is, and yet the prophetic reckoning shows us that Christ is at the door. (Letter 38, 1888)

We are not impatient. If the vision tarry, wait for it, for it will surely come; it will not tarry. Although disappointed, our faith has not failed, and we have not drawn back to perdition. The **apparent tarrying** is **not so** in reality, for at the **appointed time** our Lord will come, and we will, if faithful, exclaim, "Lo, this is our God; we have waited for Him, and He will save us" [Isaiah 25:9.] (Letter 38, 1888)

There is an exact appointed time for the vision to take place.

In like manner the types which relate to the ***second advent must be fulfilled at the time pointed out*** in the symbolic service. (GC 399.4)

The events surrounding Jesus' sacrifice were in harmony with the timing of the spring feasts. The events surrounding His second coming will be in harmony with the timing of the fall feasts. The fall feasts are Feast of Trumpets, Day of Atonement, and the Feast of Tabernacles, all of which point forward to the events surrounding the second coming of Jesus.

The time of tarrying is almost ended. The pilgrims and strangers who have so long been seeking a better country are almost home. I feel as if I must cry aloud, Homeward bound! . . . "Wherefore, beloved, seeing that ye look for such things, be diligent that ye may be found of him in peace, without spot, and blameless." 2 Peter 3:14. (OHC 367.6)

For additional information, see chapter 22 of *The Great Controversy*, pages 391 and 392.

The Days of Noah

And the Lord said, My spirit shall not always strive with man, for that he also is flesh: yet his days shall be an hundred and twenty years. (Gen. 6:3)

But as the days of Noe were, so shall also the coming of the Son of man be. (Matt. 24:37)

A 120-year time prophecy was given before the flood. Jesus said that history will repeat itself at the time of the end. If there was a time prophecy before the first destruction of the world (at the flood) then there must be another time prophecy before the final destruction of the world at Jesus' second coming.

> "Another kind of evidence that vitally affected my mind," he [Miller] says, "was the chronology of the Scriptures. ... I found that predicted events, which had been fulfilled in the past, often occurred within a given time. *The one hundred and twenty years to the flood* (Genesis 6:3); the seven days that were to precede it, with forty days of predicted rain (Genesis 7:4); the four hundred years of the sojourn of Abraham's seed (Genesis 15:13); the three days of the butler's and baker's dreams (Genesis 40:12–20); the seven years of Pharaoh's (Genesis 41:28–54); the forty years in the wilderness (Numbers 14:34); the three and a half years of famine (1 Kings 17:1); [see Luke 4:25;] ... the seventy years' captivity (Jeremiah 25:11); Nebuchadnezzar's seven times, (Daniel 4:13–16); and the seven weeks, threescore and two weeks, and the one week, making seventy weeks, determined upon the Jews (Daniel 9:24–27); the events limited by these times were all once only a matter of prophecy, and were fulfilled in accordance with the predictions."—Bliss, pages 74, 75. (GC 323.2)

Surely the Lord God will do nothing, but he revealeth his secret unto his servants the prophets. (Amos 3:7)

Isaiah 58

This chapter is critical to understand in these last days.

> My brethren, you need to study more carefully the fifty-eighth chapter of Isaiah. This chapter marks out the only course that we can follow with safety.... The prophet receives this word from the Lord—a message startling in its clearness and force:

> "Cry aloud, spare not, lift up thy voice like a trumpet, and show my people their transgression, and the house of Jacob their sins." Though they are called the people of God, the house of Jacob, though they profess to be linked with God in obedience and fellowship, they are far from Him. (Letter 76, 1902)

Where do we find the people who are thus addressed? Who is it that shall build the old waste places, and raise up the foundation of many generations? Where are the people who have had light from heaven to see that a breach has been made in the law of God?

In the Revelation, John says, "The temple of God was opened in heaven, and there was seen in his temple the ark of his testament." Revelation 11:19. John saw in vision the Lord's people looking for His coming and searching for truth. As the temple of God was opened unto His people, the light of the law of God, which was in the ark, shone forth. Those who receive this light are brought to view in the proclamation of the third angel's message.

> This angel is seen flying in the midst of heaven, "saying with a loud voice, If any man worship the beast and his image, and receive his mark in his forehead or in his hand, the same shall drink of the wine of the wrath of God, which is poured out without mixture into the cup of his indignation; and he shall be tormented with fire and brimstone in the presence of the holy angels, and in the presence of the Lamb.... Here is the patience of the saints, here are they that keep the commandments of God, and the faith of Jesus." [Rev. 14:9, 10, 12.]

> This is the people that are repairing the breach in the law of God. They see that the Sabbath of the fourth commandment has been supplanted by a spurious sabbath, a day that has no sanction in the Word of God. Amid great opposition they become loyal to their God, and take their position under the standard of the third angel. (Ms. 48, 1900)

Joel

The short book of Joel is a type of what is happening and what is about to happen in God's church and the world.

> Blow the trumpet in Zion, sanctify a fast, call a solemn assembly: ... Let the priests, the ministers of the LORD,

This is the people that are repairing the breach in the law of God. They see that the Sabbath of the fourth commandment has been supplanted by a spurious sabbath, a day that has no sanction in the Word of God.

weep between the porch and the altar, and let them say, Spare thy people, O LORD, and give not thine heritage to reproach, that the heathen should rule over them: wherefore should they say among the people, Where *is* their God? (Joel 2:15, 17)

If this prophecy of *Joel* [2:28, 29] met a *partial fulfilment* in the days of the apostles, we are living in a time when it is to be even more evidently manifest to the people of God. He will so bestow His Spirit upon His people that they will become a light amid the moral darkness; and great light will be reflected in all parts of the world. O that our faith might be increased, that the Lord might work mightily with His people. (Ms. 49, 1908)

Part 5: Key Points of Daniel and Revelation

We have no time to lose; God calls upon us to watch for souls as they that must give an account. *Advance new principles, and crowd in the clear-cut truth*. It will be as a sword cutting both ways. But be not too ready to take a controversial attitude. There will be times when we must stand still and see the salvation of God. Let Daniel speak, let the Revelation speak, and tell what is truth. But whatever phase of the subject is presented, uplift Jesus as the center of all hope, "the Root and the Offspring of David, and the bright and morning Star." (TM 118.1)

We do not dwell sufficiently upon the Revelation and the book of Daniel. These books should be published together in pamphlet form, *with a few explanations added*, and they should be circulated everywhere. The words of inspiration will do their appointed work; for the Holy Spirit will impress hearts in regard to the prophecies given. (Ms. 165, 1902)

Below are brief explanations of key points presented in the books of Daniel and Revelation in a present truth context (2023). This study is a work in progress. Please study these things with earnest prayer that God may lead you into all truth by His Spirit (John 16:13; Acts 17:11). May the thoughts below aid you in your study and preparation for the final fulfillment of prophecy that is yet to come!

Part 5: Key Points of Daniel and Revelation

Key Points of Daniel 8 through 12

Daniel 8

Many people have said that Daniel 2, 7, and 8 are parallel prophecies, and, in some regards, that is true. Daniel 8 has some similarities to Daniel 2 and 7, *but there are a number of key differences* that cannot be ignored if we are to fully understand the context and the message. Daniel begins chapter 8 by saying that he saw a vision. He uses the word "vision" three times in verses one and two that we might not miss the importance of this particular vision. The Hebrew word for "vision" that is used here is *chazôn*.

The context of the Daniel 8 vision is defined in verses 1, 2, and 17. As just mentioned, in verses 1 and 2, *three times* Daniel says that he saw a **vision**! When something is repeated in the Bible, we must pay attention! Then, in verse 17, Daniel says, "Understand, O son of man: for *at* the **time of the end** shall be the **vision**." *Chazôn* is again the word he used. *Don't miss this*! Daniel 8:1, 2, and 17, are telling us that the vision that he received by the river Ulai, which is described in this chapter, is for the "time of the end." The *chazôn* vision is referred to several times in this chapter and in succeeding chapters with specific information about **the time of the end**.

Important note: There are two different Hebrew words used for the word "vision" in Daniel 8 to 12: *chazôn* and *mareh*. The *chazôn* vision is referenced in Daniel 8:1, 2, 13, 15, 17, and 26. The *chazôn* vision relates to the final conflict between good and evil. *Mareh* is used in Daniel 8:16, 26, and 27, and is defined more completely in chapter 9. The *mareh* vision refers to the 2300 days (see Daniel 8:26) and points forward to the purification of a holy people (see chapter 9). To help you see this more clearly, in your Bible underline in red the words translated from *chazon*, and in blue the words translated from *mareh*. You will need e-Sword, BlueLetterBible.org, or a *new edition* of *Strong's Exhaustive Concordance*. Note that older Strong's editions recorded the words for "vision" incorrectly.)

The Hebrew words for "time of the end" are *eth qets*. Strong's Concordance tells us this phrase means an "extremity of time." The biblical context for the *chazôn* vision is a last-day, final events context. Daniel 8 and the remaining chapters must be understood in this last-day context. It is also important to note that the *chazôn* vision of Daniel 8 to 12 was sealed from our understanding till the time of the end (see Dan. 8:26; 12:4, 9). Additionally, it is important to realize that this vision is given in sanctuary atonement language, with sanctuary service beasts used as symbols. The final Day of Atonement, with its cleansing of the sanctuary and purification of a holy people, didn't **begin** until Oct. 22, 1844, emphasizing that this vision is for the "time of the end," which comes *after* 1844. (The Hebrew word translated as "sanctuary" in Dan. 8:14 can also be translated as "saint." See *Strong's Exhaustive Concordance* for the Hebrew word "*qôdesh*," H6944, and the section under the heading "*Our part*" under Daniel 9 later in Part 5, on p. 121)

What do the symbols of the ram and the goat mean then if they don't apply to ancient Medo-Persia or Greece? Let's take a deeper look.

The ram (Daniel 8:3, 4)

The ram is symbolic of the Medo-Persian Empire, and both the ram and the Medo-Persian Empire are symbolic of God and His people in an end-time context. The following symbols help to make this clear:

- The ram had two horns that symbolize two powers (the Medes and the Persians). God's end-time people are described as being part of one of two groups—the 144,000 and the Great Multitude. The larger group, like the higher horn, comes up last. The 144,000 preach the Word and the Great Multitude respond.

- The ram and Medo-Persian empire came from the east. This is the same direction that the sacrificial animal comes from in the sacrificial system and the same direction Jesus comes from when He returns.

- The ram of the Medo-Persian empire came from the east and took control of the four directions of the earth. *Its influence was worldwide.* The influence of Jesus, through His people, will be worldwide.

- Persia is the power that delivered Israel and decreed the restoration of Jerusalem. Jesus will restore His people to reflect His image, and He will deliver us.

- The ram is an atonement animal in the sacrificial system. Jesus is our atonement sacrifice.

- The ram was a substitute for Isaac on Mt. Moriah, which was a symbol of *Jesus, our deliverer and substitute* on the cross.

- The ram as the Medo-Persian empire came after Babylon, but Babylon is not mentioned at the beginning of chapter 8. The declaration "Babylon has fallen" is future imagery of when Babylon will fall again.

- Sheep (and a ram is a male sheep) represent those destined to inherit God's eternal kingdom (Matt. 25:32–34).

In an end-of-time context, the Medo-Persian Empire and the ram are symbols of Jesus and His people. These symbols represent God, working through His people, who are challenged to become like Him, as outlined in Daniel 9:24. They are to put away sin and be restored fully to heaven's favor. This is covenant completion imagery. When fully surrendered and under the control of Jesus, they will go out with power—just like that white horse of Revelation—to conquer the world for Jesus.

The terrible he-goat (Daniel 8:5–8)

The he-goat is symbolic of Satan and those who follow him. Consider the meaning behind these symbols:

- The goat moved so fast that it didn't touch the ground. This is symbolic of the rapid conquest of Alexander the Great and Greece. In an end-time context, the goat and Greece are symbolic of powers that will oppose God's people.
- The goat, which represented Greece, came from the West, the opposite direction from which Jesus comes.
- If the Ram is symbolic of powers that will bring deliverance to God's people, and Greece came to destroy Medo-Persia, this goat represents a power that is trying to prevent the deliverance and restoration of God's people.
- The goat, which represented Greece, "smote" the ram—the Medo-Persian Empire—and conquered it. So it will be again when Babylon persecutes God's people.
- Goats represent those prepared for everlasting fire (Matt. 25:32–34, 41).
- On the Day of Atonement, two goats were chosen. One was to represent Jesus and His blood that cleanses from sin, and the other was to represent Satan. All the sins that were cleansed by Jesus' blood were transferred to the goat representing Satan, and then that goat was led into the wilderness to die. Satan will bear the curse of the sin goat during the millennium following Jesus' second coming.
- As Greece was divided into four powers, so, in an end-time context, God's people will be opposed by four powers. Those powers

are: (1) the dragon, or Satan, (2) the sea beast, or the king of the north, which is Rome, (3) the false prophet, which is apostate Protestantism, and (4) the king of the south, which is Islam.

- Muslims make up the second largest religious group in the world and are, to a large degree, located at latitudes south of Rome. (See the commentary on Daniel 11:22–27, 40–45, and Revelation 16:13 in part 5, p.132-139, 213.)

The he-goat and Greece represent Satan, working through his agencies—especially the "little horn"—trying to prevent the covenant promise from being fulfilled in God's people. Only Medo-Persia and Greece are represented by animals in Chapter 8. Neither Babylon nor Rome are mentioned. The Persia-Greece time period serves as timing markers for the beginning of the 2300-year prophecy, which then identifies the ending point of the 2300-year prophecy. The end of the 2300-year prophecy marks the *beginning* of the judgment of the dead and paves the way for the final end-time events to take place. Gabriel said that this vision was for the time of the end (Dan. 8:17 and 8:19). Therefore, the purpose of this prophecy is different from that of Daniel 2 and 7. It adds details and becomes the continuing story from the time of the feet with ten toes in Daniel 2 and the judgment in Daniel 7. (Notice the end-time, whole earth context of Daniel 2:34, 35, 44, 45; 7:22–28.)

The "atonement ram" is contrasted with the "sin goat." It is Jesus versus Satan and God's people versus Satan's people. This vision is telling of a time when Jesus is purifying His people in an atonement process, and Satan's people, or agents, will fight them and persecute them, trying to prevent that from ever happening.

> *This vision is telling of a time when Jesus is purifying His people in an atonement process, and Satan's people, or agents, will fight them and persecute them, trying to prevent that from ever happening.*

Many have asked, "Where does the Little Horn of Daniel 8:9 come from?" The text says, "Out of one of them." The preceding noun in this verse is "winds," and the word "heaven" explains the word "winds." Grammatically, it has to be from "one" of the "winds" of heaven, meaning one of the directions—north, south, east, or west.

The "little horn" waxed exceedingly great, "towards the south and towards the east and towards the pleasant *land* [west]" ("land" is not in the original text) (Dan. 8:9b). If it went towards the south, east, and west, then it came from the "winds" of the north. By coming from the north, its power spreads throughout the world. What power comes from the north?

> For thou hast said in thine heart, I will ascend into heaven, I will exalt my throne above the stars of God: I will sit also upon the mount of the congregation, in the sides of the **north**: I will ascend above the heights of the clouds; I will be like the most High. (Isaiah 14:13, 14)

This "little horn" (of Daniel 8) is anti-God and represents the papacy, which will have power over the whole world and will come to its end "*without hand*" (Dan. 8:25) during the judgment after the 2300 evenings and mornings have ended. These are the first clues that the "little horn" power of Daniel 8 is referring to the second rise of the papacy after the deadly wound is healed.

Some say that this "little horn" (Daniel 8) represents pagan Rome first and then it represents Papal Rome. There is no animal or beast in Daniel 8 that is the bearer of the "little horn," or an associated symbol. Instead, the "little horn" came out of one of the winds of heaven in an end-time context, as defined in verses 17 and 19.

Will God tell us what is to happen at the end? He has done just that! In the context of Daniel 8, which is defined as the "time of the end," in verse 17, Gabriel tells us that he *"will* **make thee know** *what shall be in the last end of the indignation: for at the time appointed* **the end shall be**" (Dan. 8:19). Totally amazing! "At the time appointed [*môw'ed*] the end [*qets*] shall be" (Dan. 8:19).

This statement tells us that if we discover when the *môw'ed* (time appointed) is, we will know when the end of time (*qets*) is. That is exactly what Daniel 12 is all about. Look up the Hebrew word for "time" in Daniel 12:7. It is the same as "time appointed" in Daniel 8:19 (cf. v. 17). The rest of the Hebrew words for "time" in chapter 12 are different. This is another clue. The "time of the end" is here defined as the last 1260 days of persecution ("time, times and an half").

All these things also relate to the time of "indignation" (*zaam*), which is the time when God begins to pour out His wrath right at the end (v. 19).

God is giving us clues that lead to answers concerning the timing questions posed by Gabriel in verse 13. "How long *shall be* the vision *concerning* the daily *sacrifice* …?" "*Shall be,*" "*concerning,*" and "*sacrifice*" were not in the original text. It literally reads, "How long the vision, the daily." Looking up the words "How long" in Strong's Concordance, we discover some interesting information. "How long" really implies that the question is, "How long *until* ..." or "*Until when* ..." The answer is 2300+ years away. In other words, the vision wouldn't *start* for over 2300 years. Could this be why Daniel fainted in verse 27? Notice that in verse 26, the vision regarding the 2300 days is defined as the *mareh* vision. In Daniel 10:1, Daniel says he now had understanding of the *mareh* vision, but the time appointed was long!

The end of the 2300-year prophecy marks the *beginning* of the final time of judgment. Daniel 8 is teaching us that, during this time of judgment, the final events of Daniel 8 to 12 will take place. The visions given by the Ulai and the Hiddekel encompass the visions of Daniel 8 to 12 (see Dan 8:1, 2; 10:4).

> The light that Daniel received from God was given especially for these *last days*. The visions he saw by the banks of the Ulai and the Hiddekel, the great rivers of Shinar, are now in process of fulfillment, and *all the events foretold will **soon** come to pass*. (TM 112.2)

There is additional evidence that this passage points to an end-time context. Notice that Daniel 8:13 includes the words "transgression of desolation." This is referring to the same "abomination of desolation" spoken by Jesus in the Olivet discourse and by Gabriel in Daniel 12:11. God's law will be transgressed, which is an abomination in God's sight. This transgression, or abomination, will lead to the desolation of the earth at the "*extremity of time*" just as Jerusalem's transgression resulted in the desolation of the Jewish people and their city in AD 70.

Daniel 9

- Verses 1–19 portray, through Daniel's witness, the character and prayers of the saints in the last days. Daniel's prayer focuses on the forgiveness and restoration of a holy people. This is the context of the *mareh* vision.

- Verses 20–23 tell us that Gabriel came to Daniel to give us the meaning of the *mareh* vision—which began in chapter 8 with the 2300-day prophecy. The end of the 2300-day prophecy marks the *beginning* of the final, antitypical time of atonement, which began in 1844.

- Verse 24 calls Daniel's people "thy people." In an end-time time of trouble context, Daniel's people are called the "children of thy people" (Dan. 12:1), tying God's end-time people together with Daniel's people in his time.

- Verse 24 decrees "seventy weeks" of probationary time to accomplish six things that can be divided in two parts:
  - ***Our part***
    1. *Finish the transgression*—stop revolting against God and His covenant; stop living for self and the world. Jesus is pleading with us to recognize our need of Him (see Strong's definition for "transgression").
    2. *Make an end of sins*—once we recognize our need, we need to literally stop sinning by claiming God's promises for victory over every temptation and sinful thought.
        - "Those who come up to every point, and stand every test, and overcome, be the price what it may, have heeded the counsel of the True Witness, and they will receive the latter rain, and thus be fitted for translation" (1T 187.1).
        - "The heart must be emptied of every defilement, and cleansed for the indwelling of the Spirit. It was by the confession and forsaking of sin, by earnest prayer and consecration of themselves to God, that the early disciples prepared for the outpouring of the Holy Spirit on the day of Pentecost. The same work, only in greater degree, must be done now" (RH, March 2, 1897).
    3. *Make reconciliation for iniquity*—we must make our wrongs right. As a people, atonement, restitution, and turning away from wrong must occur. Repentance is to be made. All are to be reconciled back to God. We must leave Laodicea and become part of Philadelphia. We must find ourselves judged as reconciled to God. Nothing less than God's character reflected in us is acceptable to Him. Daniel 8 to 12 starts with a substitutionary atonement ram and ends with a holy people. That is what is to be accomplished within the seventy weeks-of-years, or ten cycles of forty-nine years. Ten Jubilee cycles—forty-nine years each, totaling 490 years—are given to Israel to complete the restoration and re-creation process. Daniel 8:14 states that God's judgment, cleansing, and purification of a holy

people won't be complete until after 1844. Could part of the 490 years be finished at the very end of time? The prophecy anticipates another Israel when the covenant is completed!

- **God's part**

    4. *Bring in everlasting righteousness*—God's people will be eternally holy, sinless. When He comes, Jesus will declare: "He that is righteous, let him be righteous still: and he that is holy, let him be holy still" (Rev. 22:11). During the Jubilee everything became cleansed and *restoration had occurred.* God's people, within the span of ten Jubilees must reach the moral standard of God and of Christ and be cleansed from all sin issues. Those who surrender to God and follow His plan will have their names written in the book of life.

    5. *Seal up the vision and prophecy*—the Hebrew word used for vision here is *chazôn,* which, in Daniel 8 through 12, refers contextually to the conflict between good and evil. God will seal up and "make an end" (Strong's H2856) of all the issues stated in the prophecy regarding the papal oppression and sin in our world!

    6. *Anoint the most Holy*—"anoint" (H4886) means to consecrate which is a sacred setting apart for God's service. "Most Holy" refers to something that is holy or that is purified and made holy including "saints" (H6944). The verses with the Hebrew word *qôdesh* (H6944) used in Daniel 8:14 and here in 9:24 are telling us that God will have a pure people at a point in time after the 2300 evenings and mornings are complete (cf. 8:16, 26, 27, 9:23 and 10:1). The context of Daniel's prayer, Gabriel's answer to his prayer, and the context of the mareh vision as a whole in Daniel chapters 8, 9, and 10 is the purification and setting apart of a holy people.

"In that day shall the branch of the Lord be beautiful and glorious, and the fruit of the earth shall be excellent and comely for them that are escaped of Israel. And it shall come to pass, that *he that is left* in Zion, and *he that remaineth* in Jerusalem, *shall be called holy*, even every one that is written among the living in Jerusalem" (Isaiah 4:2, 3).

- ***These six things have not yet been accomplished!*** Daniel 9:24 is a model for God's end-time people who will be restored to the image of God and will experience the final Jubilee.

- Verse 25 describes the rebuilding and restoration of literal Israel after the Babylonian captivity. More importantly, this verse symbolically describes the rebuilding and restoring of spiritual Israel and a covenant relationship with God. (See Isa. 58:12; Ps. 127:1; Jer. 24:6; 33:7, 8.) It is a call to return to God and to *restore the everlasting covenant* with God's people. Then Israel will become holy. That is what Daniel and Revelation are ultimately all about. Those six steps will be completed! At the end of time, God will have a holy people.

- There were four different decrees, or directives, related to rebuilding Jerusalem after the Babylonian captivity. (See Ezra 1:1–4; 6:1, 6–12, 15; 7:13, 25, 26; and Nehemiah.) Only one of the decrees addressed the necessary spiritual restoration issues stating that all must obey God—with the threat of death if not followed! That decree was given in 457 BC, as recorded in Ezra chapter 7. It is the decree that marks the beginning of the "seventy weeks" (490 years).

- The seventy weeks of years is divided into three parts: seven weeks, sixty-two weeks, and one week. The first seven weeks (seven weeks times seven years per week equals forty-nine years) of the seventy weeks brings us to 408 BC. Did anything significant happen then? Historically—no. Spiritually—yes. The forty-ninth year would end the first cycle of seven weeks the land would rest (Lev. 25:3–7). God's people would have enjoyed seven Sabbath years of rest during these forty-nine years, and the fiftieth year would be a holy year of liberty with full restoration (Lev. 25:8–55), a Jubilee. That first "seven" (forty-nine years) was the first of ten Jubilee cycles that was to be part of the 490-year restoration *theme* for Israel's journey to reconciliation, holiness, and everlasting righteousness. (It is important to note that the repeating cycle of seven years is never interrupted. The 50th year, the Jubilee, fell on the first year of the next cycle of seven.)

- In prophecy, "ten" means "a whole." At the beginning of the 70th week, in AD 27, Jesus came as the Messiah. Israel's probation was set on Jubilee cycles, and AD 27 does not fall on a Jubilee. *At His first coming*, Jesus did *not* come on a Jubilee. He came *in promise*—with all the *provisions* for a Jubilee restoration at His second coming.

- In the middle of a restoration context, Gabriel says, "The street shall be built again, and the wall, even in troublous times." The word for "street" can mean a broad place or area (see Strong's Concordance). A broad place or an area of a city would likely be the city square or the heart of a city. Symbolically, the center—or heart—of God's people, His church, is to be built up or restored. We will become the pure woman of Revelation 12.

- The Hebrew word for "wall" figuratively refers to a decision (see Strong's Concordance). In the context of troublous times, God's people will be spiritually brought back to holiness by decisions that will never change. Like a wall around a city, it will be a protective barrier forever.

- Verses 26 and 27 are parallel verses that add information to each other.

- After the threescore and two weeks, in the midst of the 70th week, Jesus was cut off, crucified, and that "not for himself" but for us. At that point, the sacrificial system that had pointed forward to the death of Jesus for centuries ceased to have any meaning.

- Who is the "prince" in verse 26? In Daniel 9:25, we have "Messiah the Prince." Here in verse 26 we have "Messiah" being cut off (crucified), and then we have a "prince" destroying the city and the sanctuary. This is just a breakup of the word pair and should be the "Prince" that refers to Jesus.

- The primary context of Daniel 9 is a spiritual restoration, and this verse is making it clear that Israel would fail spiritually in crucifying Jesus, and then the city would literally be destroyed as prophesied by Jesus the "Prince."

- Israel failed spiritually, and God directed Nebuchadnezzar to destroy Jerusalem. Seventy years later, God remembered His covenant and, in response to Daniel's prayer, restored Jerusalem spiritually and physically. Four hundred eighty-seven years later, Israel had again fallen spiritually, crucifying the Messiah, and, in God's providence, the city was destroyed by Titus in 70 AD.

- The last part of verse 26 and of verse 27 parallels Matthew 24. There is a partial fulfillment at the destruction of Jerusalem. But the final and complete fulfillment begins with the "abomination," which is the Sunday law, and it ends with "desolation" at the "end of the war" "even unto the consummation."
- There is only one "consummation" that takes place after the abomination of desolation. That is the consummation of God's people with Jesus at His second coming! The fulfillment of this passage will take place at the end of time.
- There are critical concepts to understand.
  - At the beginning of the seventieth week, Jesus, "the Lamb of God," was baptized, and the promise to "take away the sin of the world" was given. Our restoration will become complete!
  - In the middle of the seventieth week, the Messiah caused the ceremonial Jewish system to cease. Jesus was crucified, the veil of the temple was "rent in twain," and Jesus became that veil—the portal to the Most Holy and God's throne. (See Heb. 9:12; *The Desire of Ages*, p. 757.)
    1. "**When** Christ should hang upon the cross of Calvary, Israel's day as a nation favored and blessed of God **would be ended**" (GC 20.3).
    2. "Israel as a nation had **divorced herself from God**. The natural branches of the olive tree were broken off. Looking for the last time upon the interior of the temple, Jesus said with mournful pathos, 'Behold, your house is left unto you desolate. For I say unto you, Ye shall not see Me henceforth, till ye shall say, Blessed is He that cometh in the name of the Lord.' Hitherto He had called the temple His Father's house; but now, as the Son of God should pass out from those walls, God's presence would be withdrawn forever from the temple built to His glory. Henceforth its ceremonies would be meaningless, its services a mockery" (DA 620.4; see also DA 618–620).

- What did Jesus mean when He said:
  - The blood of the righteous will come against that generation in Jesus' day (Matt. 23:33–36) as part of a severance "woe," or curse
  - "Behold, your house is left unto you desolate" (Matt. 23:38)
  - "The kingdom of God shall be taken from you, and given to a nation bringing forth the fruits thereof" (Matt. 21:43)?
- There is no other conclusion that one can come to but that the Jewish nation would cease to be God's chosen people when Messiah the Prince was "cut off."
- Gabriel told Daniel that 490 years were "determined," or decreed, for "thy people" to become holy and have everything ready for a Jubilee restoration. Daniel's people failed. Their probation ended at the cross. That was 31 AD, three and a half years short of the 490 years. Many people are simply unaware or just ignore this point!

  When Christ upon the cross *cried out, 'It is finished' (John 19:30), and the veil of the temple was rent in twain, the Holy Watcher declared that the Jewish people had rejected Him who was the antitype of all their types, and the substance of all their shadows.* **Israel was divorced from God.** *(DA 709.4)*

- What happens to the last three and a half years? Jesus tells us in Daniel 12.
  - Many shall be purified, and made white (Dan. 12:10).
  - An abomination resulting in desolation will be set up (Dan. 12:11).
  - God's people shall be scattered by persecution until the time of deliverance and the special resurrection "shall be finished" (Dan. 12:7).
  - God promises a blessing for His people during this time (Dan. 12:12).
  - Daniel's messages will be proclaimed, and Daniel will stand in his lot during this final three and a half years, or 1260 days, of witnessing (Dan. 12:13).
- The antitypical fulfillment of the restoration of Israel comes at the end of time with the 144,000. Jesus told the Jews that the "kingdom

of God" would be taken from them and given to another people, another "nation" (Matt. 21:43). After 2300 atonement evenings and mornings, a holy people were to emerge that are forever pure and holy. The only people mentioned in the Bible that fit that description are the 144,000. They are "the firstfruits unto God and to the lamb ... they are without fault before the throne of God" (Rev. 14:4, 5). They meet the requirements of Daniel 9:24. This will be the complete fulfillment of the seventy-week prophecy, when Israel is spiritually restored.

- Confirming the covenant continues in a special way during the 70th week. *The last week is a unified whole in the context of restoration and redemption.*

- It wasn't good for the people of Ellen White's day to know all these things. By God's design, they needed to go through a testing time. But now our whole church needs to be awakened and needs to seek Jesus and His character with all our heart. We need to strive to be among the 144,000. God promises to complete the good work He has begun in us! (Phil. 1:6).

- An interesting point to notice is that the abomination that leads to desolation takes three and a half years in both cases—in Jesus' day and at the end of time.

- Another vital point is that Jerusalem was desolated and destroyed many years after the crucifixion of Jesus in the middle of the 70th week *during a three-and-a-half-year siege*. There was a delay or gap of thirty-nine years—but within a generation. (See Matt. 24:34.) A generation in the Bible is forty years (Num. 32:13; Ps. 95:10). There is also a delay or gap between the cross and the final abomination of desolation yet to come—at the end.

Jesus' Day	**End of time**
Cross	Cross
Time gap	*Time gap*
Abomination	Abomination
Flee destruction—Jerusalem	Flee destruction—Babylon
Desolation of Jerusalem	Desolation of World
End	End

- Daniel and John the Revelator talk, in several places, about the same 1260-day time period of the "abomination of desolation." Daniel 12 and Revelation 11 together, among other passages, put last-day events within a three-and-a-half-year time period. Both periods (Jesus' day and the end of time) depict a final probation. The 70 AD desolation is a metaphor of the final period of mercy before the world becomes desolate. God's people escaped Jerusalem before it was destroyed, and God's people will escape Babylon before the world is destroyed at the end.

- The complete fulfillment of the 70-week prophecy has not yet occurred. The final events of Daniel 9:24 and the following verses have yet to take place. The last three and a half years still tarry for a people to finally meet the divine objective. The everlasting covenant is not yet complete.

> *Daniel 12 and Revelation 11 together, among other passages, put last-day events within a three-and-a-half-year time period.*

> That which God purposed to do for the world through Israel, the chosen nation, *He will finally accomplish through His church on earth today.* He has "let out His vineyard unto other husbandmen," even to His covenant-keeping people, who faithfully "render Him the fruits in their seasons." Never has the Lord been without true representatives on this earth who have made His interests their own. *These witnesses for God are numbered among the spiritual Israel, and to them will be fulfilled all the covenant promises made by Jehovah to His ancient people."* (PK 713.1)

- This is plain and confirming. Spiritual Israel will be rewarded with the covenant promises. In the 144,000 will be seen the completion of Daniel 9:24.

- What did happen between the cross and 34 AD? *"Probation was lengthened."*

> "Jesus was sitting in the midst of priests, rulers, lawyers, and Pharisees,—in the midst of men who had long been favored with the heavenly invitation, and who claimed to be guests for the feast of the Lord. But when the time came when they should have entered

into the spiritual kingdom of heaven, when by believing on Christ they should have been partakers of his flesh and blood, when they should have received him whom their sacrificial offerings typified, they all with one consent began to make excuse. Mercy was extended to them, and their *probation was lengthened*, until three years and a half after the death of Christ [*if it was already part of the seventy weeks, why "lengthen" it?*], when the apostles declared:

" 'It was necessary that the word of God should first have been spoken to you; but seeing you put it from you, and judge yourselves unworthy of everlasting life, lo, we turn to the Gentiles.' The Lord gave the commission to go out into the highways and the hedges of the cities and villages, to go to the poor, the halt, the lame, and the blind, to minister to those who felt that they had need of a physician. Jesus had declared, 'I am not come to call the righteous, but sinners to repentance.' The wandering sheep must be hunted up. The Jews refused to accept the flesh and blood of the Son of God; they would not listen to his word, which he declared is spirit and life, and rejected the invitation to the gospel feast. Through their impenitence and stubbornness of heart in refusing the heavenly invitation, they themselves were rejected. The solemn words were spoken by lips that cannot lie, saying, 'None of those men that were bidden [and who have refused my invitation] shall taste of my supper" (RH, March 10, 1896).

- The 1260-day prophecies of Daniel 12 and Revelation 11–13 unfold the time period of the last probation for God's people and the time when the prince of this world (Satan, the beast) will attempt to prevent the completion of the covenant—the finishing of the last half of the last week of the covenant.

- Before the seventy weeks began, God anticipated Israel's failure by giving the 2300-year prophecy. That in itself shows that Daniel 9:24 would never be completed by Israel of old, and a delay, or gap, of time was going to occur.

- The seventy weeks of years have not been completed. Jesus said that would happen after the 2300 evenings and mornings (Dan. 8:14). There would be a long *tarrying time*.

"For the vision is yet for an appointed time, but in the end it will speak, and not lie: though it tarry, wait for it; because it will surely come, it will not tarry" (Hab. 2:3).

- At the "appointed time," the final three and a half years of earth's history will resume. Then this great prophecy will see its termination at the deliverance of God's people.

- The future understanding of this prophecy was noted by Ellen G. White:

"As Daniel's prayer is going forth, the angel Gabriel comes sweeping down from the heavenly courts to tell him that his petitions are heard and answered. This mighty angel has been commissioned to give him skill and understanding—to open before him the *mysteries of future ages*. Thus, while earnestly seeking to know and understand the truth, Daniel was brought into communion with Heaven's delegated messenger. In answer to his petition, Daniel received not only the light and truth which he and his people most needed, but a view of the great *events of the future,* **even to the advent of the world's Redeemer**" (SL 48.1, 2).

Summary of Daniel 9:20–27

- Daniel 8, defined as applying to the time of the end (vs. 1, 2, 17, 19), left off with Daniel fainting in astonishment and not understanding the *mareh* vision. In Daniel 9:23, Gabriel comes to give Daniel understanding of the *mareh* vision.

- 70 weeks, or 490 years, of probationary time are given for God's people to become holy and for God to complete His work as described in verse 24.

- By the middle of the 70th week, God's people failed to meet the holiness objectives required to fulfill the prophecy. Three and a half years short of the 490 years, at the cross, Israel was divorced from God and were no longer His chosen people.

- A delay, or gap, occurred between the cross and the abomination and desolation of Jerusalem, and a longer delay is occurring between the cross and the final abomination and desolation of the world.

- Just before and during the troublous times of the 1260 days yet to come (the final abomination of desolation time frame), God's people will be *spiritually restored*, or rebuilt, and brought back to holiness by decisions that will never change.

- The 70th week is a unified whole in the context of restoration and redemption.
- *Physical deliverance* will come at the final Jubilee at the end of the appointed time, the 1260 days of Daniel 8:19 and 12:7.
- It is during the final abomination of desolation timeframe that the last three and a half years of the 490 years will be completed, Daniel 9:24-27 will be fulfilled, and then we will soon see Jesus coming in the clouds of heaven to take us home.

Daniel 10

- Daniel 10 starts with understanding. Daniel finally understands that the *mareh* vision is "long" (2300 years long) and that the final battle between the ram (God's people made holy) and the he-goat (the apostate people) will take place after the 2300 years at the time of the end. (Dan. 8:14 is the first timing *explanation*.) Daniel understands that God's people will be made holy (Dan. 8:14; 9:24).
- Still, Daniel mourns for a lack of knowledge and fasts for three full weeks. He then sees a vision of Christ in white linen as our High Priest, King, and Judge. This is a prophecy of what Jesus will be in the future at the "time of the end."
- Gabriel comes in answer to Daniel's prayers to give him further understanding of the prophecies of chapters 8 and 9, focusing on what "shall befall thy people in the **latter days**" (Dan. 10:14, 12, 21; 11:2). Daniel 11 and 12 provide the answer, including the timing of the prophecies, the deliverance of God's people from the battle between good and evil, and how the 70-week prophecy would end.
- Gabriel came to give him understanding about the *chazôn* vision on the 24th of Abib. Daniel was fasting during the time of Passover (Abib 14) and the Feast of Unleavened Bread. This is also the time that the disciples were praying and coming into unity before the *Holy Spirit was poured out* on them at Pentecost. This is significant for us to note! *"In like manner* the types which relate to the *second advent must be fulfilled at the time pointed out* in the symbolic service" (GC 399.4).
- Daniel represents those who look up and are enraptured at seeing

Jesus the Lamb of God. The rest will flee, crying: "Hide us from the face of him that sitteth on the throne" (Rev. 6:16).

- To the sinner, a vision of Jesus lays bare the corruption of the heart. As that picture of our Savior becomes ever clearer, the soul longs for restoration—to be exactly like Him—and it yearns to come into harmony with His character. When that occurs, only celestial aid can rescue and restore.

- It was important that Daniel understand the *mareh* vision first:
  - It takes place after 2300 evenings and mornings.
  - It brings the perfection of a holy people (the ram).
  - It is within the 70-week period of probation.
  - It completes the restoration of God's people by Jesus—the Priest, Judge, and King.
  - Why? Because the *chazôn* vision is all about Satan's opposition to a holy people and the everlasting covenant. It is about persecution, conflict between good and evil, and the mystery of iniquity. But, at the end, God is victorious.

Daniel 11

- Beginning with Persia, Daniel 11 is a prophecy of the succession of nations, leaders, and events leading to the end of time. Chapters 8, 11, and 12 detail the *chazôn* vision and the conflict between good and evil. God's foresight is perfectly amazing!

- Here are some of the key timing markers in chapter 11:
  - Verses 1 and 2 foretell of the next four monarchs to rule Persia after Darius, with the fourth preparing to fight Greece.
  - Verses 3 and 4 identify Alexander the Great and the dividing of his empire to his four generals after his death.
  - Verses 5 through 15 give a long list of wars (spanning over 150 years) between the "king of the south" (primarily Egypt and surrounding areas) and the "king of the north" (Greece and surrounding areas) who took the rest of Alexander's empire that had been ruled by three of his generals.
    - It is noteworthy that God's people in Judea, during this time, are progressing through their 490-year probation of

the seventy weeks. Why is the Bible silent during this period of time regarding God's people? One must conclude that their probation was not going well. Apostasy led God to have Palestine traversed with repeated military campaigns between the kings of the north and the kings of the south. The only prophetic warning God gave is found here in Daniel 11. Each military conflict and each new king who ruled in the north or the south was a reminder of a sovereign God who had predicted it all beforehand. In the end, when Jesus came as the Messiah (and Daniel 9 clearly tells when this was), they didn't recognize Him. This is all a metaphor of what it will be like at the time of the end between the "king of the north" and the "king of the south." When Jesus comes, most of those who claim to be His followers will not have expected Him (1 Thes. 5:2).

- Verses 16 through 19 predict the transition of power to the Romans as they conquered the Greeks, the glorious land of Palestine, and nations beyond.

- Verse 20 foretells of Caesar Augustus who sent out a decree stating "that all the world should be taxed" (Luke 2:1). This decree helped fulfill prophecy by bringing Joseph and Mary to Bethlehem where the Messiah of Israel was to be born.

"As in old time Cyrus was called to the throne of the world's empire that he might set free the captives of the Lord, so Caesar Augustus is made the agent for the fulfillment of God's purpose in bringing the mother of Jesus to Bethlehem. She is of the lineage of David, and the Son of David must be born in David's city. Out of Bethlehem, said the prophet, 'shall He come forth … that is to be ruler in Israel; whose goings forth have been from old, from the days of eternity.' Micah 5:2, margin" (DA 44.2).

- Verse 21 prophesies the first rise of the papacy and of the pope (the "vile person" acting against God's will that is also symbolized by the "king of the north" and the "little horn") who entered the scene peacefully and deceitfully. He obtained the kingdom by "flatteries" and has a mouth that speaks great words (Dan. 7:11, 20, 25). He thinks to change times and laws

(Dan. 7:25).

- Verses 22 through 27 list the corruption and conquests of the papacy and its fall:
  - The papacy stood up against the prince of the covenant, which is Jesus who is also the "Prince of the host" (Dan. 8:11), the "Prince of princes" (Dan. 8:25), and "Messiah the Prince" (Dan. 9:25, 26). Through the civil governments of Europe during the dark ages, the papacy wiped out many of God's people and took the spoils from their exploits.
  - The papacy takes on the role of the King of the North and initiates the crusades against the King of the South (the Muslims). These crusades between the Christian and Muslim world are a type of the battle that will take place at the end of time.
  - French leaders (General Berthier under Napoleon's orders) removed the pope (Pope Pius VI) in 1798, and he died in France. "They that feed" with him "shall destroy him."
  - On September 20th, 1870, Rome fell to Italian troops, and the papal states became part of Italy. The papacy was reined in to just 109 acres within Rome, called the Vatican.
- Verses 28 through 31 prophesy of the second rise of the papacy.
  - Five times Scripture says that he (the vial person) shall "return." He shall be restored to what he had before. The beginning of his return became reality at the signing of the Lateran Treaty in 1929 when the papacy became, once again, a religious and civil power.
  - Recent popes have made many trips to different countries and have engaged in many exploits, raising support for the papacy and its terrible plans. Pope John Paul II alone made over 100 trips abroad with as many as one million in attendance. The world is truly "wondering after the beast."
  - Some of these papal trips abroad have been to the "king of the south," that is, to Muslim countries. These visits are not as the former actions—crusades—nor as the latter—open

warfare (Dan. 11:40). They have been "peaceful" trips.

- Since north and south portray the forces hostile to God (see verse 27), it would seem logical that east and west illustrate those who meet with God's approval. See Isaiah 43:5, 6, and Zechariah 8:7. The ships of Chittim symbolize the remnant people coming from the west, specifically beginning in the United States, who oppose the "vile person" (Dan. 11:21). Ellen G. White referred to this verse, then quoted verses 31–36 and concluded that these "scenes" "will take place" when Satan assumes "control of human minds, who have not the fear of God before them. Let all read and understand the prophecies of this book" (Letter 103, 1904). She saw these events as part of the end of time.

> *Ellen G. White concluded that these "scenes" "will take place" when Satan assumes "control of human minds, who have not the fear of God before them.*

- What is the papal power's response to God's remnant people coming from the west? He exhibits open indignation against the holy covenant. Ecumenism, which is "intelligence" between Protestants and Catholics, goes directly against God's covenant, and it promotes Sunday worship instead of honoring God's holy Sabbath.

- The completion of his rise to power will be at the "time appointed" (Dan. 8:19; 11:27, 29, 35; 12:7). This time begins with the Sunday law (the removal of the "daily" and the placing of the abomination that maketh desolate) and will last 1260 days. This appointed time is discussed in Daniel 8:19; 11:29; and 12:7. This time period parallels Revelation 17:12–14 and Revelation 12:12–17.

- "The first day of the week is to be exalted and presented to all for observance. Shall we be partakers of this *cup of abomination?* Shall we bow to the authorities of earth and despise God? The powers of darkness have been gathering their forces to bring this crisis about in the world, so that the man of sin may exalt himself above God" (RH, April 15, 1890; ST, March 3, 1890).

- Verses 32–35 contrast those who are for God's holy covenant with those who are against His holy covenant.
  - The ecumenical bond between Catholicism and Protestantism that is against God's holy law and covenant is driven by deception and spiritually seductive actions, revealing what they are not. This insight began in chapter 8. A king "understanding dark sentences, shall stand up" (Dan. 8:23), and "he shall cause craft to prosper in his hand" (Dan. 8:25).
  - In contrast to the corrupt covenant breakers are those who "know their God." They are strong and cleave to the holy principles of heaven. They follow through and act upon their convictions and loyalty to God. This parallels an amazing prophecy found in Revelation 6, which depicts the unswerving dedication of the 144,000 of the white horse period. At that time, when the history of the world is coming to a close, God's remnant will be active, going out "conquering, and to conquer." These white horse people will be teachers spreading the final message of Jesus and His imminent return around the world crescendoing into the "loud cry."

> *These white horse people will be teachers spreading the final message of Jesus and His imminent return around the world crescendoing into the "loud cry."*

  - Those who understand the message will instruct many, but they will fall by the sword and flame, be imprisoned, and have their belongings taken away. This persecution parallels the second, fourth, and fifth seals of Revelation 6 in which a group of revengeful people (represented by the red horse) are associated with others to harm and kill (represented by the pale horse) resulting in martyrdom.
  - When God's people shall fall (Heb. *kawshal*, suggesting

someone who stumbles or totters from weakness or weariness from the pursuit of persecution), they will be assisted by God who sustains His people. He never leaves or forsakes them.

- Sadly, many of those who claim loyalty to God, when under threat, will join with, or cleave to, those who have been deceived by "smooth" teaching.

- Thankfully, at the very end, some backsliders will return to the loyalty of the remnant. The dross of this world will be purged out, and they will become white—just like the 144,000.

- In verses 36-39, the "vile person," the "king of the north," who is the "little horn" of Daniel 8, exalts himself and claims to be above God.

  - What God has already decreed in Daniel 9:26, 27 will be done! The "vile person," the "little horn" who is the "king of the north," is destined for destruction. God has foretold his final demise.

  - The "king of the north," the papacy, has no regard for the God of his fathers, nor any god. The apostolic church had a pure faith and unswerving interest to uphold the God of truth. As Rome gradually became the center of Christian power, pagan influences tainted the truth. The disregard for women is reflected in the rule of celibacy and prohibition of marriage for the priesthood.

  - The papacy honors gods of gold, silver, precious stones, and pleasant things. Within Catholicism, the massive system of idols, icons, expensive ornaments, luxurious clothing, jewelry, and lavish churches transfers worship from the God of heaven to man himself—that is, to the pope. In many different places in Catholic literature, the pope is seen as, is worshiped as, and is declared to be *"god on earth"* (reminiscent of the "strange god" of the passage).

  - "Who is like the beast? Who can make war against him?" (Rev. 13:4). The papacy so intrigues the minds of the world that they submit to it, feeling that it is all-powerful.

- In verses 40–45, the "vile person," or "king of the north," although seemingly triumphant for a time, comes to his end.
  - During the Dark Ages, the conflict, as described earlier in this chapter, was between the "Christian" papacy and the Muslim world through the wars of the Crusades. The center of the conflict was Palestine. That was a "type" of what was to come.
  - There is only one significant world power that wars specifically against Christianity, and that is the Muslim world.
  - The Koran identifies all non-Islamicists as "unbelievers." Islam is the opposite force opposing the "symbolic center" of Christianity—the papacy and the Protestantism of the United States. Ayatollah Khomeini convinced the Islamic world that the United States was the "Great Satan." In over fifty of the world's 184 countries, there are 1.9 billion followers that make up the house of Islam.
  - The papacy and its ally, apostate Protestantism of the United States (Revelation 13), will fight back and enter many Islamic countries and Palestine as well.
  - *Strong's Exhaustive Concordance* suggests that the word "countries" means "the earth." From this perspective, the "king of the north" shall stretch his hand of power over the earth, and the world will not escape his grip. This parallels the symbolic description of the Sea Beast (the papacy) and the Earth Beast (Protestant America) in Revelation 13 (note the word "all" in Rev. 13:7, 12). This also parallels the time of the ten kings of Revelation 17:12.
  - The "king of the north" will be in control of the world's financial system.
  - The "east" was where the tribe of Judah was camped in relation to the tabernacle (Num. 2:3). That tribe is represented by the first of the living creatures in heaven (Rev. 4:7) and by the white horse of the first seal (Rev. 6:1, 2). Those symbols are associated with the last work of the 144,000. Since we know this setting in Daniel 11 is in the end-time (*eth qets*), "tidings" (verse 44) must represent the power of the Holy Spirit in the "latter rain," giving power

to the "loud cry" of the 144,000 coming from the "east." It is having an effect that "shall trouble him" (the "king of the north").

- The papacy is troubled by what is occurring and, in his fury, sets out to destroy God's people. The papacy, with its supporting "host" (Dan. 8:12), fixes its authority between the people of the world and God's holy people.

- God has the last word. The "king of the north" comes to his end (*qets*)—his final end—and no one will help him. When does that occur? It *begins* when the River Euphrates is dried up under the sixth plague (Rev. 16:12). Babylon's support will be finished. God remembers (Rev. 16:19) the hatred and treachery of the papacy, the earth-beast, and the dragon. They will finally be subject to His wrath (Rev. 6:16, 17; 16:19), and then *the battle will be over*.

- That is exactly where Daniel 8:1–13 and the promised timed prophecy of Daniel 12:7 point to—the end of papal power and the deliverance of God's people (Dan. 12:1–3, 6–13).

Daniel 12

- The appointed "time, times, and an half," or 1260 days of witnessing and forty-two months of persecution, take place inside a 1335-day window at the very end of time. Then, deliverance of God's people comes.

- See Part 2 of this book for details.

Daniel 8 through 12 in review

- The *ram symbol* of Daniel 8 represents Jesus and those who claim to be His people—the remnant, His church.

- The ram is persecuted by the he-goat, representing Satan and his people.

- Daniel 8:14 comes in response to Gabriel's question as to when that persecution would occur. There, Jesus promised it would be after **spiritual** *deliverance, when restoration* would come.

- Daniel 9:24 tells us what the remnant must do to experience that deliverance.
- Daniel 11 gives greater information about the he-goat opposition and persecution.
- Daniel 12:7 defines *when **physical** deliverance* and restoration will occur.

Key Points of Revelation 1 through 18

Revelation is a sealed book, but it is also an opened book. It records marvelous events, that are to take place in the last days of this earth's history. The teachings of this book are definite, not mystical and unintelligible. In it the same line of prophecy is taken up as in Daniel. Some prophecies God has repeated, this showing that *importance must be given to them.* The Lord does not repeat things that are of no great consequence. (Ms. 107, 1897)

Revelation 1

- This book is "The Revelation of Jesus Christ."
- Revelation shows us things "which must *shortly come to pass*" (v. 1). This book is a book of future events relative to when Jesus gave the information to John on the island of Patmos.

> *The Lord does not repeat things that are of no great consequence.*

- On the Sabbath, John hears a voice like a trumpet. This is a clue that the timing is related to the Feast of Trumpets, which takes place in the fall on a "Sabbath." The underlying message of the Feast of Trumpets is: Get Ready! Get Ready! Get Ready!
- John sees a vision of seven golden candlesticks and Jesus walking among them. Here John is receiving a "revelation of Jesus Christ" walking among His churches and holding His "angel" messengers in His hand. John falls "at his feet as dead. And he [Jesus] laid his right hand upon me, saying unto me, Fear not …" Jesus' care for His people is close and intimate.
- This is all sanctuary imagery. The Feast of Trumpets is a call to

prepare for the judgment and atonement of His people taking place in the heavenly sanctuary.

- "The instruction to be communicated to John was *so important that Christ came from heaven to give it to His servant*, telling him to send it to the churches. *This instruction is to be the object of our careful and prayerful study*" (Ms. 129, 1905).
- "Now he [John] was permitted again to behold his risen Lord, clothed with as much glory as a human being could behold, and live. What a Sabbath was that to the lonely exile, always precious in the sight of Christ, but now more than ever exalted! Never had he learned so much of Jesus. Never had he heard such exalted truth" (YI April 5, 1900).

Revelation 2 and 3

- When reviewing the attributes of each of the seven churches, it is important to remember that Jesus loves His people and that He is walking among His churches (Rev. 1:12, 13, 20).
- Each of the seven churches are judged in these chapters.
- All seven churches were in existence during the first century.
- Each of the seven churches is symbolic of a time period during the Christian dispensation.
- The characteristics of the seven churches also describe the characteristics of the Christian church in existence today. They are not sequentially numbered like the seals, trumpets, or plagues since they all existed at the same time at the beginning of the Christian dispensation, and, in an end-time context, they all exist at the same time as well.
- Notice that, in an end-time context, five of the seven churches have apostatized and two of the seven churches are loyal to Jesus.
- The two faithful churches are encouraged to stay true to God no matter the cost.
  - God has nothing against Smyrna (Rev. 2:8–11). He encourages Smyrna to be "faithful unto death." Their reward for the ultimate sacrifice is a crown of life.
  - God has nothing against Philadelphia (Rev. 3:7–13). He tells

them they have kept His word, and He instructs them to hold fast to the truth so that no man take their crowns.
- Crowns are a symbol of victory in their Christian experience with Jesus. By faith in Jesus, they have overcome self and the powers of darkness in our world!
- The enemies of God's people will worship at their feet.
- Notice that there are several patterns of two in Daniel and Revelation, *symbolizing the two groups* of God's faithful, end-time people.
  - two horns on the ram in Daniel 8,
  - two loyal churches in Revelation 2 and 3,
  - two of the beasts and two of the horses in Revelation 4 and 6,
  - the 144,000 and the great multitude in Revelation 7,
  - two witnesses, two olive trees, two candlesticks, and two prophets in Revelation 11.
- The five unfaithful churches are encouraged to overcome.
  - Thyatira represents the papacy and the Catholic Church (Rev. 2:18–29).
    - Among the positive attributes listed, charity is one thing for which Thyatira is recognized.
    - On the negative side, Jezebel represents the Antichrist and the character of the pope who is declared to be God on earth. He teaches many falsehoods, and many commit spiritual adultery with the papacy and the Catholic Church.
    - Those who stay in Thyatira will be destroyed, while God will use in mighty ways those who leave and overcome.
    - "The apostasy today is similar to that which overspread Israel in Elijah's day. In *exalting the human above the divine*, in the praise of popular leaders, in the worship of mammon, and in the placing of science above the truths of revelation, multitudes today are following Baal. Many are substituting for the oracles of God the theories of men. It is taught that human reason should

be exalted above the teachings of the Word. The law of God is declared to be of no effect. The enemy is working to cause men and women to forget that which was ordained for the happiness and salvation of mankind" (SS 89.7).

- The remaining churches, Ephesus, Pergamum, Sardis, and Laodicea represent Apostate Protestantism.
    - They have many good works that the Lord recognizes. Sadly, they have many things that God is against, and, unless they repent, overcome, and choose to join Smyrna or Philadelphia, they will be lost (James 2:10–12).
    - "The losing of the first love is specified as a moral fall. The loss of this love is represented as something that will affect the entire religious life. Of those who have lost this love, God says that unless they repent, He will come to them, and remove their candlestick out of its place" (Ms. 1, 1906)
    - "The doctrine is now largely taught that the gospel of Christ has made the law of God of no effect; that by 'believing' we are released from the necessity of being doers of the Word. But this is the doctrine of the Nicolaitans, which Christ so unsparingly condemned" (ST, Jan. 2, 1912).
    - "In the Laodicean state of the church at the present time, how little evidence is given of the direct, personal guidance of God! Men place themselves in positions of temptation, where they see and hear much that is contrary to God, and detrimental to spirituality. They lose their warmth and fervor, and become lukewarm Christians, who are, in a great measure, indifferent to the glory of God, and the advancement of his work" (RH, June 19, 1888).
    - "Today there is need of the voice of stern rebuke; for grievous sins have separated the peo-

ple from God. Infidelity is fast becoming fashionable. 'We will not have this man to reign over us,' is the language of thousands. The smooth sermons so often preached make no lasting impression. The trumpet does not give a certain sound. Men are not cut to the heart by the plain, sharp truths of God's Word" (RH, Sept. 11, 1913).

- "He [Jesus] stands at the door of the heart as a heavenly merchantman; he knocks there, saying, Open unto me, buy of me the heavenly wares, buy of me the *gold tried in the fire, which is faith and love*, the precious, beautiful attributes of our Redeemer, which will enable us to melt our way into the hearts of those who do not know him, those who are cold and alienated from him through unbelief and sin. He invites us to buy of him the *white raiment, which is his glorious righteousness,* and the *eyesalve, that we may discern spiritual things.* Oh, shall we not open the heart's door to this heavenly voice? He says, 'Behold, I stand at the door and knock; if any man hear my voice, and open the door, I will come in to him, and will sup with him, and he with me'" (ST, Feb. 8, 1892).

Revelation 4

1. *After this I looked, and, behold, a door was opened in heaven: and the first voice which I heard was as it were of a trumpet talking with me; which said, Come up hither, and I will shew thee things which must be hereafter.*

    - John again hears the voice of a trumpet (as he did in Rev. 1:10–12), a sound that ties back to the Feast of Trumpets, announcing that it is time to "Get Ready! Get Ready! Get Ready!" He identifies the timing as taking place after a door has been opened in heaven. The door to the most holy place was opened in the heavenly sanctuary in 1844 (Rev. 3:8). This scene takes place after that time when He says, "Behold I come quickly," as the saints, or 144,000, *already have a crown* (for they are victorious!), and they anticipate being sealed (Rev. 3:11).

- The Feast of Trumpets represented the final preparation for the Day of Atonement when all of sin's issues will be resolved. It was a time of judgment.
- The *final* anti-typical Day of Atonement and its judgment of the living will begin in the fall of the year at the time of the fall feasts—just before the Sunday law is passed—and will continue until probation closes right before the seven last plagues. Judgment begins with God's people, His church (Rev. 11:1).
- In this verse, Jesus says that He will show John the things that will take place after the trumpet warning begins. This portion of Revelation encompasses Revelation chapters 4 through 6 and the first part of chapter 8.

2. *And immediately I was in the spirit: and, behold, a throne was set in heaven, and one sat on the throne.*

3. *And he that sat was to look upon like a jasper and a sardine stone: and there was a rainbow round about the throne, in sight like unto an emerald.*

4. *And round about the throne were four and twenty seats: and upon the seats I saw four and twenty elders sitting, clothed in white raiment; and they had on their heads crowns of gold.*

5. *And out of the throne proceeded lightnings and thunderings and voices: and there were seven lamps of fire burning before the throne, which are the seven Spirits of God.*

6. *And before the throne there was a sea of glass like unto crystal: and in the midst of the throne, and round about the throne, were four beasts full of eyes before and behind.*

- These verses portray a judgment scene with a throne, twenty-four thrones with the elders seated on them, the sound of thunder and of voices, seven lamps of fire, and a sea of glass. These are all elements of the sanctuary in heaven where the final judgment is taking place. The imagery is amazing! Compare Isaiah 6:1–4; Ezekiel 1:26–28.
- This scene has *new elements* not found in the judgment scene that *began* in Daniel 7:9, 10. Here we are seeing a new scene related to the second coming.

- The four beasts representing the end-time players are part of this scene.
- The twenty-four elders, men redeemed from the earth, are part of this judgment scene. They are called "elders," which applies to positions of men. They are clothed in white, a symbol that is used for those who are translated (Rev. 7:13–15). They have crowns showing that they have gained the victory—likely over sin. Those who overcome are promised white garments, crowns, and thrones (Rev. 3:5, 11, 21). They sing about their redemption and about reigning on the new earth (Rev. 5:9, 10).
- The emerald rainbow reveals God's mercy. Jasper and sardine were stones on the High Priest's breastplate. Our High Priest, Jesus, is bringing the judgment to a close and seeking to extend mercy to as many as possible.
- The seven Spirits of God in this passage and in Revelation 1:4 and 5:6 relate to Zechariah 4:1–10. Their inclusion suggests that this is the time of the complete manifestation of the Holy Spirit in the "latter rain."

7. *And the first beast was like a lion, and the second beast like a calf, and the third beast had a face as a man, and the fourth beast was like a flying eagle.*

8. *And the four beasts had each of them six wings about him; and they were full of eyes within: and they rest not day and night, saying, Holy, holy, holy, Lord God Almighty, which was, and is, and is to come.*

- The four beasts are angelic beings with six wings. Each beast has specific characteristics that relate to the seal that each one opens in chapter 6.
- The four beasts around the throne in heaven represent the four lead tribes that were around the sanctuary in the wilderness, and the lead tribes, with their symbol or standard, are symbols of last-day groups who claim to be God's people (Num. 2:2; compare with Ezek. 1:10).
- The first beast, the lion, opens the white horse seal.
  - The lion is symbolic of the tribe of Judah (Rev. 5:5).
  - The lion was the lead standard of the tribes on the east side of the sanctuary in the wilderness (Num. 2:3; Ezek. 1:10).

- Jacob, who prophesied what would happen to his sons in the "last days" (Gen. 49:1) said, "The sceptre shall not depart from Judah, nor a lawgiver from between his feet, *until Shiloh come*" (Gen. 49:10). The lion and Judah are symbols of the 144,000 and the church of Philadelphia who have the character of Jesus and proclaim the law of God *"until Shiloh come"* (Gen. 49:1; compare Rev. 6:1, 2).

- The second beast, the calf, opens the red horse seal.
  - The calf is symbolic of the tribe of Ephraim.
  - The calf (or ox) was the lead standard of the tribes on the west side of the sanctuary in the wilderness (Num. 2:18; Ezek. 1:10; the Hebrew word for "ox" in Ezek. 1:10 also means cow; see Strong's OT 7794).
  - The tribe of Ephraim joined with the other tribes of the *northern kingdom* of Israel (reached her hand across the gulf) and made Jeroboam, an Ephraimite, their king. Jeroboam instituted a false system of worship in Israel, uniting the ten tribes (1 Kings 11:26–13:34; Hosea 4:17). Who does Ephraim represent in an end-time context? It represents Apostate Protestantism, which unites with Babylon, the "king of the north," and enforces an idolatrous system of worship, the replacement of the Sabbath by Sunday.
  - Revelation 17 states that ten kingdoms will unite with Babylon for a short period of time "until the words of God shall be fulfilled" (Rev. 17:17).

- The third beast, the man, opens the black horse seal.
  - The man is symbolic of the tribe of Reuben.
  - The man was the lead standard of the tribes on the south side of the sanctuary in the wilderness (Num. 2:10).
  - Jacob said that Reuben was "unstable as water" (Gen. 49:4). Reuben lost his birthright as firstborn son because he laid with his father's concubine (Gen. 35:22). In the last days, those symbolized by Reuben are *associated* with a prostitute woman, Babylon, the mother of harlots (Rev. 17:1–5). Yet, they respond to the "loud cry," and they "come out of her" and join with Smyrna. Reuben is the second tribe in Revelation 7. They

are listed after Judah, and they are sealed. They will overcome!

- The fourth beast, the eagle, opens the pale horse seal.
    - The eagle is symbolic of the tribe of Dan.
    - The eagle was the lead standard of the tribes on the north side of the sanctuary in the wilderness (Num. 2:25).
    - Jacob said: "Dan shall be a serpent by the way, an adder in the path, that biteth the horse heels, so that his rider shall fall backward" (Gen. 49:17).
    - God's throne is in the "north" (Ps. 48:2; Ezek. 1:4), but Satan *claims* that his throne is in the north, and he gives his power to Babylon, the "king of the north," to persecute and destroy God's people (Isa. 14:13, 14; Jer. 6:22, 23; 1:14).
    - Dan represents the papacy and is synonymous with the church of Thyatira in Revelation 2, the sea beast of Revelation 13, and Babylon the Great in Revelation 17.
        - The calf and the eagle are on opposing sides from the lion and the man. The red horse opposes the white horse, and the pale horse opposes the black horse in end-time events (Rev. 6).
        - In the list of the 144,000 in Revelation 7, the tribes of Dan and Ephraim are missing (the second and fourth beasts). They are lost.
        - In the sanctuary, there were images of cherubs and palm trees, and each cherub had two faces, as we see in Ezekiel: "The face of a man was toward the palm tree on the one side, and the face of a young lion toward the palm tree on the other side" (Ezek. 41:19). The symbolism of the palm can be seen in the Psalms: "The righteous flourish like the palm tree" (Ps. 92:12).
        - Here, God's end-time people, in a sanctuary judgment setting, are depicted. The lion represents the white horse and the 144,000. The man represents the black horse and the great multitude who are waiting in darkness to hear the message of the 144,000 and respond in faith.

9. *And when those beasts give glory and honour and thanks to him that sat on the throne, who liveth for ever and ever,*

10. *The four and twenty elders fall down before him that sat on the throne, and worship him that liveth for ever and ever, and cast their crowns before the throne, saying,*

11. *Thou art worthy, O Lord, to receive glory and honour and power: for thou hast created all things, and for thy pleasure they are and were created.*

- The beasts and the twenty-four elders give glory and honor to our Creator and Savior.

Revelation 5

This scene, a continuation of the sanctuary scene in chapter 4, is one of mercy and justice. Jesus, the Lamb that was slain, is pleading His blood on our behalf and is at the right hand of God who is sitting on the mercy seat throne. Under the mercy seat is the law of God.

1. *And I saw in the right hand of him that sat on the throne a book written within and on the backside, sealed with seven seals.*

2. *And I saw a strong angel proclaiming with a loud voice, Who is worthy to open the book, and to loose the seals thereof?*

- God is holding a scroll with writing on both sides, similar to the scroll in Ezekiel 2:9, 10. The context of this passage suggests that this scroll contains the documentation of judgments decreed against a rebellious people.
- This scroll is sealed with the seven seals. It is "completely" sealed with a numbered sequence. Therefore, it cannot be reviewed until after all the seals are removed. That won't take place until we are in heaven after the removal of the seventh seal during the 1000 years. It is then that we can review the "books."
- A "loud voice" is recorded a number of times in Revelation. Each time it relates to the time just before or during the loud cry. This is the "appointed time" of Daniel 8:19 and Habakkuk 2:2, 3. During this time, Jesus is pleading with the people of the world effectively saying, "This is the *last chance* before the end."

3. *And no man in heaven, nor in earth, neither under the earth, was able to open the book, neither to look thereon.*

4. *And I wept much, because no man was found worthy to open and*

to read the book, neither to look thereon.

5. *And one of the elders saith unto me, Weep not: behold, the Lion of the tribe of Juda, the Root of David, hath prevailed to open the book, and to loose the seven seals thereof.*

- "There in His open hand lay the book, the roll of the history of God's providences, the prophetic [written beforehand] history of nations and the church. Herein was contained the divine utterances, His authority, His commandments, His laws, the whole symbolic counsel of the Eternal, and the history of all ruling powers in the nations. In symbolic language was contained in that roll the influence of every nation, tongue, and people from the *beginning* of earth's history to its *close*.

  "This roll was written within and without. John says: 'I wept much, because no man was found worthy to open and to read the book, neither to look thereon' [verse 4]. The vision as presented to John made its impression upon his mind. *The destiny of every nation was contained in that book.* John was distressed at the utter inability of any human being or angelic intelligence to read the words, or even to look thereon. His soul was wrought up to such a point of agony and suspense that one of the strong angels had compassion on him, and laying his hand on him assuringly said, 'Weep not: behold, the Lion of the tribe of Judah, the Root of David, hath prevailed to open the book, and to loose the seven seals thereof'" (Letter 65, 1898).

- "Thus the Jewish leaders made their choice. Their decision was registered in the book which John saw in the hand of Him that sat upon the throne, the book which no man could open. In all its vindictiveness this decision will appear before them in the day *when* this book is unsealed by the Lion of the tribe of Judah" (COL 294.1).

6. *And I beheld, and, lo, in the midst of the throne and of the four beasts, and in the midst of the elders, stood a Lamb as it had been slain, having seven horns and seven eyes, which are the seven Spirits of God sent forth into all the earth.*

- Jesus, the Lamb that was slain for us, is the only being in the universe worthy to open the scroll. In His humanity, He was victorious over all principalities and powers. He is worthy to remove each seal according to His timing. He is in control of all the final end-time events. He will vindicate to the universe God's character of love, mercy, and justice.

- This verse mentions the "seven Spirits of God *sent forth into all the earth*." This is a complete manifestation of the Spirit, adding information to Revelation 1:4 and 4:5. The "latter rain" is being poured out into all the earth.

- The lamb that stood "as it had been slain" is symbolized as still bleeding. His blood is still pleading for us. There is still a small period of probationary time remaining!

- "Christ is our Mediator and officiating High Priest in the presence of the Father. He was shown to John as a Lamb that had been slain, *as in the very act of pouring out His blood in the sinner's behalf*. When the law of God is set before the sinner, showing him the depth of his sins, he should then be pointed to the Lamb of God, that taketh away the sin of the world. He should be taught repentance toward God and faith toward our Lord Jesus Christ. Thus will the labor of Christ's representative be in harmony with His work in the heavenly sanctuary" (4T 395.2).

7. *And he came and took the book out of the right hand of him that sat upon the throne.*

8. *And when he had taken the book, the four beasts and four and twenty elders fell down before the Lamb, having every one of them harps, and golden vials full of odours, which are the prayers of saints.*

    - Christ's taking the scroll marks the beginning of the final proceedings necessary to open the scroll.

    - While the judgment of the living is underway, it is a time of intense prayer by the saints as they prepare for a terrible time of trouble just ahead.

    - There is now a group of morally pure people in the making. The 144,000, the white horse people, will carry the final message of salvation to the world under the power of the Holy Spirit.

9. *And they sung a new song, saying, Thou art worthy to take the book, and to open the seals thereof: for thou wast slain, and hast*

redeemed us to God by thy blood out of every kindred, and tongue, and people, and nation;

10. And hast made us unto our God kings and priests: and we shall reign on the earth.

11. And I beheld, and I heard the voice of many angels round about the throne and the beasts and the elders: and the number of them was ten thousand times ten thousand, and thousands of thousands;

12. Saying with a loud voice, Worthy is the Lamb that was slain to receive power, and riches, and wisdom, and strength, and honour, and glory, and blessing.

13. And every creature which is in heaven, and on the earth, and under the earth, and such as are in the sea, and all that are in them, heard I saying, Blessing, and honour, and glory, and power, be unto him that sitteth upon the throne, and unto the Lamb for ever and ever.

14. And the four beasts said, Amen. And the four and twenty elders fell down and worshipped him that liveth for ever and ever.

- The angels and representatives from earth around the throne are praising the Lamb for His wisdom and sacrifice. The universe understands the great controversy. Jesus receives all the honor and glory and initiates the final events with the removal of the seals.

Revelation 6

1. And I saw when the Lamb opened one of the seals, and I heard, as it were the noise of thunder, one of the four beasts saying, Come and see.

- This chapter starts out with the noise of "thunder." A judgment takes place at this point. What judgment would be complete at the beginning of the seals when the "latter rain" is poured out? It is the judgment leading to the determination of the 144,000. This also relates to the beginning of the judgment of the living (see Rev. 10:3 and 11:1–3).

- The seven seals are numbered and take place in a specific sequence, just as the trumpets and the plagues. The sequence contains a break between the sixth and seventh event, adding important information that we need to understand.

- "Here were *scenes* presented to John that were not in reality but that which would be in a *period of time in the future*. [Rev. 6:1-4 quoted]" (Letter 65, 1898).
  - This statement was written in 1898 and points to a future fulfillment from when it was written.
  - In what period of time will these scenes take place? At the "appointed time" of Daniel 8 and Habakkuk 2.
- "The same spirit is seen today that is represented in Revelation 6:6-8. *History is to be repeated. That which has been will be again*" (Letter 65, 1898).
- Jesus the Lamb who was portrayed, in Revelation 5, as still bleeding and as slain is initiating the final events. Jesus is the center of the prophecies.

2. *And I saw, and behold a white horse: and he that sat on him had a bow; and a crown was given unto him: and he went forth conquering, and to conquer.*

   - White is a symbol of purity and the perfect righteousness of Jesus (Rev. 7:14; 19:8). The horse and the bow are weapons of war, and the crown symbolizes victory.
   - This horse symbolizes God's pure people, the 144,000, who are judged worthy to ride forward in conquest, and nothing can stop them from being empowered by the "latter rain" (Zech. 10:3; Joel 2:1-4). They are fully under the control of their rider and leader, Jesus.
   - Each of the four beasts of Revelation 4 relate to the first four seals, and, at the opening of each seal, they each say, "Come and see." The first beast represents the lead tribe on the east of the sanctuary. East is the direction from which Jesus will come. Thus, east symbolizes deliverance. The 144,00 will bring the final message of deliverance to the world.
   - "At the commencement of the time of trouble, we were filled with the Holy Ghost as we went forth and proclaimed the Sabbath more fully.… 'The commencement of the time of trouble,' here mentioned does not refer to the time when the plagues shall begin to be poured out, but to a short period just be-

fore they are poured out, while Christ is in the sanctuary. At that time, while the work of salvation is closing, trouble will be coming on the earth, and the nations will be angry, yet held in check ..." (EW 33.2; 85.3).

3. *And when he had opened the second seal, I heard the second beast say, Come and see.*

4. *And there went out another horse that was red: and power was given to him that sat thereon to take peace from the earth, and that they should kill one another: and there was given unto him a great sword.*

- The red horse people are depicted using red, which is a symbol of sin and under the control of their rider and leader, Satan.
- The conflict begins in the United States of America and spreads to the rest of the world. When the Sunday law is passed in the United States, God's 144,000 go out to teach the Sabbath truth more fully. Apostate Protestantism, the red horse under Satan's leadership, responds with a vengeance.

5. *And when he had opened the third seal, I heard the third beast say, Come and see. And I beheld, and lo a black horse; and he that sat on him had a pair of balances in his hand.*

6. *And I heard a voice in the midst of the four beasts say, A measure of wheat for a penny, and three measures of barley for a penny; and see thou hurt not the oil and the wine.*

- The removal of the third seal releases the black horse. This horse is sitting still and his rider has a pair of balances in his hand. A warning from heaven is given to not hurt the oil and the wine.
- The black horse people, who are still in Babylon, are sitting in darkness waiting for the white horse to give the three angels' messages to the whole world.
- Their rider, Jesus, has a pair of balances. Judgment is taking place.
- This period is also a time of famine. In Bible times, a day's wages was a "penny" and the amount of grain that could be purchased for a day would barely sustain a person or possibly a family, let alone other expenses. Grain is symbolic of the Word of God. This is a time of famine for the truth of Jesus.

- Hurt not the oil (the Holy Spirit's influence) or the wine (the blood of Jesus). There is a work going on in the lives of the black horse people. In response to the white horse messages given by the 144,000, the Holy Spirit will work to wash their characters in the blood of the Lamb. They, the great multitude, will come out of Babylon and join God's people.

> *The black horse people, who are still in Babylon, are sitting in darkness waiting for the white horse to give the three angels' messages to the whole world.*

7. *And when he had opened the fourth seal, I heard the voice of the fourth beast say, Come and see.*

8. *And I looked, and behold a pale horse: and his name that sat on him was Death, and Hell followed with him. And power was given unto them over the fourth part of the earth, to kill with sword, and with hunger, and with death, and with the beasts of the earth.*

   - Power is given to this horse to kill.
   - Satan claims his throne in the north (symbolized by the fourth beast and the tribe of Dan in Rev. 4), and he gives his power to the papal power, the "king of the north" (Dan. 11:28–45).
   - Ephraim and Dan, who represent the red and pale horses, the calf and the eagle, are not listed among the twelve tribes in Revelation 7. They join together to make up the people and power of Babylon.
   - Anciently, Ephraim, Dan, and eight other tribes joined to form the northern kingdom. The northern kingdom had ten of the twelve tribes. The pattern of ten and two is significant.
     - Ten spies rebelled after spying out Canaan, and two were loyal (Joshua and Caleb).
     - There were ten rebellious northern tribes (Israel) and two loyal southern tribes (Judah).
     - There are ten divisions ("kings") of our world at the very end (Rev. 17:12) that receive power along with the beast,

and there are two groups that are loyal—the 144,000 and the great multitude.

- The eagle (the fourth beast) is a bird of prey.
- The mission of the pale horse is death and hell, not persecution. Martyrdom will be the result.
- One third represents the wicked (Revelation 8), and a fourth (or a "fourth part") represents God's people willing to sacrifice all for Jesus (2 Tim. 4:6-8; Exod. 29:39-41; Num. 23:10). This horse has power over God's people "to kill with the sword."
- "Not only was Balaam shown the history of the Hebrew people as a nation, but he beheld the increase and prosperity of the *true Israel of God to the close of time*. He saw the special favor of the Most High attending those who love and fear Him. He saw them supported by His arm as they enter the dark valley of the shadow of death. And he beheld them coming forth from their graves, crowned with glory, honor, and immortality. He saw the redeemed rejoicing in the unfading glories of the earth made new. Gazing upon the scene, he exclaimed, 'Who can count the dust of Jacob, and the number of the *fourth part* of Israel?' And as he saw the crown of glory on every brow, the joy beaming from every countenance, and looked forward to that endless life of unalloyed happiness, he uttered the solemn prayer, 'Let me die the death of the righteous, and let my last end be like his!' " (PP 447.3).

9. *And when he had opened the fifth seal, I saw under the altar the souls of them that were slain for the word of God, and for the testimony which they held:*

10. *And they cried with a loud voice, saying, How long, O Lord, holy and true, dost thou not judge and avenge our blood on them that dwell on the earth?*

11. *And white robes were given unto every one of them; and it was said unto them, that they should rest yet for a little season, until their fellowservants also and their brethren, that should be killed as they were, should be fulfilled.*

- Removal of the fifth seal reveals souls symbolically under the altar who were slain for the Word of God and their testimony.
- Those who are martyred are symbolically crying out to God

for the vindication of His character that they fearlessly stood for. They want to know, "How long?"

- God replies with a message to wait. This message to the living faithful tells us that the work has not yet been completed but will be fulfilled in a "little season."
- The altar is another piece of the sanctuary scene that has continued since chapter 1. There are two altars associated with the sanctuary. One is in the courtyard, and the other is in the Holy Place.
    - The courtyard altar:
        - That it is outside the sanctuary implies that it is "in the world," where the saints are martyred as Jesus was.
        - The blood of the victim is poured out at the base of the altar (Lev. 4:7; Exod. 29:12).
    - The incense altar:
        - Some of the blood of the victim was put on the horns of the altar of sweet incense before the Lord (Lev. 4:7).
        - The blood of the martyrs is symbolically crying out, or praying, to God (Gen. 4:10).
        - When we pray, our prayers are purified by Jesus in His mediation for us at the altar of incense (1 Chron. 6:49; Rev. 8:3).
        - "By blood and by incense God was to be approached—symbols pointing to the great Mediator, through whom sinners may approach Jehovah, and through whom alone mercy and salvation can be granted to the repentant, believing soul" (PP 353.2).
- These saints are martyred for the word of God and the testimony they hold (Rev. 6:9). What is the testimony of Jesus? It is the character of Jesus revealed in their lives and the prophetic truths they speak. They are just like Jesus who revealed His character while speaking the prophetic word of God. The testimony of Jesus is the "spirit of prophecy" (Rev. 19:10).
    - Their characters and the truth they speak cry out with a

"loud voice" to all the world.

- The first four trumpets are a direct response to this cry to avenge their blood, bring in justice, and vindicate the character of Jesus.

12. *And I beheld when he had opened the sixth seal, and, lo, there was a great earthquake; and the sun became black as sackcloth of hair, and the moon became as blood;*

13. *And the stars of heaven fell unto the earth, even as a fig tree casteth her untimely figs, when she is shaken of a mighty wind.*

14. *And the heaven departed as a scroll when it is rolled together; and every mountain and island were moved out of their places.*

15. *And the kings of the earth, and the great men, and the rich men, and the chief captains, and the mighty men, and every bondman, and every free man, hid themselves in the dens and in the rocks of the mountains;*

16. *And said to the mountains and rocks, Fall on us, and hide us from the face of him that sitteth on the throne, and from the wrath of the Lamb:*

17. *For the great day of his wrath is come; and who shall be able to stand?*

    - The opening of the sixth seal reveals the events that take place at the return of Jesus.
    - Verses 12 to 14 list similar events as does Matthew 24:29 that take place "after the tribulation of those days." The sun and moon are darkened, the stars fall, and the powers of the heavens are shaken.
    - Those who have rejected the love and mercy of their Creator and Savior will flee in terror.
    - Jesus returns, the wicked are slain by the brightness of His coming, and the faithful declare, "Lo, this this is our God. We have waited for Him!"

Revelation 7

Chapter 7 is a pause in between the sixth and seventh seal with new and important information about the work of our Savior in the heavenly sanctuary and those who will be victorious in the battle just described in the seals.

1. *And after these things I saw four angels standing on the four corners of the earth, holding the four winds of the earth, that the wind should not blow on the earth, nor on the sea, nor on any tree.*
2. *And I saw another angel ascending from the east, having the seal of the living God: and he cried with a loud voice to the four angels, to whom it was given to hurt the earth and the sea,*
3. *Saying, Hurt not the earth, neither the sea, nor the trees, till we have sealed the servants of our God in their foreheads.*

    - The four angels "*standing* on the four corners of the earth" are holding back the winds of strife so that God's faithful may be sealed with the seal of the living God.
    - "Only those who, in their attitude before God, are filling the position of those who are repenting and confessing their sins in the great anti-typical day of atonement, will be recognized and marked as worthy of God's protection. The names of those who are steadfastly looking and waiting and watching for the appearing of their Saviour—more earnestly and wishfully than they who wait for the morning—will be numbered with those who are sealed" (TM 445.1).
    - The seal of the living God is placed upon those who conscientiously keep the Sabbath of the Lord. (See Isa. 58:12–14.)
    - The seal is a mark of redemption that is placed on all those who are obedient and faithful to all God's commandments, including the seventh-day Sabbath. These faithful ones have humbled themselves before Jesus and, by faith, have trusted in Him and His promises to make their characters spotless (Phil. 1:6).
    - The seal of the living God will be placed on those who bear a likeness to Christ in character. The seal is our passport to the Holy City.

4. *And I heard the number of them which were sealed: and there were sealed an hundred and forty and four thousand of all the tribes of the children of Israel.*

    - "Let us strive with all the power that God has given us to be among the hundred and forty-four thousand" (RH, March 9, 1905).

- Evidence suggests that the 144,000 are sealed just before the final three and a half years begins (Rev. 1:10; 4:1–4; 11:1–4; 6:1, 2).

- Additionally, notice the sequence of events. Verses 4 through 8 detail the sealing of the 144,000. In verse 9, John states, "After this …" Sequentially, we have the sealing of the 144,000 and then, as the result of their work, we have a great multitude "of all nations" who end up standing before God in heaven.

- "Especially in the closing work for the church, *in the sealing time of the one hundred and forty-four thousand* who are to stand without fault before the throne of God, will they feel most deeply the wrongs of God's professed people. This is forcibly set forth by the prophet's illustration of the last work under the figure of the men each having a slaughter weapon in his hand. One man among them was clothed with linen, with a writer's inkhorn by his side. 'And the Lord said unto him, *Go through the midst of the city, through the midst of Jerusalem,* and *set a mark upon the foreheads* of the men that *sigh and that cry* for all the abominations that be done in the midst thereof.' [Ezek. 9:4.]" (3T 266.2).

- The sealing time of the 144,000 is a distinct time.

- The seal of God will be placed upon the foreheads of those only who sigh and cry for the abominations done in the land.

- Now is the time to prepare. Not one of us will ever receive the seal of God while our characters have one spot or stain upon them.

- *Then*, when our characters are spotless, the "latter rain" will fall upon us as the early rain fell upon the disciples on the *Day of Pentecost*.

- Those who receive the seal of the living God and are protected in the time of trouble must reflect the image of Jesus fully.

5. *Of the tribe of Juda were sealed twelve thousand. Of the tribe of Reuben were sealed twelve thousand. Of the tribe of Gad were sealed twelve thousand.*

- Judah and Reuben were the lead tribes of the east and south sides of the camp of Israel in the wilderness. They are synonymous with the lion and the man in Revelation 4:7, the white and the black horses in Revelation 6, and the 144,000 and the great multitude.

6. *Of the tribe of Aser were sealed twelve thousand. Of the tribe of Nepthalim were sealed twelve thousand. Of the tribe of Manasses were sealed twelve thousand.*

7. *Of the tribe of Simeon were sealed twelve thousand. Of the tribe of Levi were sealed twelve thousand. Of the tribe of Issachar were sealed twelve thousand.*

8. *Of the tribe of Zabulon were sealed twelve thousand. Of the tribe of Joseph were sealed twelve thousand. Of the tribe of Benjamin were sealed twelve thousand.*

   - The original tribes of Dan and Ephraim are missing. They were the lead tribes on the west and north sides of the camp of Israel in the wilderness and are synonymous with the calf and eagle in Revelation 4 and the red and the pale horses in Revelation 6. They oppose God's faithful people in the last days and are lost.

9. *After this I beheld, and, lo, a great multitude, which no man could number, of all nations, and kindreds, and people, and tongues, stood before the throne, and before the Lamb, clothed with white robes, and palms in their hands;*

   - The great multitude are described as unnumberable, coming from all nations, pure (symbolized by the white robes), having gained the victory (symbolized by the palms in their hands), and giving all credit to Jesus (the Lamb).

10. *And cried with a loud voice, saying, Salvation to our God which sitteth upon the throne, and unto the Lamb.*

11. *And all the angels stood round about the throne, and about the elders and the four beasts, and fell before the throne on their faces, and worshipped God,*

12. *Saying, Amen: Blessing, and glory, and wisdom, and thanksgiving, and honour, and power, and might, be unto our God for ever and ever. Amen.*

    - All heaven is in awe and worships God for his incredible mercy toward sinful man.

13. *And one of the elders answered, saying unto me, What are these which are arrayed in white robes? And whence came they?*
14. *And I said unto him, Sir, thou knowest. And he said to me, These are they which came out of great tribulation, and have washed their robes, and made them white in the blood of the Lamb.*
15. *Therefore are they before the throne of God, and serve him day and night in his temple: and he that sitteth on the throne shall dwell among them.*
16. *They shall hunger no more, neither thirst any more; neither shall the sun light on them, nor any heat.*
17. *For the Lamb which is in the midst of the throne shall feed them, and shall lead them unto living fountains of waters: and God shall wipe away all tears from their eyes.*
    - The great multitude are identified as those who came out of the great tribulation during the last three and a half years of earth's history and who have become pure through the sacrifice of Jesus, symbolized by the blood of the Lamb. (See also Matt. 24:21 and Rev. 2:22.)
    - The reward of the great multitude is the privilege of serving Jesus, the King of the New Jerusalem, and dwelling with Him forever.
    - They are also assured that they will not suffer ever again.

Revelation 8

1. *And when he had opened the seventh seal, there was silence in heaven about the space of half an hour.*
    - At the opening of the seventh seal, all of heaven will be emptied, and there will be silence for about half an hour (Zech. 2:13).
    - Calculating the time of half an hour, using a symbolic day for a year, all heaven will be emptied for about seven days while they are on the mission of rescuing God's faithful from earth.
    - Then the scroll will be open for our review!
2. *And I saw the seven angels which stood before God; and to them*

were given seven trumpets.

- Verse 2 begins with the activities of our God and His angels in the sanctuary just before the trumpets are poured out in His last effort to get the attention of every soul on earth.

3. *And another angel came and stood at the altar, having a golden censer; and there was given unto him much incense, that he should offer it with the prayers of all saints upon the golden altar which was before the throne.*
4. *And the smoke of the incense, which came with the prayers of the saints, ascended up before God out of the angel's hand.*
5. *And the angel took the censer, and filled it with fire of the altar, and cast it into the earth: and there were voices, and thunderings, and lightnings, and an earthquake.*
6. *And the seven angels which had the seven trumpets prepared themselves to sound.*

- The last time the altar was in view, martyrs were crying out to Jesus. Now, Jesus, our high priest, who is interceding for us, is standing before the altar which is before the throne of God. He is given much incense so that he can offer the merits of His righteousness with the prayers of the saints to His Father.
- What is taking place at this point, right at the end of time, just before the close of probation? The fifth seal is taking place, Sunday laws have become almost universal, and people everywhere are being killed for their faith. Also, the amount of prayer ascending to our God from a great multitude of people will be unimaginable. Jesus will need "much incense," representing His cleansing blood, to cover the great number of prayers from His people (Num. 16:47).
- It is at this point, *when* the Sunday laws are almost universal and God's people are crying out in prayer to Him to vindicate His character and truth, that *Jesus will act.*
- Jesus takes the censer filled with coals of fire from the altar and casts it to the earth. The coals of fire represent judgment fire to the wicked (see Ezek. 10:2). Coals also symbolize the purification of God's people (Isa. 6:6–8).
- Voices, thunderings, lightnings, and earthquakes in Revelation tell us that a judgment is taking place!

- Verses 7 through 13 (below) describe the first four trumpets. The context of these trumpets is the judgment of God against those who have rebelled against Him and who have persecuted and killed His people, similar to the way that God's judgments fell upon Egypt before the Exodus.
- It is important to note that God is doing all he can to reach every soul possible before probation closes. He has no pleasure in the death of the wicked (Ezek. 33:11).
- The destruction of one third usually applies to the wicked, including those who have strayed from God (Ezek. 5:2, 12). The symbol of the third is used twelve times in the trumpets alone.
- During the trumpets, Jesus sends *partial destruction* upon the earth in mercy. He destroys a third of the land or of the sea at a time, and as a result, He removes a third of those who have hardened their hearts against Him and His people. He does this *in mercy, in order to give the remaining two thirds every opportunity possible to know and make a choice to follow Him.* The trumpets show His great desire to save as many as possible. The love of our God is amazing!

7. *The first angel sounded, and there followed hail and fire mingled with blood, and they were cast upon the earth: and the third part of trees was burnt up, and all green grass was burnt up.*

    - A plague of hail and fire was one of the plagues inflicted upon Egypt. Egypt had enslaved God's people, and God used this plague and the others to lead His people to freedom (Exod. 9:23, 24).
    - During this trumpet, about a third of the vegetation and, likely, a third of the population of those who have hardened their hearts against God are destroyed. The two thirds that remain through the mercy of God will be in awe of the power of God and see that they have a decision to make.
    - "The time of God's destructive judgments is the time of mercy for those who have had no opportunity to learn what is truth. Tenderly will the Lord look upon them. His heart of mercy is touched; His hand is still stretched out to save, while the door is closed to those who would not enter" (9T 97.2; ChS 56.2).

8. *And the second angel sounded, and as it were a great mountain*

burning with fire was cast into the sea: and the third part of the sea became blood;

9. *And the third part of the creatures which were in the sea, and had life, died; and the third part of the ships were destroyed.*

    - Each time Revelation uses the word "mountain" it is referring to a literal mountain.
    - There is only one humanly imaginable object that meets John's description and that is an asteroid falling to the earth in glowing fire.
    - The third of the ocean that becomes blood will no longer sustain life.
    - The tidal waves that result from the impact will destroy all the ships in the affected area, and the ocean will pass its borders to an unimaginable degree.
    - "The tempest is coming, and we must get ready, for its fury by having repentance toward God and faith toward our Lord Jesus Christ. The Lord will arise to shake terribly the earth. … lives will be sacrificed by the millions" (MYP 89.2; LDE 24.1).
    - The four angels that are holding back the four winds of strife are partially releasing the winds in *destructive warnings* (Luke 21:25, 26).
    - This horrible event will be used by God's people to warn the world that the end is in sight. Jesus' return is imminent!

10. *And the third angel sounded, and there fell a great star from heaven, burning as it were a lamp, and it fell upon the third part of the rivers, and upon the fountains of waters;*

11. *And the name of the star is called Wormwood: and the third part of the waters became wormwood; and many men died of the waters, because they were made bitter.*

    - The word "lamp" means a "torch."
    - Wormwood is a plant and bitter herb that can be poisonous. God warned Israel that He would feed them with wormwood if they rebelled against Him (Jer. 9:15).
    - The result of this great star is the poisoning of a third of the

fresh water on earth. There is no human way to explain this event. It can only happen by divine power.

- At this point, much of the earth's food supply is gone, many of the ships are gone along with the coastal cities they sailed to, and now fresh water is unavailable to a third of the earth.

12. *And the fourth angel sounded, and the third part of the sun was smitten, and the third part of the moon, and the third part of the stars; so as the third part of them was darkened, and the day shone not for a third part of it, and the night likewise.*

    - The plague of darkness before the Exodus fell on the Egyptians, not on the people of God (Exod. 10:21–23).
    - This trumpet will display God's power and judgment against those in rebellion. It gives overwhelming evidence and encouragement to the remaining survivors to repent before Him who has total control over His creation (Amos 8:9).

13. *And I beheld, and heard an angel flying through the midst of heaven, saying with a loud voice, Woe, woe, woe, to the inhabiters of the earth by reason of the other voices of the trumpet of the three angels, which are yet to sound!*

    - This message of woes to the world is a warning of what will happen to those who reject the three angel's messages, which God's faithful are still preaching during this time.
    - God's faithful people can claim the Lord's kind care and protection through these judgments (Deut. 32:11, 12; Exod. 19:4).
    - God is crying out to His people to choose life! (Deut. 30:19, 20).

Revelation 9

1. *And the fifth angel sounded, and I saw a star fall from heaven unto the earth: and to him was given the key of the bottomless pit.*
2. *And he opened the bottomless pit; and there arose a smoke out of the pit, as the smoke of a great furnace; and the sun and the air were darkened by reason of the smoke of the pit.*
3. *And there came out of the smoke locusts upon the earth: and unto them was given power, as the scorpions of the earth have power.*
4. *And it was commanded them that they should not hurt the grass of*

the earth, neither any green thing, neither any tree; but only those men which have not the seal of God in their foreheads.

5. *And to them it was given that they should not kill them, but that they should be tormented five months: and their torment was as the torment of a scorpion, when he striketh a man.*
6. *And in those days shall men seek death, and shall not find it; and shall desire to die, and death shall flee from them.*
7. *And the shapes of the locusts were like unto horses prepared unto battle; and on their heads were as it were crowns like gold, and their faces were as the faces of men.*
8. *And they had hair as the hair of women, and their teeth were as the teeth of lions.*
9. *And they had breastplates, as it were breastplates of iron; and the sound of their wings was as the sound of chariots of many horses running to battle.*
10. *And they had tails like unto scorpions, and there were stings in their tails: and their power was to hurt men five months.*
11. *And they had a king over them, which is the angel of the bottomless pit, whose name in the Hebrew tongue is Abaddon, but in the Greek tongue hath his name Apollyon.*

- John sees a star fall to the earth (Rev. 12:7–9; Luke 10:18).
- This star is Satan who is given the key of power. Satan uses his key to loose his demons to work in a very powerful way (Eph. 6:12).
- Smoke is compared to an invading army from the north (Isa. 14:31). Spiritual darkness, symbolized by smoke from Satan and his demons, covers the earth.
- Locusts can cause great destruction. Power is given these locusts to cause harm like scorpions due to their scorpion-like tails. Tails represent those who teach lies (Isa. 9:15; Deut. 28:15, 44, 45).
- Power was given to harm only those people who are not sealed in their foreheads. God's faithful will be protected during this time (Luke 10:19).
- Power will be granted to Satan's demonic forces for five months

right before the close of probation. God is controlling each event! God allows this plague to give the remaining two thirds a chance to see the difference between Christ and Satan. This is one more chance to choose Jesus.

> *God allows this plague to give the remaining two thirds a chance to see the difference between Christ and Satan.*

- Similarly, waters covered the earth for five months after the flood. God's faithful were protected during that time in the ark (Gen. 7:24; 8:3).

- The torment will be so mentally and emotionally painful that people will want to die.

- These locusts have many evil character traits.

- Words "like" or "as" are used because John is unable to describe them in any other way that we could understand.
    - *Like* horses prepared for battle (Prov. 21:31)
    - *As* crowns *like* gold, where crowns represent victory or power to rule, and Satan is claiming victory and ruling his subjects
    - Faces *as* of men signifies intelligence
    - Hair *as* of a women, which, in this context, represents false teaching, a false church, and spiritual seduction
    - Teeth *as* of lions points to Satan who goes about like a ravenous lion (1 Peter 5:8)
    - Breastplates *as* of iron, which is a symbol of Rome, and iron protects hard hearts
    - Wings "*as* the sound of chariots of many horses running to battle" (see Joel 2:4, 5) means that a fierce conflict is underway
    - Tails *like* scorpions means false ideas and teaching (Isa. 9:14, 15)

- Power given to hurt men for five months means 150 days of suffering

- A king over them named Abaddon and Apollyon, which means "destroyer," and the destroyer is Satan
  - God calls us to prayer when the locusts invade (1 Kings 8:37–40; Joel, chapters 1–3).

12. *One woe is past; and, behold, there come two woes more hereafter.*

    One woe is past, and two more are yet to come. Link by link the chain of events is given to tell us where we are in history. All that prophecy has foretold in the past has taken place. We may be assured that all that is yet to come will be fulfilled in its order (Isa. 46:9–11; 48:3).

13. *And the sixth angel sounded, and I heard a voice from the four horns of the golden altar which is before God,*

14. *Saying to the sixth angel which had the trumpet, Loose the four angels which are bound in the great river Euphrates.*

15. *And the four angels were loosed, which were prepared for an hour, and a day, and a month, and a year, for to slay the third part of men.*

16. *And the number of the army of the horsemen were two hundred thousand thousand: and I heard the number of them.*

17. *And thus I saw the horses in the vision, and them that sat on them, having breastplates of fire, and of jacinth, and brimstone: and the heads of the horses were as the heads of lions; and out of their mouths issued fire and smoke and brimstone.*

18. *By these three was the third part of men killed, by the fire, and by the smoke, and by the brimstone, which issued out of their mouths.*

19. *For their power is in their mouth, and in their tails: for their tails were like unto serpents, and had heads, and with them they do hurt.*

20. *And the rest of the men which were not killed by these plagues yet repented not of the works of their hands, that they should not worship devils, and idols of gold, and silver, and brass, and stone, and of wood: which neither can see, nor hear, nor walk.*

21. *Neither repented they of their murders, nor of their sorceries, nor of their fornication, nor of their thefts.*

- John hears a voice from the four horns of the golden altar.
- This is the third time we have seen the golden altar.
  - The martyrs under the altar are symbolically crying to God for him to vindicate His character.
  - Jesus is standing at the altar interceding for His people and initiating judgment in the form of the trumpets.
  - After that, we hear a voice from the horns of the altar.
- These horns symbolize power and strength (Deut. 33:17; Zech. 1:18–21) and God's intercessory power extending to the four corners of the earth. Jesus, personified by the horns, is responding to the trumpet blast of the sixth angel, commanding judgment on the wicked. The time of God's wrath and a final response to the persecuted saints (Rev. 6:9, 10) has come.
- These four angels are evil angels that were "bound" (restrained from killing) at the "great river Euphrates." The Euphrates river represents people of the earth who support Babylon (Rev. 16:12; 17:15). These four angels are different from the four angels on the four corners of the earth holding the four winds of the earth (Rev. 7:1–3).
- These angels were "prepared" but held back until the very hour of God's design and purpose. Not until that hour of that day of that month of that year would Satan be permitted to fully express his hatred and evil character through his demonic forces and his deceived people to kill a third of humankind.

> *These four angels are different from the four angels on the four corners of the earth holding the four winds of the earth*

- The same destructive power exercised by holy angels when God commands them to use it will be exercised by evil angels when He permits them to use it. Evil forces are ready and waiting to spread desolation everywhere.

Part 5: Key Points of Daniel and Revelation   171

- John hears the number of a vast army of 200 million.
- John sees the horses and them that sat on them and all their evil characteristics:
  - The breastplates of the riders were of fire, jacinth, and brimstone.
  - The heads of the horses were *as* the heads of lions.
  - Out of their mouths came fire, smoke, and brimstone.
    - Fire and brimstone are God's instruments of wrath. And the result is that their smoke rises for ever and ever. Satan always has his counterpart twisting God's truths, symbols, and methods for his own evil purposes.
    - Similarly, Satan claims the Lion symbol of King Jesus as his own (1 Peter 5:8).
    - What comes out of their evil mouths is destructive.
    - Similar to the red and pale horses of Revelation 6, the horses here personify the wicked world after probation closes and the riders typify Satan's millions of angels leading the wicked forward to the worst conflict ever seen.
    - A third part of men were killed by the fire, smoke, and brimstone, and by the power that came out of their mouths and tails (representing lies—see Isa. 9:15), which lead to world war.
    - "The wicked shall do wickedly: and none of the wicked shall understand" (Dan. 12:10).
    - Jesus promises to protect His people from "all the power of the enemy" (Luke 10:19).
    - Those not killed by the trumpet judgments "repented not." Though God has allowed the character of Satan to be made perfectly clear, they still choose to hang onto their idols and wicked ways. What more could Jesus have done?

Revelation 10

Chapter 10 is a pause between the sixth and seventh trumpets, giving us information about the "little book."

1. *And I saw another mighty angel come down from heaven, clothed with a cloud: and a rainbow was upon his head, and his face was as it were the sun, and his feet as pillars of fire:*

   - This portion of Revelation begins with a wonderful image of Jesus "clothed with a cloud" and his "feet as pillars of fire." God led his people in the wilderness with a cloud by day and a pillar of fire by night. He will lead us and carry us through the final events in our deliverance from "Egypt."
   - His face is lit with the "sun" as the whole earth will soon be lit with His glory (Rev. 18:1; Ezek. 43:2).
   - The rainbow is a token of the everlasting covenant between God and every living creature and a covenant of His peace. God's promises bring us peace! (Gen. 9:11–17).

2. *And he had in his hand a little book open: and he set his right foot upon the sea, and his left foot on the earth.*

3. *And cried with a loud voice, as when a lion roareth: and when he had cried, seven thunders uttered their voices.*

   - The mighty Angel (which means "messenger") is in this case Jesus, who has "His right foot on the sea, and His left foot upon the dry land," showing "His supreme power and authority over the whole earth" and the part that He is acting in the *closing scenes* of the great controversy with Satan (*The Truth About Angels*, p. 243).
   - He has a "little book open" in his hand. The little book is "open." What things that were sealed at the time John wrote Revelation are now unsealed? What book, which was closed when John wrote Revelation, is now open? It is the end-time portion of prophecy revealed in Daniel 8 to12.
   - Jesus, the Lion of the Tribe of Judah, holds the unsealed portion of Daniel and gives a "loud cry" revealing the seven thunders to John.

4. *And when the seven thunders had uttered their voices, I was about to write: and I heard a voice from heaven saying unto me, Seal up those things which the seven thunders uttered, and write them not.*

Part 5: Key Points of Daniel and Revelation

- John is told to seal up what the seven thunders uttered. We can know what those seven thunders say by first studying the portion of Daniel that is now open.

- The seven thunders are a delineation of events that take place within and around the prophetic framework revealed in Daniel 8 to 12. These events are to be presented as part of the final proclamation of the three angel's messages of Revelation 14.

- "John heard the mysteries which the thunders uttered, but he was commanded not to write them. The special light given to John which was expressed in the seven thunders was a *delineation of events* which *would transpire* under the first and second angels' messages" (Ms. 59, 1900).

- "*It was not best for the people to know these things*, for their *faith* must necessarily be *tested* [in 1844]. In the order of God, most *wonderful and advanced truths* would be proclaimed" (Ms. 59, 1900).

- The seven thunders and most of Revelation are a supplement to the framework given in the *chazôn* vision of Daniel 8–12, which was sealed until the time of the end. Daniel's prophecies relating to the last days and the seven thunders are to be understood at the time of the end.

- Delineation of the seven thunders within and around Daniel's three-and-a-half-year time prophecy given in Daniel chapter 12.

    1. The seals begin. The judgment of the living is underway, and the 144,000 (symbolized by the white horse) go forth giving the warning: Soon, time will no longer be delayed!

    2. The 1290/1335 days begin. The "Daily" is taken away by the removal of God's Sabbath, and the abomination of desolation begins with the passing of the Sunday law.

    3. The 1260 days begin. Enforcement of Sunday laws begin, and the scattering during the 1260 days of witnessing and 42 months of persecution begins. The seals continue.

    4. Trumpets begin. The martyrs under the altar symbolically cry out when the Sunday laws are almost universal, and God responds with the sounding of the trumpet judgments. This is also the time when the loud cry goes forth.

5. Close of probation. Michael stands up; the seven last plagues begin; the death decree and the time of Jacobs trouble follow.

6. 1260/1335 days end. The special resurrection and deliverance of God's people take place.

7. The second coming of Jesus. The time of the seventh seal and the seventh trumpet takes place sometime after the final time prophecies are complete when Jesus returns to take His faithful home. (See chart at the end of Part 5 on page 227.).

5. And the angel which I saw stand upon the sea and upon the earth lifted up his hand to heaven,

6. And sware by him that liveth for ever and ever, who created heaven, and the things that therein are, and the earth, and the things that therein are, and the sea, and the things which are therein, that there should be time no longer:

- Jesus swears by His *Father*, *Creator* of *heaven and earth*. This is the seal of God given to us in the fourth commandment showing His *name*, *title*, and *dominion*.

    o The Sabbath commandment is the central issue and is presented here as the seal of God (Exod. 20:11).

    o The first thunder begins with the white horse of Revelation 6 riding with power to conquer. The conflict over the true day of worship, Sunday worship versus Sabbath worship, is the focus of the conflict. See Daniel 8 and 12, and Revelation 6.

- Then Jesus says there shall be "time no longer."

    o *Strong's Exhaustive Concordance* says that the word for "time" implies, "delay." The NKJV says that there will be "delay no longer," and many translations other than the KJV say, "There will be no more delay."

    o What delay comes to an end? Habakkuk 2:2, 3 tells us that the "vision" is for an "appointed time" at the "end," and, though it "tarry," we are to wait for it. Habakkuk's word for vision (*chazôn*) is the same Hebrew word used for the sealed vision in Daniel 8 to 12.

- In Daniel 8:17, we are told that the vision is to take place "at the time of the end." Daniel 8:19 gives us more information telling us that the end shall take place at "the time appointed" and we shall "know" what shall be during that time of "indignation" (when God's wrath is poured out).
    - Daniel 8:26; 12:4, 9 tell us that the words and the book are sealed "for many days," "even to the time of the end."
    - There is a tarrying time, a delay, until that final vision takes place at the end, and we need to wait for it.
    - What is the message of Daniel 12? The message of Daniel 12 conveys the timing framework of events to take place during the final three-and-a-half-year time period of earth's history. Soon after this final time period is complete, at some unrevealed point in time, Jesus' coming takes place. Eternity is in view!
- Taking the phrase as it reads in the KJV: "time no longer."
    - As discussed in Part 3, the proclamation that there should be "time no longer," "announces the end of the prophetic periods" (2SM 108.1). The final time periods contained in the "little book" ("time, times, and an half a time," 1290 days, and 1335 days of Daniel 12) and highlighted in the seven thunders will be proclaimed to the world! After these time frames are complete, there will be "time no longer"! Time to make a choice to follow Jesus is at an end! Then Jesus will return in the clouds of glory to take His faithful servants home.

7. *But in the days of the voice of the seventh angel, when he shall begin to sound, the mystery of God should be finished, as he hath declared to his servants the prophets.*

    - When the seventh angel begins to sound, the mystery of God's character reflected in us and our oneness with Jesus will be finished (Eph. 3:9; Col. 1:27; 2:2; 1 Tim. 3:16; Zech. 13:9; Mal. 3:1–4). Then the everlasting covenant shall be complete. The end of the sin issue is in sight! The Day of Atonement, the cleansing of the heavenly sanctuary, will come to an end!

8. *And the voice which I heard from heaven spake unto me again, and said, Go and take the little book which is open in the hand of the angel which standeth upon the sea and upon the earth.*

9. *And I went unto the angel, and said unto him, Give me the little book. And he said unto me, Take it, and eat it up; and it shall make thy belly bitter, but it shall be in thy mouth sweet as honey.*
10. *And I took the little book out of the angel's hand, and ate it up; and it was in my mouth sweet as honey: and as soon as I had eaten it, my belly was bitter.*
11. *And he said unto me, Thou must prophesy again before many peoples, and nations, and tongues, and kings.*

- The command to take the little book tells us that it is not understood *until the command comes* to "take it" and "eat it up." We must study the open book, understand the new light it contains, internalize it, and then share it with the world.
- The truths contained in the little book are sweet as honey but the experience during those three and a half years will be bitter.
- We are then told that we must "prophesy again" before the whole world. God's faithful people prophesied at the beginning of the heavenly day of Atonement in the 1840s. We must all prophesy again, as part of the 144,000 and of the white horse, at its close.
- Sequence of Revelation 10
    1. John sees Jesus come to Earth with the "little book" (Daniel 8 to 12) "open."
    2. He cries with a "loud voice" and the sequence of final events is revealed through the seven thunders.
    3. He tells John, "Seal up" what the seven thunders uttered. Don't reveal the sequence of final events … yet.
    4. Then, swearing by the Creator of the Sabbath, he says that there will be no more delay. In other words, we are out of time!
    5. The mystery of final events revealed to John and His servants the prophets will now be revealed and come to an end.
    6. Eat (which means study) the little open book. Understand the sequence of final events.
    7. Then, prophesy again. Teach these things to the world!

Revelation 11

- In Revelation 10:9–11, the voice of God tells John to take the little book from the hand of the Angel (that is, from Jesus) who was protecting the little book truths until that point in time. The book is released *when* John asks for it! Then, John is instructed to eat it (study the *new light* and understand it), and prophesy again (share it with others). *John's activity of eating the book represents the 144,000 preparing to give the last message.*
- Here, in the next verse (Rev. 11:1), our prophesying, or sharing, begins with the house of God. The *straight truth of Daniel 8 to 12* will be shared with God's church and then with the world as part of the three angel's messages.

1. *And there was given me a reed like unto a rod: and the angel stood, saying, Rise, and measure the temple of God, and the altar, and them that worship therein.*

    - To measure means gathering information, and in this case, the information is compared with a *spiritual standard*. John is asked to evaluate the "temple of God" and those who worship there (compare Eph. 4:13).
        - The temple of God symbolizes His church.
        - The altar symbolizes where God's leaders, teach, preach and intercede for His people.
        - Those who worship are the congregation, who claim to belong to God.
    - This is a judgment of living people, a judgment of people who are in the act of worshiping. The judgment of the living begins with the house of God. (See 1 Peter 4:17.)
    - The sequential information given in Revelation 10 and 11 reveal several events that mark the *beginning* of the judgment of the living—
        - *When* "time is no longer delayed" is almost upon us
        - *When* the "loud cry" is about to go out to the world
        - *When* the final time periods of Daniel 12 are about to be proclaimed with the three angel's messages

- These time periods begin with the removal of the Sabbath (the "daily") and the replacement of Sabbath with Sunday under penalty of law.
  - *Then*, the straight truth will be shared with God's church and the judgment of His church and His people will begin.
    - Some will not accept this straight truth; they shall rise up against it, and a shaking of God's last day people will result. Those who remain standing for truth will receive Holy Spirit power to go on and share the final proclamation of the three angel's message and its timing message with the world. (See *Christian Experience and Teachings of Ellen G. White*, pp. 175–178.)

2. *But the court which is without the temple leave out, and measure it not; for it is given unto the Gentiles: and the holy city shall they tread under foot forty and two months. [Their judgment will come later.]*

    - John is told not to worry about the "outer court" (the rest of the world) at this point. He is to focus instead on the inner court, those who claim to be God's people. This is a sanctuary atonement scene focusing on the lives of God's professed people who are being weighed in the balance.
    - During the time of Jesus, only God's "chosen" people were allowed in the inner court of the sanctuary.
    - 42 months equals 1260 days. This three-and-a-half-year time frame is given seven times in prophecy in an end-time context. (These time frames have a partial application to the 1260 years of papal rule from 538 AD to 1798 AD. They have a final and complete fulfillment, in literal time, yet to come.)
    - Whenever timing is described in terms of months, the focus is on the wicked.
    - This is the "appointed time" of scattering for a "time, times, and an half" because of the persecution from the red and the pale horses (Dan. 12:7; 8:9–12). It is the same time as the "forty and two months" of persecution in Revelation 13:5–7. This is also the same time period given in Daniel 7:25; Revelation 11:3; 12:6, 14.

- Jesus suffered for three and a half years at the hands of His own people, but, at the end, He arose! (Mark 9:31). God's faithful will follow in the same footsteps of their Savior for three and a half years. Then we too will arise! (Rev. 11:12).

3. *And I will give power unto my two witnesses, and they shall prophesy a thousand two hundred and threescore days, clothed in sackcloth.*

    - Although God is allowing evil to manifest its true colors, He has his eye on those who are loyal to him—His two witnesses. Why "two witnesses"? Judgment of God's people and the world is in progress. Two witnesses are required to validate any testimony (Deut. 19:15).

    - God shall pour out His Holy Spirit "latter rain" power on His faithful remnant at this time (after the shaking with its judgment of God's church) to strengthen us to give the messages of Daniel's little open book with the three angel's messages to the world. Jesus will not leave us alone during this trying time.

    - Their work will continue during a 1260-day timeframe. Whenever the three-and-a-half-year timeframe is given in terms of days, the focus is on God's faithful.

    - Clothed in humility, their characters and testimony will shine for Jesus.

    - God is seeking to bring His covenant to completion, and Satan is fighting to keep that from happening. God sets a three-and-a-half-year time limit on Satan's efforts to stop God's covenant from becoming reality (Dan. 9:24–27).

    "If we can bear persecution for His dear name's sake, His love becomes a ruling power in our hearts, for we have the assurance that nothing can separate us from the love of Christ. Never is the tempest-tried soul more dearly loved by His Savior than when he is suffering reproach for the truth's sake" (TMK 275.3).

4. *These are the two olive trees, and the two candlesticks standing before the God of the earth.*

    - His two witnesses are the two candlesticks that symbolize Philadelphia and Smyrna, His two faithful churches who represent the 144,000 and the great multitude. These two witnesses are fed with golden oil from the two olive trees which represent God's Holy Spirit feeding His truth to the hearts of His faithful candlesticks to keep their lights shining for Jesus during earth's final hours.

- The two witnesses, the two anointed ones (Zech. 4:12–14), God's human instrumentalities who *stand* before their loving God, are to "prophesy" with the most important message ever given to men. This message contains the everlasting gospel, the three angels' messages, and that which is in the little open book. That little open book solemnly states that probation will close within three and a half years. Noah, Elijah, and John the Baptist prophesied the same way. Sighing and crying over the sins of the people, they plead with the people to turn their hearts to God in anticipation of impending judgment.

- The two witnesses who seek after and plead for God's Holy Spirit and "latter rain" will receive the *Word*, represented by the golden oil. This is the baptism of the Holy Spirit with fire. This power from above will open the soul of unbelievers who hear the *Word* and will bring conviction to their hearts. (See Ms. 109, 1897.)

- Daniel was one of two witnesses to the timing prophecies in Daniel 12:5. The sweetness of the little book kindles a fire within the two witnesses to "prophesy again."

5. *And if any man will hurt them, fire proceedeth out of their mouth, and devoureth their enemies: and if any man will hurt them, he must in this manner be killed.*

    - When they tried to kill Jesus, no one touched Him because His time had not yet come (John 7:30). The same will be true for God's 144,000.

    - Smyrna represents the great multitude. The True Witness tells them to be faithful unto death, and He will give them a crown of life (Rev. 2:10). Their enemies will receive the wages of sin, which is death (Rom. 6:23).

    - The truth of God's Word will fall like fire from the mouths of God's faithful on their enemies (Jer. 23:29).

    - In spite of three and a half years of persecution, nothing will stop the work of the two witnesses.

- "When for the truth's sake the believer stands at the bar of earthly tribunals, Christ stands by his side. When he is confined within prison walls, Christ manifests Himself to him and cheers his heart with His love. When he suffers death for Christ's sake, the Saviour says to him, They may kill the body, but they cannot hurt the soul. 'Be of good cheer; I have overcome the world.' 'Fear thou not; for I am with thee: be not dismayed; for I am thy God: I will strengthen thee; yea, I will help thee; yea, I will uphold thee with the right hand of My righteousness.' John 16:33; Isaiah 41:10)" (AA 85.1).

6. *These have power to shut heaven, that it rain not in the days of their prophecy: and have power over waters to turn them to blood, and to smite the earth with all plagues, as often as they will.*

    - This verse reinforces the timing in verse 3. Power will be given to the two witnesses for 1260 days.
    - Elijah had power to stop the rain for three years and six months (James 5:17). Moses had power to turn water to blood and to smite the earth with plagues (Exod. 7:17–21). God's 144,000 will have these powers plus the authority to exercise their power "as often as they will."

7. *And when they shall have finished their testimony, the beast that ascendeth out of the bottomless pit shall make war against them, and shall overcome them, and kill them.*

    - The work of the two witnesses will be complete! They will finish their testimony to the world. From town to town, from city to city, from country to country, the message of present truth will be proclaimed in the power of the Spirit.
    - God's faithful will be sealed, and Jesus will finish His intercessory work in the heavenly sanctuary.
    - The four angels will let go of the winds of strife, and the seven last plagues will fall during a forty-five-day time period right at the end of the 1260 days (see Daniel 12). The time of trouble such as never was, will begin (Dan. 12:1), and Satan will make war on God's faithful (Rev. 16:14).
    - The seven last plagues enrage the wicked who believe that God's faithful have caused the judgments of God to fall on them, and a death decree goes forth to slay the saints. The

saints cry day and night for deliverance. This is the time of Jacob's trouble, and they shall be saved out of it (Jer. 30:5–7).

- God's remaining faithful are symbolically killed. In other words, their witness is silenced.

  "By condemning the people of God to death, they have as truly incurred the guilt of their blood as if it had been shed by their hands" (GC 627.3; LDE 245.2).

8. *And their dead bodies shall lie in the street of the great city, which spiritually is called Sodom and Egypt, where also our Lord was crucified.*

9. *And they of the people and kindreds and tongues and nations shall see their dead bodies three days and an half, and shall not suffer their dead bodies to be put in graves.*

   - Sodom the immoral city and Egypt the pagan anti-God kingdom represent the world in general. The world will have no respect for the fate of God's faithful ones, who are symbolically represented as not allowing their "dead bodies to be put in graves."
   - Jesus' voice was silenced after His death, so the voices of God's elect will be silenced for "three days and a half."
   - Jacob wrestled with the angel all night as impending doom approached him. When his wrestling was over, God gave him peace and delivered him from the wrath of his brother. God's two witnesses will wrestle with God, apparently for three and a half days, before God gives them peace and deliverance from those seeking to kill them.

10. *And they that dwell upon the earth shall rejoice over them, and make merry, and shall send gifts one to another; because these two prophets tormented them that dwelt on the earth.*

    - The "loud cry" warning of the three angels' message contain the last warning that men will ever receive, and, for this reason, it will be given with the strong terrible language of the threatening of judgment in the form of the trumpets, and then the plagues that will fall on those who reject the mercy and love of Jesus. This message has tormented the world, and now they will "make merry" that their voice has been silenced.

- John calls the two witnesses "prophets." In Revelation 10:11, we are told to "prophesy again." When our prophesying is complete, the world will rejoice (John 16:20).

11. *And after three days and an half the Spirit of life from God entered into them, and they stood upon their feet; and great fear fell upon them which saw them.*

    - After the three and a half days of wrestling and pleading with God for their lives, God's faithful come out of the "time of Jacob's trouble" with peace and strength, and the assurance that He will protect them from the world's death decree during the remainder of the forty-five days of plagues.
        o "With shouts of triumph, jeering, and imprecation, throngs of evil men are about to rush upon their prey, when, lo, a dense blackness, deeper than the darkness of the night, falls upon the earth. Then a rainbow, shining with the glory from the throne of God, spans the heavens, and seems to encircle each praying company. The angry multitudes are suddenly arrested. Their mocking cries die away. The objects of their murderous rage are forgotten. With fearful forebodings they gaze upon the symbol of God's covenant, and long to be shielded from its overpowering brightness" (LDE 246.2).
    - As the three and a half years nears the end, God will deliver His people, and there will be a special resurrection (Dan. 12:1, 2; Ezek. 37:5, 10; Luke 18:7, 8).
    - It will be impossible to describe the horror and despair of those who have trampled upon God's holy requirements. Those in despair will include those who pierced Him.
    - Glorious will be the deliverance of those who have patiently waited for His coming and whose names are written in the book of life. Their voices will rise triumphantly! (Ps. 46:1–3).
    - The Smyrna church, representing those who were martyred, are raised to eternal life (Rev. 1:7; Ezek. 37:12).

12. *And they heard a great voice from heaven saying unto them, Come up hither. And they ascended up to heaven in a cloud; and their enemies beheld them.*

- A cloud represents God's presence (Exod. 16:10; Lev. 16:2).
- God's two witnesses are delivered and called to join their master in a "cloud." Jesus returns in a cloud (Luke 21:27; Acts 1:9–11).
- God allows the witnesses' enemies to witness their ascension heavenward, so they become "witnesses" themselves.

13. *And the same hour was there a great earthquake, and the tenth part of the city fell, and in the earthquake were slain of men seven thousand: and the remnant were affrighted, and gave glory to the God of heaven.*
    - The "same hour" is a timing statement tying these events to the previous verse.
    - A "great" earthquake takes place under the sixth seal. That is the same event describing the return of Jesus in this verse (Rev. 6:12–17).
    - The earth will be utterly destroyed. The tenth part of that great city called "Babylon," which was all that remained, was destroyed, and the 7000 who represent the *whole* of the wicked that remain are slain by the brightness of His coming.
    - The remnant, God's redeemed, give glory to God!

14. *The second woe is past; and, behold, the third woe cometh quickly.*
    - God, in His love for us, continues to tell us of every significant waypoint on the way to heaven. He does nothing without telling His servants the prophets what He is going to do. Those who share the three angels' messages are His prophets (Amos 3:7; Rev. 11:10, 18).

15. *And the seventh angel sounded; and there were great voices in heaven, saying, The kingdoms of this world are become the kingdoms of our Lord, and of his Christ; and he shall reign for ever and ever.*
    - **When** Jesus comes in His glory, **then** He shall sit upon the throne of His glory, and we will receive our inheritance! (Matt. 25:31, 34; Rev. 3:21).
    - At the voice of the seventh angel, the mystery of God is finished (Rev. 10:7). The "last trump" sounds, the jubilee begins,

the Day of Atonement is complete, God's people are delivered, the Feast of Tabernacles begins (seven days), and then the marriage supper of the Lamb takes place.

- This final "woe" is a woe to those left on earth. It is victory and deliverance for those who have stood for Jesus!

16. *And the four and twenty elders, which sat before God on their seats, fell upon their faces, and worshipped God,*

17. *Saying, We give thee thanks, O Lord God Almighty, which art, and wast, and art to come; because thou hast taken to thee thy great power, and hast reigned.*

18. *And the nations were angry, and thy wrath is come, and the time of the dead, that they should be judged, and that thou shouldest give reward unto thy servants the prophets, and to the saints, and them that fear thy name, small and great; and shouldest destroy them which destroy the earth.*

    - The twenty four elders, redeemed from the earth, are worshiping God who has brought the plan to rid the universe of sin to its climax. Soon the redeemed will be joining them!
    - In their worship and gratitude, they summarize who God is and all He has done to bring the universe to this point as described in this chapter. The 6000-year wait is over. The millennial sabbath is now here.
    - The dead will now, during the 1000 years, be judged by the redeemed (1 Cor. 4:5; 6:2; Dan. 7:22; Rev. 20:4, 6).
    - Revelation 6:12–17 and chapters 18–22 describe the events of this time in more detail.

19. *And the temple of God was opened in heaven, and there was seen in his temple the ark of his testament: and there were lightnings, and voices, and thunderings, and an earthquake, and great hail.*

    - When God's temple in heaven is opened, what a triumphant time that will be for all who have been faithful and true!
    - Jesus says to His faithful, "My grace is sufficient for you." The love of Jesus for His people is unfathomable.
    - A storm, described in more detail in the seventh plague, draws all the judgments of God and the final events to a close (Rev. 16:17–21).

Revelation 12

- Like many other portions of Revelation, there is a historical perspective and also an end-time perspective in the passages given by Jesus to John on the island of Patmos. This chapter is no exception. The end-time perspective, the perspective that is most pertinent to us today, continues to be our focus here.

1. *And there appeared a great wonder in heaven; a woman clothed with the sun, and the moon under her feet, and upon her head a crown of twelve stars:*

2. *And she being with child cried, travailing in birth, and pained to be delivered.*

   - The pure woman (God's church) is clothed with the sun (Jesus and the gospel) and has the moon (permanent faithful witness—Ps. 89:36, 37) under her feet and a crown (symbolizing victory) of twelve stars (twelve messengers of the twelve tribes of spiritual Israel—compare with Rev. 1:20; 2:1; 7:4–8) on her head.

   - This great wonder of the image of a holy woman symbolizes *God's end-time church* consisting of the church of *Philadelphia* (the 144,000 who are born from the Laodicean church), the church of *Smyrna* (the persecuted and martyred church), and the overcomers of the other five churches of Revelation 2 and 3 who will join the Smyrna church.

   - The Smyrna church, also called the "great multitude," are made up of those who will hear the final and complete proclamation of the three angels' messages calling them out of "Babylon" and will be converted.

   - She is in pain and about to give birth. God's remnant church is about to go through painful travail—the shaking—and, out of her, the 144,000 will be born.

   - She is standing on the moon, travailing in birth, at the same time as the woman of Revelation 17 is riding the beast.

   - Israel, during the time of Gideon, was under the judgment of God. God used Gideon to raise up a small group of 300 faithful men to deliver Israel. Like Gideon and his small army, the

144,000, which are made up of the twelve spiritual tribes of Israel, will spearhead the completion of the work God has given His people to do.

- The twelve sons of Jacob, who formed the twelve tribes of literal Israel, had some serious defects of character as do today's tribes of spiritual Israel. But God will complete the good work He has begun in us. Claim the promise in Philippians 1:6!
- God's true church, feeble as she may be through all her ups and downs, is the light of God to the world.

3. *And there appeared another wonder in heaven; and behold a great red dragon, having seven heads and ten horns, and seven crowns upon his heads.*

4. *And his tail drew the third part of the stars of heaven, and did cast them to the earth: and the dragon stood before the woman which was ready to be delivered, for to devour her child as soon as it was born.*

- The Devil and Satan is red, symbolizing his sinfulness. This description ties to the scarlet-colored beast of Revelation 17:3.
- With his seven heads, ten horns, and seven crowns, the scarlet-colored beast has direct parallels to the sea beast of Revelation 13:1–10 and Babylon the Great in Revelation 17:1–14. The dragon gives his power to the sea beast, which is also designated as "Babylon."
- During the second rise of the papacy, beginning in 1929, there have been "seven kings" (Rev. 17:7, 9, 10). These represent the seven popes that reigned before Pope Francis.
- The ten horns represent the ten divisions of the world right at the end, as depicted on the feet with ten toes in the statue of Daniel 2 and the ten horns in Daniel 7:23, 24; Revelation 13:1; 17:12.
- This verse (Rev. 12:3) is a timing statement. The dragon, who gives his power to the sea beast and Babylon, is appearing at a time when all seven heads, or popes, have reigned prior to Pope Frances. That they are reigning is symbolized by the *seven crowns* that are on their heads. We are now in the time of the "eighth" (Rev. 17:11).

- Another timing element shown here is that the ten horns do not yet have crowns. The ten divisions of the world do not yet have power to rule.
- The dragon, who is deceiving a "third part" of God's professed leaders (represented by stars) with his lies (represented by his tail—see Isa. 9:15), is ready to devour the 144,000 as soon as they are born. As noted in Revelation 8, a "third" usually applies to the wicked including those who have strayed from God (Ezek. 5:2,12).

5. *And she brought forth a man child, who was to rule all nations with a rod of iron: and her child was caught up unto God, and to his throne.*

    - Like Paul who was caught up to paradise and heard unspeakable words (2 Cor. 12:4; 1 Cor. 2:9), the 144,000 will be caught up spiritually to God and His throne, entering into the Most Holy Place (in their thoughts, feelings, and beliefs) where Jesus is interceding for us at His Father's throne in the Most Holy Place of the sanctuary (Heb. 10:19–22).
    - The 144,000, born of God's people, will be intimately connected with Him and will rule all nations with the truth of Jesus (Rev. 2:26, 27; Judges 7:19, 20; Rev. 19:15).
    - The statue of Daniel 2 represents the deterioration of religion and morality among the people of the nations represented by the different metals of the statue. The iron and clay of the feet in Daniel 2 represent the mixing of church and state. We are living in the time when church and state will unite to enforce a false sabbath on a worldwide scale, and the rock, representing the 144,000, will proclaim the truth of Jesus and His infinite love for us. By the power of the Holy Spirit working through the 144,000 and the judgments of God, the powers of earth will be broken, and truth will prevail. (Study Dan. 2:34, 35, 44, 45.)

6. *And the woman fled into the wilderness, where she hath a place prepared of God, that they should feed her there a thousand two hundred and threescore days.*

    - God's people will flee to a place of safety that God has prepared for them, and He will take care of them for three and a half years.

- The place of safety is in total surrender to Jesus. As Jesus walked the earth under the perfect direction of His Father, His enemies constantly plotted to kill him. Each time they planned or tried to get rid of Him prior to the end of His three and a half years of ministry, their plans and intents were overruled. God's remnant, will walk just as Jesus did. They will be under the direct leadership of Jesus, and He will protect them and provide for them.
- God cherishes His faithful and will strengthen them during the final three and a half years.
- A thousand, two hundred, and three score days is literally 1260 days, which is about three and a half years.
- The timing of this verse ties directly to the 1260 days of witnessing in Revelation 11:3, which ties to the forty-two months of Revelation 11:2 and 13:5 and other references.
- This time period begins with the enforcement of the Sunday law in the United States and ends with God's deliverance of His people. (Study Matthew 24 and Daniel 12 for the foundation of this prophecy.)

7. *And there was war in heaven: Michael and his angels fought against the dragon; and the dragon fought and his angels,*

8. *And prevailed not; neither was their place found any more in heaven.*

9. *And the great dragon was cast out, that old serpent, called the Devil, and Satan, which deceiveth the whole world: he was cast out into the earth, and his angels were cast out with him.*

- Opposition to the law of God had its beginning in the courts of heaven. Satan and his angels were cast out of heaven, and the earth became the theater of the conflict.
- The war begun in heaven is now being fought on earth between Jesus and His angels and Satan and his angels and between God's people and Satan's people (Rev. 19:11). It is a battle between truth and error. During the final three and a half years, truth will be exalted. Satan will lose the war and will be cast down with all his lies.

- The devil seeks to efface from man the image of God and to impress his character in human hearts. (See ST, April 4, 1895, par. 2.)

- The minds of human beings are either controlled by evil angels or by the angels of God. We must make every preparation within our power to resist the enemy of souls. True religion is the imitation of Christ. To imitate Jesus' love, tenderness, and compassion will require that we draw near to Him daily. God's power is far greater than Satan's, and God will impress His character on the hearts of all who are yearning to be like Christ (Phil. 1:6).

- The contest between God's people and Satan's people is ultimately between God and Satan spiritually in "high places" (Eph. 6:12). As God's people pray, like Sampson prayed to be "avenged of the Philistines" (Judges 16:28), the Lord will move to assert His almighty power and His supreme authority (Eph. 6:10, 12; Rev. 8:4–6).

- Satan will ultimately be cast down into the lake of fire on this earth (Rev. 19:20; 20:10).

10. *And I heard a loud voice saying in heaven, Now is come salvation, and strength, and the kingdom of our God, and the power of his Christ: for the accuser of our brethren is cast down, which accused them before our God day and night.*

    - Jesus, who is called Michael (meaning "Who is like God?"), fights against Satan and His angels through the 144,000 who will exalt the truth of salvation and proclaim that the kingdom of heaven is at hand! The lies of Satan will be cast down to the ground.

    - A proclamation with *timing* is being given. What is the timing context of this chapter?

        - God's Laodicean church is shaken and in travail.

        - The 144,000 who stand for the straight truth during the shaking are "born."

        - The seven heads of the dragon have ruled (see Rev. 17).

        - God has "fed" (Rev. 10:10) and prepared His faithful 144,000 for the final 1260 days of witnessing.

- During the 1260 days of witnessing, the three angels' messages are proclaimed (Rev. 14:6–12).
- "Christ is our High Priest. Satan stands before Him night and day as an accuser of the brethren. With his masterly power he presents every objectionable feature of character as sufficient reason for the withdrawal of Christ's protecting power, thus allowing Satan to discourage and destroy those whom he has caused to sin. But Christ has made atonement for every sinner. Can we by faith hear our Advocate saying, 'The Lord rebuke thee, O Satan; even the Lord that hath chosen Jerusalem rebuke thee: is not this a brand plucked out of the fire?' [Zech. 3:2]" (4BC 1178.3).
- During this time, Satan is seeking to kill the 144,000 just like he tried to kill Jesus, but they are under the power of God's protecting hand (Rev. 12:4–6).

11. *And they overcame him by the blood of the Lamb, and by the word of their testimony; and they loved not their lives unto the death.*

    - God's faithful ones overcome Satan by the blood of the Lamb and by the word of their testimony. They are willing to give their lives for their Savior and the people He died for.
    - "Those whom the Lamb shall lead by the fountains of living waters, and from whose eyes he shall wipe away all tears, will be those now receiving the knowledge and understanding revealed in the Bible, the Word of God" (RH, March 9, 1905).
    - "By the increase of knowledge, a people is to be prepared to stand in the latter days" (2SM 105; Dan. 12:4; 1 John 4:4–6).
    - The testimony of Jesus, given by God's 144,000, is the spirit of prophecy (Rev. 19:10). The 144,000 will give the final three angels' message to the world, which includes the final end-time understanding of the prophecies of Daniel and Revelation. Like the proclamation given by Noah, the final chance to accept truth and God's salvation will be preached.
        - "The fourteenth chapter of Revelation is a chapter of the deepest interest. *This scripture will soon be understood* in all its bearings, and the messages given to John the revelator will be repeated with distinct utterance" (RH, Oct. 13, 1904).

- "*Daniel shall stand in his lot at the end of the days. John sees the little book unsealed.* **Then** *Daniel's prophecies have their proper place in the first, second, and third angels' messages to be given to the world. The unsealing of the little book was the message in relation* **to time**" (Ms. 59, 1900).

- The testimony is also the law of the Lord, which is perfect, converting the soul (Ps. 19:7). The law of God, including the Sabbath commandment, will be proclaimed throughout the world (Isa. 58:12–14).

- God's end-time people, those who proclaim the final messages to the world and those who will accept the messages, will love Jesus, their Savior, more than life itself.

12. *Therefore rejoice, ye heavens, and ye that dwell in them. Woe to the inhabiters of the earth and of the sea! For the devil is come down unto you, having great wrath, because he knoweth that he hath but a short time.*

    - God's people who dwell spiritually in the heavens will rejoice! (Ps. 91:1). But there is only woe for those whose thoughts, feelings, and beliefs are controlled by the devil, for his wrath is great, knowing that his time is short.

    - See Psalms 91 and comments on Revelation 12:5.

    - The devil knows the time prophecies of Daniel 12 and the delineation of events within those prophecies proclaimed by the seven thunders. His end is in sight, and he wants to take as many with him as he possibly can (Rev. 10:3, 4).

13. *And when the dragon saw that he was cast unto the earth, he persecuted the woman which brought forth the man child.*

14. *And to the woman were given two wings of a great eagle, that she might fly into the wilderness, into her place, where she is nourished for a time, and times, and half a time, from the face of the serpent.*

    - The dragon (the serpent, the devil, and Satan, Rev. 12:9), who is cast to the earth, understands his hopeless condition outside of Jesus, and he takes out his wrath on God's faithful, the 144,000, and the great multitude who respond to the proclamation of the three angels' messages (Rev. 12:13).

- God's faithful will be given strength, power, nourishment, and a place of safety in Jesus during the final three and a half years of this earth's history.
  - The time, and times, and half a time in this verse ties to Daniel 8:19; 7:25; and 12:7. The final fulfillment of this prophecy is a literal three-and-a-half-year time period.
  - Daniel 8:19 tells us that there is an appointed time for God's indignation at the very end of time. The Hebrew word for "time appointed" is *môw'ed* (Strong's H4150). The same Hebrew word is used for "time" in the phrase "time, times and an half" in Daniel 12:7. God is tying all the final three-and-a-half-year prophecies together in this chapter.
  - As God guided and provided for the children of Israel in the wilderness for forty years, God will guide and provide for his faithful during the final time of trouble during three and a half years.

15. *And the serpent cast out of his mouth water as a flood after the woman, that he might cause her to be carried away of the flood.*
16. *And the earth helped the woman, and the earth opened her mouth, and swallowed up the flood which the dragon cast out of his mouth.*

- The serpent, Satan, will send a flood of people all over the earth to try to entice or force the remnant people of God to come back to the world in their thoughts and actions.
- Natural disasters come upon the earth in increasing measure—especially during the trumpet disasters—resulting in the destruction of Satan's people who have hardened their hearts against God (Revelation 8). In this way, the earth helps the woman by giving her relief from those who are seeking to destroy her.
- As the battle between good and evil intensifies between God's people and Satan's people at the end of the appointed time, God will provide solitary places of refuge for His faithful ones.
- "As the decree issued by the various rulers of Christendom against commandment keepers shall withdraw the protection of government and abandon them to those who desire their destruction, the people of God will flee from the cities and villages and associate together in companies, dwelling in the

most desolate and solitary places. Many will find refuge in the strongholds of the mountains. Like the Christians of the Piedmont valleys, they will make the high places of the earth their sanctuaries and will thank God for 'the munitions of rocks.' Isaiah 33:16" (GC 626.1).

17. *And the dragon was wroth with the woman, and went to make war with the remnant of her seed, which keep the commandments of God, and have the testimony of Jesus Christ.*

    - Satan is enraged at his hopeless condition, so he intensifies his war against God and His people, culminating in a death decree against God's faithful ones.

    - God will protect His 144,000 who proclaim the truths of the three angels' messages, and He will strengthen those who will be His faithful martyrs that keep the commandments of God.

    - "Soon we heard the voice of God like many waters, which gave us the day and hour of Jesus' coming. *The living saints*, 144,000 in number, knew and understood the voice, while the wicked thought it was thunder and an earthquake. When God spake the time, He poured upon us the Holy Spirit, and our faces began to light up and shine with the glory of God, as Moses' did when he came down from Mount Sinai" (1T 59.1).

Revelation 13

1. *And I stood upon the sand of the sea, and saw a beast rise up out of the sea, having seven heads and ten horns, and upon his horns ten crowns, and upon his heads the name of blasphemy.*

    - A "beast," which represents a kingdom, government or political power (Dan. 7:23), comes out of the "sea," which represents an inhabited area of people, nations, and languages (Rev. 17:15; 12:15).

    - This beast has seven "heads," or leaders (Rev. 17:9, 10), and it has ten "horns," which represent ten powers, or kings (Ps. 89:17, 24; Rev. 17:12). The ten horns have "crowns" indicating that, at this point in the prophecy, they are ruling and victorious (1 Chron. 20:2).

    - This beast is blasphemous, for it claims to be God and to forgive sins (John 10:33; Mat. 9:2, 3).

2. *And the beast which I saw was like unto a leopard, and his feet were as the feet of a bear, and his mouth as the mouth of a lion: and the dragon gave him his power, and his seat, and great authority.*

- In Daniel chapter 7, God gave Daniel a dream that began with four beasts—representing four kingdoms that rise in succession. The first beast was a lion, representing Babylon; the second was a bear, representing Medo-Persia; next came a leopard, representing Greece; and lastly came a dreadful and terrible beast, representing Rome. From the perspective of Revelation 13, we are looking back in history and seeing the symbols in reverse order beginning with the leopard, then the bear, and finally the lion.

- In Daniel 7:21, 22, God tells Daniel that the terrible beast, representing Rome, will continue "until" the end of time when the saints possess the kingdom. Additionally, in 7:12, He declares that the rest of the beasts had their dominion taken away though their lives were "prolonged." Therefore, the symbols representing these beasts, or powers, have another application.

- The *leopard*, which is symbolic of Greece in Daniel 7, is the same beast power represented by the goat in Daniel 8. The *bear* is symbolic of the Medo-Persian power in Daniel 7, and the ram in Daniel 8 represents the same world power. In an end-time context, the leopard (Dan. 7) and the goat (Dan. 8) are symbolic of Satan and his people who fight against the bear (Dan. 7) and the ram (Dan. 8), which are symbolic of Jesus and His people.

- In Daniel 7, the *lion* is symbolic of Babylon. In an end-time context, Babylon is symbolic of Rome, the "MOTHER OF HARLOTS" (Rev. 17:5). The lion is often used as a symbol of a destroyer in Scripture (Jer. 4:7).

Tying the symbols of this leopard-like beast all together, we have a power that is made up of *Satan and his people*, of *Jesus' people who have apostatized and joined with the north* (five of the seven churches in Revelation 2 and 3 apostatized), and of the *voice of Rome* (with the mouth of a lion) that leads the **whole world** astray. It's ... Satan's people + Jesus' apostatized people + Rome.

- The beast here in Revelation 13 has similarities to the terrible beast of Daniel 7 and uses some of the same symbols, but there are some key differences. The fourth beast of Daniel 7 begins with the rise of the Roman Empire and progresses from there until the saints possess the kingdom. In contrast, when all the details of Revelation 13 are taken together as a whole, it becomes apparent that the rise of the beast out of the sea, the makeup of its power (seven heads, Satan's people, apostatized people, and Rome), its direct relationship to Revelation 12 and 17 (seven heads and ten horns), and its scope of influence (worldwide) are different from the beast power in Daniel 7. This beast represents a power that has a final and complete fulfillment that is still future. More details are added in the verses that follow.

- Revelation 13 has a partial application to the 1260 years of papal rule, since some of the symbols fit, but the final and *complete* fulfillment of Revelation 13, where all of the symbols apply at the same time, is still future. The seven heads have already ruled (they have crowns—see Revelation 17) and we are in a tarrying time, waiting for the image of the beast to be set up, with the Sunday law being enforced in the United States, and the ten kings emerging.

3. *And I saw one of his heads as it were wounded to death; and his deadly wound was healed: and all the world wondered after the beast.*

    - Revelation 17 explains the second rise of the papacy that began in 1929. Since 1929, seven heads, or kings, or popes, have reigned, and we are living during the reign of the "eighth."

    - The seventh pope, Pope John Paul II received a deadly wound (was shot), and the wound was healed. No other previous pope traveled so extensively and was followed, or worshiped, by so much of the world. The world has and is wondering after the beast.

    - Notice that Revelation 13 describes a seven-headed beast with one of the heads receiving a deadly wound. Daniel 7 does not depict a seven-headed beast or a deadly wound. The two descriptions are different.

4. *And they worshipped the dragon which gave power unto the beast:*

and they worshipped the beast, saying, Who is like unto the beast? Who is able to make war with him?

- When the world follows the dictates of the beast of Rome, they are effectively worshiping the beast and the dragon, or Satan, who gives Rome her power.
- Rome has over a billion people who give her their allegiance. Additionally, there are many more who follow her dictates on different political subjects such as global warming. Sunday worship is being presented as a solution to this and other problems.
- Who can make war against Rome when all the world is increasingly following what the pope has to say?

5. *And there was given unto him a mouth speaking great things and blasphemies; and power was given unto him to continue forty and two months.*

    - Blasphemy is when a human being claims the prerogatives of God (John 10:33). The pope claims to have the power to change God's day of worship, written with His own finger in the fourth commandment, to a different day, and he claims to be able to forgive sins through the confessional.
    - Once the pope achieves his goal and the leaders in the USA agree that rest and worship on Sunday should be enforced, he will have power for forty-two months, or three and a half years. The rest of the world will follow the example of the United States and enforce Sunday worship laws.
    - There are three different expressions for the final three-and-a-half-year time frame given in prophecy, and each of them has a specific meaning:
        - time, times and an half = the final "appointed time" right at the extremity of time, and the border of eternity
        - 1260 days = the final time of witnessing for God's people
        - 42 months = the final time of persecution by Satan's people.

6. *And he opened his mouth in blasphemy against God, to blaspheme his name, and his tabernacle, and them that dwell in heaven.*

    - Titles for the pope include "Vicar of Christ" and "His Holiness." There is only one who walked this planet that can be considered "holy," and that one was Jesus. The pope is not holy, but he claims the place of Jesus Christ on earth.

- The pope, through his false teachings, has obscured all elements of the sanctuary, or heavenly tabernacle, and their meaning (see "Angel 2" in Part 6 of this book).

7. *And it was given unto him to make war with the saints, and to overcome them: and power was given him over all kindreds, and tongues, and nations.*

- Power will be given to the pope for forty-two months, and he will dictate Sunday worship to the **entire world**. He will persecute all who do not follow his dictates.

8. *And all that dwell upon the earth shall worship him, whose names are not written in the book of life of the Lamb slain from the foundation of the world.*

- Those who love Jesus and desire to keep *all* His commandments will be written in the Lamb's book of life. Everyone else who worships the papal power by following his false teachings and his false sabbath will lose eternal life.

9. *If any man have an ear, let him hear.*

- Jesus is pleading with us to listen to Him and receive His infinite love and care for us and turn to Him.
- We desperately need to know these things and to seek a deep and intimate relationship with Jesus with all our heart. When we surrender all to Him, then we can walk in peace—now and for all eternity.
- "In perfect acquiescence there is perfect rest" (DA 331.2).

10. *He that leadeth into captivity shall go into captivity: he that killeth with the sword must be killed with the sword. Here is the patience and the faith of the saints.*

- Persecution and martyrdom will come and God's people must be patient and trust Him completely. Their reward will be resurrection and eternal life with Jesus.
- The reward of the wicked will come. They will receive the same punishment that they inflicted on the innocent. However, their punishment will be eternal, everlasting death.

11. *And I beheld another beast coming up out of the earth; and he had two horns like a lamb, and he spake as a dragon.*

   - This beast power comes up out of the earth, not out of the sea. The sea, or water, represents peoples, multitudes, nations, and languages (Rev. 17:15). The opposite of the sea then would be a relatively uninhabited place where very few people live.

   - This power has two divisions of power within it (represented by two horns), and it has the appearance of a lamb (pointing to Jesus) at its beginning. But in the end, it will speak like the dragon Satan.

   - There is only one power in our world that fits these characteristics. That power is Protestant America. It came up in a relatively uninhabited area. Its beginning was initiated by Christian lamblike people, looking for a place where they could worship in freedom. The lamblike horns represent a character of innocence and gentleness expressed by the government in its two fundamental principles, republicanism and Protestantism. However, the nation's lamb-like Christian character is quickly disappearing, and the attributes of Satan are emerging instead (see 7BC 975).

   - "Religious powers, allied to heaven by profession, and claiming to have the characteristics of a lamb, will show by their acts that they have the heart of a dragon" (Mar 183.4).

12. *And he exerciseth all the power of the first beast before him, and causeth the earth and them which dwell therein to worship the first beast, whose deadly wound was healed.*

   - There is a partial historical application of the deadly wound, and there is a final and complete fulfilment of the deadly wound that leads to the final events just ahead.

     - Looking at the historical perspective, the papal power received a deadly wound in 1798, and its civil power was brought to an end in 1870 with the confiscation of the Papal States. In 1929, the Lateran Treaty gave civil power back to the papacy, and now the wound is healing.

     - Looking at the final fulfillment application, one of the seven heads of the beast (one of seven popes), which ruled since 1929, received a deadly wound. Pope John Paul II was shot, but his deadly wound healed, and all the world wondered after the beast like never before in history.

- "The man of sin [the pope], who thought to change times and laws, and who has always oppressed the people of God, will cause laws to be made enforcing the observance of the first day of the week. But God's people are to stand firm for Him. And the Lord will work in their behalf, showing plainly that He is the God of gods" (9T 229.3).

- Soon, Protestant America, influenced by the papacy, will *force all the world to worship* the beast by enforcing Sunday worship, for which there is no scriptural authority. Sunday worship is nothing more than an invention and tradition of the Catholic Church, which most Protestants have continued to follow contrary to the law of God.

13. *And he doeth great wonders, so that he maketh fire come down from heaven on the earth in the sight of men,*

    - This lamblike power, Protestant America, will work great miracles by the power of Satan working through them.

14. *And deceiveth them that dwell on the earth by the means of those miracles which he had power to do in the sight of the beast; saying to them that dwell on the earth, that they should make an image to the beast, which had the wound by a sword, and did live.*

    - Satan will work miracles through his people in Protestant America to confirm minds in the belief that he is God and that the world should worship on Sunday. Protestant America will push Sunday worship on the rest of the world.

    - God created man in His image with His character (Col. 3:10). Satan's goal is to destroy the image of God and implant his image, meaning his character, in the hearts of men and women. Satan's image is falsehood (Jer. 10:14).

    - "The image of the beast will be formed before probation closes; for it is to be the great test for the people of God, by which their eternal destiny will be decided. This is the test that the people of God must have before they are sealed. All who prove their loyalty to God by observing His law, and refusing to accept a spurious Sabbath, will rank under the banner of the Lord God

Jehovah, and will receive the seal of the living God. Those who yield the truth of heavenly origin, and accept the Sunday Sabbath, will receive the mark of the beast" (Letter 11, 1890).

15. *And he had power to give life unto the image of the beast, that the image of the beast should both speak, and cause that as many as would not worship the image of the beast should be killed.*

- "History will be repeated. False religion will be exalted. The first day of the week, a common working day, possessing no sanctity whatever, will be set up as was the image at Babylon. All nations and tongues and peoples will be commanded to worship this spurious sabbath. This is Satan's plan to make of no account the day instituted by God, and given to the world as a memorial of creation.

  "The decree enforcing the worship of this day is to go forth to all the world. In a limited degree, it has already gone forth. In several places the civil power is speaking with the voice of a dragon, just as the heathen king spoke to the Hebrew captives.

  "Trial and persecution will come to all who, in obedience to the Word of God, refuse to worship this false sabbath. Force is the last resort of every false religion. At first it tries attraction, as the king of Babylon tried the power of music and outward show. If these attractions, invented by men inspired by Satan, failed to make men worship the image, the hungry flames of the furnace were ready to consume them. So it will be now. The papacy has exercised her power to compel men to obey her, and she will continue to do so. We need the same spirit that was manifested by God's servants in the conflict with paganism. Giving an account of the treatment of the Christians by the emperor of Rome, Tertullian says, 'We are thrown to the wild beasts to make us recant; we are burned in the flames; we are condemned to prisons and to mines; we are banished to islands,—such as Patmos,—and all have failed.' So it was in the case of the three Hebrew worthies; their eye was single to the glory of God; their souls were steadfast; the power of the truth held them firmly to their allegiance to God. It is in the power of God alone that we shall be enabled to be loyal to him.

  " 'If ye love me,' said Christ, 'keep my commandments.' 'He that hath my commandments, and keepeth them, he it is that loveth me; and he that loveth me shall be loved of my Father, and I will love him, and will manifest myself to him.' And has not Christ manifested himself to his faithful children? Did he not walk in the furnace with the captives who refused to yield to the golden image one tittle of the reverence which belonged to God? Did he not manifest himself to John, banished to the Isle of Patmos for his faithfulness? Have not those who have been persecuted for righteousness' sake, who, tho they have been compelled to suffer, have refused to worship the institution of the papacy, realized the presence of the divine Comforter in their lonely prisons?

"The commandments of finite, sinful men are to sink into insignificance beside the Word of the eternal God. Truth is to be obeyed at any cost, even tho gaping prisons, chain-gangs, and banishment stare us in the face. If you are loyal and true, that God who walked with the three Hebrew children in the fiery furnace, who protected Daniel in the lions' den, who manifested himself to John on the lonely island, will go with you wherever you go. His abiding presence will comfort and sustain you; and you will realize the fulfilment of the promise, 'If a man love me, he will keep my words; and my Father will love him, and we will come unto him, and make our abode with him'" (ST, May 6, 1887).

16. *And he causeth all, both small and great, rich and poor, free and bond, to receive a mark in their right hand, or in their foreheads.*

- Sunday keeping becomes the mark of the beast *when the decree goes forth* causing men to worship this idol sabbath. Some will receive the mark in the hand, symbolizing the works of their hands (Eccl. 9:10). They will take the easy road and just go along with it. Some will receive the mark in their forehead, symbolizing their thoughts and where their loyalty is (Deut. 11:18).

17. *And that no man might buy or sell, save he that had the mark, or the name of the beast, or the number of his name.*

- Economic pressure will be put upon those who refuse to worship on Sunday. They will not be allowed to buy or sell.

18. *Here is wisdom. Let him that hath understanding count the number of the beast: for it is the number of a man; and his number is Six hundred threescore and six.*

- 666 is made up of the number six, representing *man* who was made on the sixth day of the first week. The number three represents the three persons of the Godhead—the Father, Son, and the Holy Spirit.

- 666, therefore, represents man putting himself in God's place. The pope claims to be God on earth, having the power to change God's holy day of worship and to forgive sins, among many other errors that he teaches.

- To "count the number of the beast," we add up the Roman numerals in the pope's name. They equal the number 666.

V	5	F	0	D	500		
I	1	I	1	E	0		
C	100	L	50	I	1		
A	0	I	1				
R	0	I	1				
I	1						
U	5						
S	0						
	112	+	53	+	501	=	666

* Until recent centuries the letter "V" was the same as the letter "U." The Romans wrote the letter "V" for both U and V sounds, similar to the way that today we write the letter "C" for both the "K" and the "S" sound. Later, medieval scholars began using "U" for a vowel and "V" for a consonant. See an encyclopedia for the history of the letters U and V.

- Our eternal destiny depends on who we choose to follow. Will it be Jesus and His eternal truth based in love or Satan and his selfish falsehoods forced on his subjects?

Revelation 14

1. *And I looked, and, lo, a Lamb stood on the mount Sion, and with him an hundred forty and four thousand, having his Father's name written in their foreheads.*

> *Our eternal destiny depends on who we choose to follow.*

- John sees the 144,000 who triumph over the beast and his image standing on mount Sion in heaven with Jesus, the Lamb of God.

- "They [144,000] bore the signet of heaven. They reflected the image of God. They were full of the light and the glory of the Holy One. If we would have the image and superscription of God upon us, we must separate ourselves from all iniquity. We must forsake every evil way, and then we must trust our cases in the hands of Christ. While we are working out our own salvation with fear and trembling, God will work in us to will and to do of his own good pleasure" (RH, March 19, 1889).

- "Why were they [the 144,000] so specially singled out? Because they had to stand with a wonderful truth right before the whole world, and receive their opposition, and while receiving this opposition they were to remember that they were sons and daughters of God, that they must have Christ formed within them the hope of glory" (1SAT 72.3).

- "While we are working out our own salvation with fear and trembling, God will work in us to will and to do of His own good pleasure" (RH, March 19, 1889).

- "Let us strive with all the power that God has given us to be among the hundred and forty-four thousand" (RH, March 9, 1905).

- "In this world their minds were consecrated to God; they served Him with the intellect and with the heart; and now He can place His name in their foreheads. And they shall reign for ever and ever. Revelation 22:5" (AA 590.4).

2. *And I heard a voice from heaven, as the voice of many waters, and as the voice of a great thunder: and I heard the voice of harpers harping with their harps:*

3. *And they sung as it were a new song before the throne, and before the four beasts, and the elders: and no man could learn that song but the hundred and forty and four thousand, which were redeemed from the earth.*

    - "But all who follow the Lamb in heaven will first have followed Him on earth, in trustful, loving, willing obedience, followed Him not fretfully and capriciously, but confidently, truthfully, as the flock follows the shepherd" (3SM 424.2).

    - "While Satan has been urging his accusations, holy angels, unseen, have been placing on the faithful ones the seal of God. These stand on Mount Zion, having the Father's name written in their foreheads. They sing that song which no one can learn save the 144,000 redeemed from the earth. 'In their mouth was found no guile: for they are without fault.' Revelation 14:5.

    "Now is reached the complete fulfillment of the words of the Angel to Joshua: 'I will bring forth My Servant the Branch.' Christ is revealed as the Redeemer and Deliverer of His people. Now are the remnant 'men wondered at' (Zechariah 3:8) as the tears and humiliation of their pilgrimage give place to joy and honor in the presence of God and the Lamb. See Isaiah 4:2, 3" (*From Splendor to Shadow*, p. 305).

4. *These are they which were not defiled with women; for they are virgins. These are they which follow the Lamb whithersoever he goeth. These were redeemed from among men, being the firstfruits unto God and to the Lamb.*

    - "The vision of the prophet pictures them as standing on Mount Zion, girt for holy service, clothed in white linen, which is the righteousness of the saints" (AA 591.1).

    - The 144,000 are the firstfruits of God's new kingdom. See Daniel 2:34, 35, 44, and 45, for a parallel passage.

5. *And in their mouth was found no guile: for they are without fault before the throne of God.*

    - "This Scripture [Revelation 14:1–5] represents the character of the people of God for these last days" (Ms. 139, 1903).

    - "Upon the 'sea of glass as it were mingled with fire' are gathered the company that have 'gotten the victory over the beast, and over his image, and over his mark, and over the number of his name.' The hundred and forty and four thousand were redeemed from among men, and they sing 'a new song,' the song of Moses and the Lamb. Revelation 15:2, 3. None but the hundred and forty-four thousand can learn that song, for it is the song of an experience such as no other company ever had. 'These are they which follow the Lamb whithersoever he goeth.' These, having been translated from among the living, are 'the firstfruits unto God and to the Lamb.' Revelation 14:4, 5. They passed through the time of trouble such as never was since there was a nation; they endured the anguish of the time of Jacob's trouble; they stood without an intercessor through the final outpouring of God's judgments.

"They 'washed their robes, and made them white in the blood of the Lamb.' 'In their mouth was found no guile: for they are without fault' before God. 'They shall hunger no more, neither thirst any more; neither shall the sun light on them, nor any heat. For the Lamb which is in the midst of the throne shall feed them, and shall lead them unto living fountains of waters: and God shall wipe away all tears from their eyes.' Revelation 7:14; 14:5; 7:16, 17" (*From Here to Forever*, pp. 392, 393).

6. *And I saw another angel fly in the midst of heaven, having the everlasting gospel to preach unto them that dwell on the earth, and to every nation, and kindred, and tongue, and people,*

7. *Saying with a loud voice, Fear God, and give glory to him; for the hour of his judgment is come: and worship him that made heaven, and earth, and the sea, and the fountains of waters.*

8. *And there followed another angel, saying, Babylon is fallen, is fallen, that great city, because she made all nations drink of the wine of the wrath of her fornication.*

9. *And the third angel followed them, saying with a loud voice, If any man worship the beast and his image, and receive his mark in his forehead, or in his hand,*

10. *The same shall drink of the wine of the wrath of God, which is poured out without mixture into the cup of his indignation; and he shall be tormented with fire and brimstone in the presence of the holy angels, and in the presence of the Lamb:*

11. *And the smoke of their torment ascendeth up for ever and ever: and they have no rest day nor night, who worship the beast and his image, and whosoever receiveth the mark of his name.*

12. *Here is the patience of the saints: here are they that keep the commandments of God, and the faith of Jesus.*
    - See Part 6 of this book for a discussion of Revelation 14:6–12.

13. *And I heard a voice from heaven saying unto me, Write, Blessed are the dead which die in the Lord from henceforth: Yea, saith the Spirit, that they may rest from their labours; and their works do follow them.*
    - With Paul, they can say, "I have fought a good fight, I have finished my course, I have kept the faith: Henceforth there is laid up for me a crown of righteousness, which the Lord, the righteous judge, shall give me at that day: and not to me only, but unto all them also which love his appearing" (2 Tim. 4:7, 8).

14. *And I looked, and behold a white cloud, and upon the cloud one sat like unto the Son of man, having on his head a golden crown, and in his hand a sharp sickle.*

15. *And another angel came out of the temple, crying with a loud voice to him that sat on the cloud, Thrust in thy sickle, and reap: for the time is come for thee to reap; for the harvest of the earth is ripe.*

16. *And he that sat on the cloud thrust in his sickle on the earth; and the earth was reaped.*
    - The day will soon come when Jesus, the Son of man, with His golden crown of victory on His head, will reap the earth and bring His faithful, ripened harvest to be with Him for eternity.
    - There is a set time, *after* the "appointed time," for Jesus to reap the earth (Matt. 24:29–36).

17. *And another angel came out of the temple which is in heaven, he also having a sharp sickle.*

18. *And another angel came out from the altar, which had power over fire; and cried with a loud cry to him that had the sharp*

> *The day will soon come when Jesus, the Son of man, with His golden crown of victory on His head, will reap the earth and bring His faithful, ripened harvest to be with Him for eternity.*

sickle, saying, Thrust in thy sharp sickle, and gather the clusters of the vine of the earth; for her grapes are fully ripe.

19. And the angel thrust in his sickle into the earth, and gathered the vine of the earth, and cast it into the great winepress of the wrath of God.

20. And the winepress was trodden without the city, and blood came out of the winepress, even unto the horse bridles, by the space of a thousand and six hundred furlongs.

> "When the storm of God's wrath breaks upon the world, it will be a terrible revelation for souls to find that their house is being swept away, because it is built upon the sand. Let the warning be given them before it is too late. We should now feel the responsibility of laboring with intense earnestness to impart to others the light we have received. We can not be too much in earnest. *Even those who have felt much have not felt enough. They must feel still more deeply.*
>
> "The heart of God is moved. Souls are very precious in his sight. It was for this world that Christ wept in agony, for this world He was crucified. God gave His only begotten Son to save sinners, and he desires us to love others as He has loved us. He desires to see those who have had great light flashing that light upon the pathway of their fellow-men" ("An Appeal for Missions," pp. 13, 14).

Revelation 15

1. And I saw another sign in heaven, great and marvellous, seven angels having the seven last plagues; for in them is filled up the wrath of God.

    - "The rabbis had a saying that there is rejoicing in heaven when one who has sinned against God is destroyed; but Jesus taught that to God the work of destruction is a strange work. That in which all heaven delights is the restoration of God's own image in the souls whom He has made" (COL 190.1).

2. And I saw as it were a sea of glass mingled with fire: and them that had gotten the victory over the beast, and over his image, and over his mark, and over the number of his name, stand on the sea of glass, having the harps of God.

3. *And they sing the song of Moses the servant of God, and the song of the Lamb, saying, Great and marvellous are thy works, Lord God Almighty; just and true are thy ways, thou King of saints.*

4. *Who shall not fear thee, O Lord, and glorify thy name? for thou only art holy: for all nations shall come and worship before thee; for thy judgments are made manifest.*

    - "What a song that will be when the ransomed of the Lord meet at the gate of the Holy City, which is thrown back on its glittering hinges and the nations that have kept His word—His commandments—enter into the city, the crown of the overcomer is placed upon their heads, and the golden harps are placed in their hands! All heaven is filled with rich music, and with songs of praise to the Lamb. Saved, everlastingly saved, in the kingdom of glory! To have a life that measures with the life of God—that is the reward" (Heaven 178.3; Ms. 92, 1908).

5. *And after that I looked, and, behold, the temple of the tabernacle of the testimony in heaven was opened:*

6. *And the seven angels came out of the temple, having the seven plagues, clothed in pure and white linen, and having their breasts girded with golden girdles.*

7. *And one of the four beasts gave unto the seven angels seven golden vials full of the wrath of God, who liveth for ever and ever.*

8. *And the temple was filled with smoke from the glory of God, and from his power; and no man was able to enter into the temple, till the seven plagues of the seven angels were fulfilled.*

    - "God's judgments will be visited upon those who are seeking to oppress and destroy His people. His long forbearance with the wicked emboldens men in transgression, but their punishment is nonetheless certain and terrible because it is long delayed. 'The Lord shall rise up as in Mount Perazim, He shall be wroth as in the valley of Gibeon, that He may do His work, His strange work; and bring to pass His act, His strange act.' Isaiah 28:21. To our merciful God the act of punishment is a strange act. 'As I live, saith the Lord God, I have no pleasure in the death of the wicked.' Ezekiel 33:11. The Lord is 'merciful and gracious, long-suffering, and abundant in goodness and truth, … forgiving iniquity and transgression and sin.' Yet He will 'by no means clear the guilty.' 'The Lord is slow to anger, and great in power, and will not at all acquit the wicked.' Exodus 34:6, 7; Nahum 1:3. By terrible things in righteousness He will vindicate the authority of His downtrodden law. The severity of the retribution awaiting the transgressor may be judged by the Lord's reluctance to execute justice. The nation with which He bears long, and which He will not smite until it has filled up the measure of its iniquity in God's account, will finally drink the cup of wrath unmixed with mercy" (GC 627.2).

Revelation 16

1. And I heard a great voice out of the temple saying to the seven angels, Go your ways, and pour out the vials of the wrath of God upon the earth.

> *To our merciful God the act of punishment is a strange act.*

- "When our High Priest has finished his work in the sanctuary, He will stand up, put on the garments of vengeance, and then the seven last plagues will be poured out.... the four angels will hold the four winds until Jesus' work is done in the sanctuary, and then will come the seven last plagues" (EW 36.1, 2).

- "When Christ ceases his intercession in the sanctuary, the unmingled wrath threatened against those who worship the beast and his image and receive his mark (Revelation 14:9, 10), will be poured out. The plagues upon Egypt when God was about to deliver Israel were similar in character to those more terrible and extensive judgments which are to fall upon the world just before the final deliverance of God's people" (GC 627.3).

- "The wrath of Satan increases as his time grows short, and his work of deceit and destruction reaches its culmination in the time of trouble. God's long-suffering has ended. The world has rejected His mercy, despised His love, and trampled upon His law. The wicked have passed the boundary of their probation, and the Lord withdraws His protection, and leaves them to the mercy of the leader they have chosen. Satan will have power over those who have yielded themselves to his control, and he will plunge the inhabitants of the earth into one great, final trouble. As the angels of God cease to hold in check the fierce winds of human passion, all the elements of strife will be let loose. The whole world will be involved in ruin more terrible than that which came upon Jerusalem of old" (Mar 275.3).

2. *And the first went, and poured out his vial upon the earth; and there fell a noisome and grievous sore upon the men which had the mark of the beast, and upon them which worshipped his image.*

3. *And the second angel poured out his vial upon the sea; and it became as the blood of a dead man: and every living soul died in the sea.*

   - "When Christ ceases His intercession in the sanctuary, the unmingled wrath threatened against those who worship the beast and his image and receive his mark (Revelation 14:9, 10), will be poured out. The plagues upon Egypt when God was about to deliver Israel were similar in character to those more terrible and extensive judgments which are to fall upon the world just before the final deliverance of God's people" (GC 627.3; LDE 244.1).

4. *And the third angel poured out his vial upon the rivers and fountains of waters; and they became blood.*

5. *And I heard the angel of the waters say, Thou art righteous, O Lord, which art, and wast, and shalt be, because thou hast judged thus.*

6. *For they have shed the blood of saints and prophets, and thou hast given them blood to drink; for they are worthy.*

7. *And I heard another out of the altar say, Even so, Lord God Almighty, true and righteous are thy judgments.*

   - "I saw that the four angels would hold the four winds until Jesus' work was done in the sanctuary, and then will come the seven last plagues. These plagues enraged the wicked against the righteous; they thought that we had brought the judgments of God upon them and that if they could rid the earth of us the plagues would then be stayed. A decree went forth to slay the saints, which caused them to cry day and night for deliverance" (EW 36.2; LDE 245.1).

   - "And 'the rivers and fountains of waters ... became blood.' Terrible as these inflictions are, God's justice stands fully vindicated. The angel of God declares: 'Thou art righteous, O Lord, ... because Thou hast judged thus. For they have shed the blood of saints and prophets, and Thou hast given them blood to drink; for they are worthy.' Revelation 16:2–6. By condemning the people of God to death, they have as truly incurred the guilt of their blood as if it had been shed by their hands" (GC 627.3; LDE 245.2).

8. *And the fourth angel poured out his vial upon the sun; and power was given unto him to scorch men with fire.*

9. *And men were scorched with great heat, and blasphemed the name of God, which hath power over these plagues: and they repented not to give him glory.*

   - "These plagues are not universal, or the inhabitants of the earth would be wholly cut off. Yet they will be the most awful scourges that have ever been known to mortals" (GC 628.2; LDE 246.1).

10. *And the fifth angel poured out his vial upon the seat of the beast; and his kingdom was full of darkness; and they gnawed their tongues for pain,*

11. *And blasphemed the God of heaven because of their pains and their sores, and repented not of their deeds.*

    - "With shouts of triumph, jeering, and imprecation, throngs of evil men are about to rush upon their prey, when, lo, a dense blackness, deeper than the darkness of the night, falls upon the earth. Then a rainbow, shining with the glory from the throne of God, spans the heavens, and seems to encircle each praying company. The angry multitudes are suddenly arrested. Their mocking cries die away. The objects of their murderous rage are forgotten. With fearful forebodings they gaze upon the symbol of God's covenant, and long to be shielded from its overpowering brightness" (GC 635.3; LDE 246.2).

    - "It is at midnight that God manifests His power for the deliverance of His people. The sun appears, shining in its strength. Signs and wonders follow in quick succession. The wicked look with terror and amazement on the scene, while the righteous behold with solemn joy the tokens of their deliverance" (GC 636.2; LDE 246.3).

12. *And the sixth angel poured out his vial upon the great river Euphrates; and the water thereof was dried up, that the way of the kings of the east might be prepared.*

- Anciently, the river Euphrates flowed through the seemingly impregnable city of Babylon. Cyrus diverted the river and conquered the city. He "dried up the Euphrates." At the end of time, God will effectively do the same. Water, representing peoples, multitudes, nations, and languages, will be "dried up," and Babylon's support will be gone.
- This plague is at least partially a result of the sixth trumpet, when Satan is permitted to fully express his hatred and evil character. Through his demonic forces and his deceived people, he is allowed to kill a third of humankind remaining in the world at the very end. An army of 200,000,000 is seen in this final worldwide battle in Revelation 9:16.

13. *And I saw three unclean spirits like frogs come out of the mouth of the dragon, and out of the mouth of the beast, and out of the mouth of the false prophet.*

14. *For they are the spirits of devils, working miracles, which go forth unto the kings of the earth and of the whole world, to gather them to the battle of that great day of God Almighty.*
    - "The spirits of devils will go forth to the kings of the earth and to the whole world, to fasten them in deception, and urge them on to unite with Satan in his last struggle against the government of heaven" (GC 624.1; LDE 248.3).
    - "Little by little he [Satan] has prepared the way for his masterpiece of deception in the development of spiritualism. He has not yet reached the full accomplishment of his designs; but it will be reached in the last remnant of time. … Except those who are kept by the power of God, through faith in His word, the whole world will be swept into the ranks of this delusion. The people are fast being lulled to a fatal security, to be awakened only by the outpouring of the wrath of God" (GC 561.2).

15. *Behold, I come as a thief. Blessed is he that watcheth, and keepeth his garments, lest he walk naked, and they see his shame.*
    - "After the transgression of Adam and Eve they were naked, for the garment of light and security had departed from them" (LDE 249.2).

- "The days of our probation are fast closing. The end is near. To us the warning is given, 'Take heed to yourselves, lest at any time your hearts be overcharged with surfeiting, and drunkenness, and cares of this life, and so that day come upon you unawares.' Luke 21:34. Beware lest it find you unready. *Take heed lest you be found at the King's feast without a wedding garment*" (COL 319.2).

16. *And he gathered them together into a place called in the Hebrew tongue Armageddon.*

    - "Four mighty angels hold back the powers of this earth till the servants of God are sealed in their foreheads. The nations of the world are eager for conflict, but they are held in check by the angels. When this restraining power is removed there will come a time of trouble and anguish. Deadly instruments of warfare will be invented. Vessels with their living cargo will be entombed in the great deep. All who have not the spirit of truth will unite under the leadership of Satanic agencies, but they are to be kept under control *till the time shall come* for the great battle of Armageddon" (LDE 238.3).

17. *And the seventh angel poured out his vial into the air; and there came a great voice out of the temple of heaven, from the throne, saying, It is done.*

18. *And there were voices, and thunders, and lightnings; and there was a great earthquake, such as was not since men were upon the earth, so mighty an earthquake, and so great.*

19. *And the great city was divided into three parts, and the cities of the nations fell: and great Babylon came in remembrance before God, to give unto her the cup of the wine of the fierceness of his wrath.*

20. *And every island fled away, and the mountains were not found.*

21. *And there fell upon men a great hail out of heaven, every stone about the weight of a talent: and men blasphemed God because of the plague of the hail; for the plague thereof was exceeding great.*

    - "We need to study the pouring out of the seventh vial.

      "The powers of evil will not yield up the conflict without a struggle. In the midst of the angry heavens is one clear space of indescribable glory, whence comes the voice of God like the sound of many waters, saying: 'It is done.' Revelation 16:17.

"That voice shakes the heavens and the earth. There is a mighty earthquake, 'such as was not since men were upon the earth, so mighty an earthquake, and so great.' Verses 17, 18. The firmament appears to open and shut. The glory from the throne of God seems flashing through. The mountains shake like a reed in the wind, and ragged rocks are scattered on every side. There is a roar as of a coming tempest. The sea is lashed into fury. There is heard the shriek of a hurricane like the voice of demons upon a mission of destruction. The whole earth heaves and swells like the waves of the sea. Its surface is breaking up. Its very foundations seem to be giving away. Mountain chains are sinking. Inhabited islands disappear. The seaports that have become like Sodom for wickedness are swallowed up by the angry waters. Babylon the great has come in remembrance before God, 'to give unto her the cup of the wine of the fierceness of his wrath.' Great hailstones, every one 'about the weight of a talent,' are doing their work of destruction. Verses 19, 21. The proudest cities of the earth are laid low. The lordly palaces, upon which the world's great men have lavished their wealth in order to glorify themselves, are crumbling to ruin before their eyes. Prison walls are rent asunder, and God's people, who have been held in bondage for their faith, are set free" (Mar 280.2–4).

- "Soon there appears in the *east* a small black cloud, about half the size of a man's hand. It is the cloud which surrounds the Saviour, and which seems in the distance to be shrouded in darkness. The people of God know this to be the sign of the Son of man. In solemn silence they gaze upon it as it draws nearer the earth, becoming lighter and more glorious, until it is a great white cloud, its base a glory like consuming fire, and above it the rainbow of the covenant. *Jesus rides forth as a mighty conqueror, and the armies of Heaven follow him*" (4SP 458.2).

Revelation 17

1. *And there came one of the seven angels which had the seven vials, and talked with me, saying unto me, Come hither; I will shew unto thee the judgment of the great whore that sitteth upon many waters:*

- This chapter begins with one of the seven angels, which had the seven vials for the plagues, coming to give John more information about what leads up to the seven last plagues and the wrath poured out on the "great city" of Babylon.
- This "great whore" (representing an impure church involved in spiritual adultery—see Isa. 1:21; Num. 15:39; Ezek. 23:4, 5, 7, 30, 35–38, 49) is the apostate church power that "sits," or rules (see Rev. 18:7), on many "waters," which is "peoples, multitudes, nations, and tongues" (see Rev. 17:15).

2. *With whom the kings of the earth have committed fornication, and the inhabitants of the earth have been made drunk with the wine of her fornication.*

- The "kings of the earth" and the "inhabitants of the earth" represent the *whole world*, which has followed the great whore. (See Rev. 13:3.)
- "Committed fornication" is equivalent to religious prostitution that alters and interferes with the true covenant relationship between God and His people (James 4:4; Rev. 14:4).
- The whole world commits spiritual fornication by accepting the "wine," which are the false doctrines and teachings that she promotes (see Isa. 29:9–13; Jer. 51:7).
- By contrast, God is betrothed to his saints (Hosea 2:19) in a covenant relationship in which God's people strive to get self off the throne (surrendering to God), stop sinning (the breaking of the Ten Commandments) and making all their wrongs right (Dan. 9:24).

> *The whole world commits spiritual fornication by accepting the "wine," which are the false doctrines and teachings that she promotes*

3. *So he carried me away in the spirit into the wilderness: and I saw a woman sit upon a scarlet coloured beast, full of names of blasphemy, having seven heads and ten horns.*

- In a spiritually desolate and protected place (symbolized as a wilderness), this impure church rules (sits) over a power (symbolized by a beast) that is scarlet-colored, or red. Red is a symbol of sin (Isa. 1:18), representing its complete guiltiness. Additionally, it is full of names of blasphemy, indicating its claims to take the place of God (see Rev. 13:1). This is deep rebellion! The harlot church and the beast are the supreme enemy of God.
- This beast has seven heads and ten horns, which will be described in verses 9–14.
    - *A beast* is symbolic of an earthly kingdom (Dan. 7:17, 23).
    - *Heads* are symbolic of leaders, rulers, or governments (Dan. 7:6; Isa. 7:8, 9; 9:14, 15).
    - *Horns* are symbolic of a king or kingdom or power that gives power to the beast (Ps. 89:17, 24; Dan. 8:5, 21, 22).
- This is a picture of an apostate *church* that rules over a sinful *state* or a unique *nation* with support or power coming from *ten kingdoms* (Rev. 17:12), having power to rule.
- The scene presented is one of great apostasy from truth so this church must be a fallen Christian church.

4. *And the woman was arrayed in purple and scarlet colour, and decked with gold and precious stones and pearls, having a golden cup in her hand full of abominations and filthiness of her fornication:*

- This impure church is symbolized as royalty, represented by purple, and very wealthy as well as sinful, represented by scarlet (Lam. 4:5; Dan. 5:7).
- She is "decked with gold, precious stones, and pearls" and has "a golden cup in her hand full of abominations," representing sins against God. She looks good on the outside but is filthy on the inside.

5. *And upon her forehead was a name written, MYSTERY, BABYLON THE GREAT, THE MOTHER OF HARLOTS AND ABOMINATIONS OF THE EARTH.*

- The thoughts of her mind and heart, represented by the forehead, are corrupt (Deut. 6:6–8, 11:18; 1 John 2:4; Ezek. 3:8, 9).

- Her name, "Babylon the Great," is symbolic of religious apostasy, rebellion, and confusion (Gen. 10:8–10; 11:3–9, since "Babel" in the Greek Old Testament is *babulôn*; Rev. 17:1–5).
- Babylon the Great is "the *mother* of *harlots*," indicating that she has daughters (meaning churches) that came out of her.
  - Daughters are not born harlots. They become harlots by choice when they follow after the abominable practices of their mother.
  - God has faithful people who truly love Him in these churches, and He doesn't condemn people for what they don't know. There is a time coming, however, when God will call his people out of these churches and each person will have to make a decision for or against God (Rev. 18:4).
- Who is the power described? There is only one power that fits all the evidence given so far as well as the rest of the evidence yet to be given in this chapter. That power is the papal power that leads the Roman Catholic Church.
  - She has growing power over the people of the world.
  - According to Wikipedia, "The Holy See ... maintains formal diplomatic relations with ... 183 sovereign states." (See the darker portions on the chart below from https://1ref.us/jbet4.)

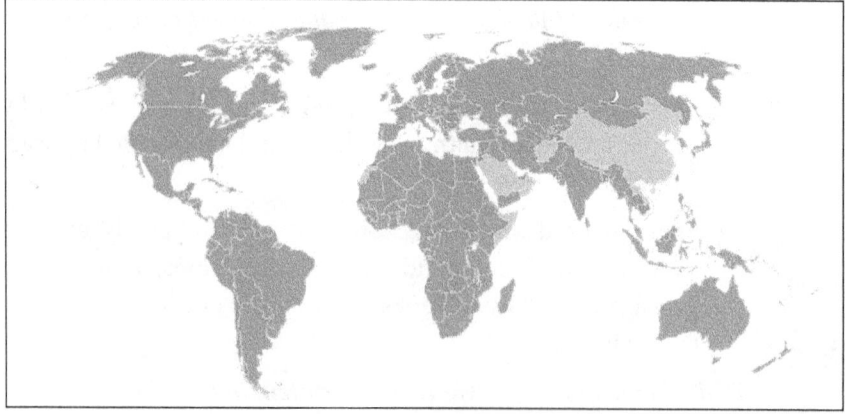

Holy See Diplomatic Relations

  - The leaders of the world have made themselves subject to her false doctrines, symbolized by "wine."

- o She is blasphemous, spiritually corrupt, and has controlling power over the state called "the Vatican."
- o She is incredibly wealthy.
- o Her cup is full of false teachings and she has churches that have come out of her who follow some of the same false teachings.

6. *And I saw the woman drunken with the blood of the saints, and with the blood of the martyrs of Jesus: and when I saw her, I wondered with great admiration.*

   - Revelation 13:15 tells us that those who don't worship this beast will be killed. Millions who will stand up for their faith will soon be put to death for it. Revelation 6:9–11 tells us of the cry of the martyrs who symbolically call from under the altar, seeking God's justice.
   - However, in Revelation 13:10, God gives us assurance that He will avenge our blood and He encourages us to have patience.

7. *And the angel said unto me, Wherefore didst thou marvel? I will tell thee the mystery of the woman, and of the beast that carrieth her, which hath the seven heads and ten horns.*

   - The angel promises to explain the mystery of the apostate church, the power that supports her, the seven leaders that led to her rise to power, and the ten powers that unite with her. (In Amos 3:7, God promises to reveal His actions through prophecy.)

8. *The beast that thou sawest was, and is not; and shall ascend out of the bottomless pit, and go into perdition: and they that dwell on the earth shall wonder, whose names were not written in the book of life from the foundation of the world, when they behold the beast that was, and is not, and yet is.*

   - The prophecy here shifts the focus from the "woman" to the "beast" power, adding additional information to that of Revelation 13:12.
     - "Was"
       - The papal power reigned over Europe from 538 to 1798 AD. In 1798, Napoleon's General

Berthier took Pope Pius VI captive, and the pope died in exile. Thus, the papal power received a "deadly wound." Nonetheless, new popes were elected and continued to reign.

- "Is Not"
    - On September 20, 1870, the Italian army under General Cadorna captured Rome. Shortly thereafter, the Papal States were confiscated.
    - Until this attack, there had been a church-state empire ruled by the papal power for centuries. The Catholic Church was reduced to an ecclesiastical body. Its civil power was broken.
- "Shall Ascend"
    - On February 11, 1929, Benito Mussolini, Prime Minister of Italy, on behalf of King Victor Emmanuel, III, and Cardinal Pietro Gasparri, Secretary of State for Pope Pius XI, signed three Lateran Accords. These restored the Church-State union. The Vatican City State was formed.
- "Go Into Perdition"
    - The Holy See power has almost finished its rise to power from the "bottomless pit" (place of evil, Rev. 9:1–3; Rev. 11:7), and it is soon to enter perdition (Rev. 19:20; 2 Thess. 2:3, 4).
- The opposite of this beast power is the power of Jesus, "the Almighty" (Rev. 1:8; 11:17) and His life, death, and resurrection (Rev. 1:18).

9. *And here is the mind which hath wisdom. The seven heads are seven mountains, on which the woman sitteth.*

10. *And there are seven kings: five are fallen, and one is, and the other is not yet come; and when he cometh, he must continue a short space.*

- The seven heads of the beast represent seven mountains. It is well known that Rome, where the Vatican is located, is called the city of seven hills. God is giving us geographical evidence.

- The seven heads also represent the seven kings of the beast. These are seven kings (or heads) that are *on the beast.*
- The context given in this passage has been building in detail and timing and has narrowed in on the time of the beast power's ascension (papal Rome's ascension). These seven kings must be understood in that end-time context.
- The seven kings (in sequence) since 1929 are:
  1. Pope Pius XI (1922–1939)
     - He played a considerable role in the negotiations and signing of the Lateran Treaty, which reunited the Catholic Church and State.
  2. Pope Pius XII (1939–1958)
     - He introduced the doctrine of the Assumption of Mary.
     - He began influencing modern governments including Nazi Germany.
  3. Pope John XXIII (1958–1963)
     - He convened Vatican II.
     - He promoted ecumenism.
  4. Pope Paul VI (1963–1978)
     - He completed the work of Vatican II.
     - He improved ecumenical relations.
  5. Pope John Paul I (August through September 1978)
     - He was possibly murdered as a result of delving too deeply into the corruption inside the Vatican Bank.
  6. Pope John Paul II (1978–2005)
     - He made 104 trips abroad during his pontificate, visiting 129 countries, covering enough distance to circle the world about thirty times. He was one of the most travelled world leaders in history.
     - He was the first pope to visit a mosque.

- He was one of the most published popes in history.
- Nobody in the history of mankind has been seen by more people. He captivated the world.
- He was shot—received a deadly wound—and the deadly wound was healed!

7. Pope Benedict XVI (2005 to his resignation on February 28, 2013)
    - Benedict's reign was brief—"a short space."

11. *And the beast that was, and is not, even he is the eighth, and is of the seven, and goeth into perdition.*
    - The symbol of the "eighth" is tied to the beast power *and* its rise during the time of the seven kings. Therefore, this eighth power (or "beast") represents the Holy See, which is a combination of both the papal power *and* the pope (or popes) that lead it after Pope Benedict XVI.
    - The Holy See is the eighth and final power presented, and it goes into perdition! (Rev. 19:20; 20:10).
    - There are no more powers after this eighth power. We are living in the extreme time of the end.
        - *Key Point: The "eighth" is not identified as a "head" but as "the beast"!*
        - We are living in the time of **the beast**!

12. *And the ten horns which thou sawest are ten kings, which have received no kingdom as yet; but receive power as kings one hour with the beast.*

13. *These have one mind, and shall give their power and strength unto the beast.*
    - Horns usually represent kings or kingdoms who give their authority or power to the beast they are on (see Dan. 7:7, 24; 8:8).
    - The timing presented in this verse describes and anticipates the time when the horns will have received their crowns or power. Revelation 13:1 shows the ten kings (or horns) when they have received power (or crowns) and the events that take place at that point.

- "Ten" represents fullness or completion.
- Ten powers shall give their support and power to the beast right at the end of time.
- The UN and the "Club of Rome" have both divided the world into ten divisions.
- *See end of Part 2 (on pages 81- 82) for maps from the UN and the Club of Rome that divide the world into ten divisions.*
- *" 'These have one mind.' There will be a universal bond of union, one great harmony, a confederacy of Satan's forces. 'And shall give their power and strength unto the beast.' Thus is manifested the same arbitrary, oppressive power against religious liberty, freedom to worship God according to the dictates of conscience, as was manifested by the papacy, when in the past it persecuted those who dared to refuse to conform with the religious rites and ceremonies of Romanists.*

    "In the warfare to be waged in the last days there will be united, in opposition to God's people, all the corrupt powers that have apostatized from allegiance to the law of Jehovah. In this warfare the Sabbath of the fourth commandment will be the great point at issue, for in the Sabbath commandment the great Lawgiver identifies Himself as the Creator of the heavens and the earth" (3SM 392.5).

14. *These shall make war with the Lamb, and the Lamb shall overcome them: for he is Lord of lords, and King of kings: and they that are with him are called, and chosen, and faithful.*

15. *And he saith unto me, The waters which thou sawest, where the whore sitteth, are peoples, and multitudes, and nations, and tongues.*
    - These ten divisions of the world will give their support and power to the beast and make war on God's people globally.
    - Jesus the Lamb and His called, chosen, and faithful shall overcome them!

16. *And the ten horns which thou sawest upon the beast, these shall hate the whore, and shall make her desolate and naked, and shall eat her flesh, and burn her with fire.*

17. *For God hath put in their hearts to fulfil his will, and to agree, and give their kingdom unto the beast, until the words of God shall be fulfilled.*

    - In the end, the ten powers will realize they have been deceived, and they will turn on the whore and fight against her until she is destroyed. God's words are perfect and true and shall not return unto Him void (Isa. 55:11).

18. *And the woman which thou sawest is that great city, which reigneth over the kings of the earth.*

    - The "great city" that "was," "is not" (that is, it was conquered), and "yet is" (that is, it is rising to power a second time to rule the whole earth), as wholistically described in this chapter, is Rome.

Revelation 18

Verses 1 through 5 are covered in Part 6 of this book, following the third angel's message. Verses 10, 17, 19, and 20 are covered below.

10. *Standing afar off for the fear of her torment, saying, Alas, alas, that great city Babylon, that mighty city! for in one hour is thy judgment come.*

17. *For in one hour so great riches is come to nought. And every shipmaster, and all the company in ships, and sailors, and as many as trade by sea, stood afar off,*

19. *And they cast dust on their heads, and cried, weeping and wailing, saying, Alas, alas, that great city, wherein were made rich all that had ships in the sea by reason of her costliness! for in one hour is she made desolate.*

    - Three times God tells us that Babylon will be judged and destroyed in "one hour." When God repeats Himself, it is important.
    - If a day equals a year in this case, the ratio reveals that one hour equals fifteen days.
    - 24 hours per day over 360 days in a biblical year equals one hour over x number of days.

$$\frac{24}{360} = \frac{1}{X}$$

- Solving for *x* gives us 15 days, and multiplying 15 days by the three times God has told us that Babylon will be destroyed in one hour equals forty-five days—15 x 3 = 45.
- Forty-five days matches with the final time period given for the plagues in Daniel chapter 12! (See timing chart in Part 2, p. 77)
- This chapter details the complete destruction of Babylon—economically, socially, and politically.
- This is the time of the "great tribulation" (Matt. 24:21; Rev. 2:22) and the "time of trouble, such as never was" (Dan. 12:1).
- Like the children of Israel during the plagues in Egypt, Noah in the flood, Shadrach, Meshach, and Abednego in the fiery furnace, Daniel in the lion's den, Joseph in Egypt, and Job in his great trials, God will be with His people and take them through that terrible time of trouble.
- God does not enjoy the destruction of His creation at all. "It is His strange act" (Isa. 28:21). He wants "to do" for us "exceedingly abundantly above all that we ask or think" (Eph. 3:20).

20. *Rejoice over her,* thou *heaven, and ye holy apostles and prophets; for God hath avenged you on her.*

- God will vindicate, avenge, and deliver His faithful people from the oppression of Babylon and reward them with the glories of eternity with Jesus.

"When sinful man can discern the inexpressible love of God in giving His Son to die upon the cross, we shall better understand that it is infinite gain to overcome as Christ overcame. And we shall understand that it is eternal loss if we gain the whole world, with all its pleasure and glory, and yet lose the soul. Heaven is cheap enough at any cost. (Con 78.1)

"Christ bids you bring all of heaven you can into your life. Talk of the great reward that awaits the overcomer. Set your face as a flint heavenward, saying, as you advance, Hear what the Lord has wrought for me. Shall we not come up to the help of the Lord against the mighty? Shall we not work with all the power that God has given us to oppose the work of Satan? An eternal weight of glory awaits the overcomer. If we gain heaven, we gain everything. Shall we not put away sin, and let Christ abide in our hearts by faith? Not until we have the mind of Christ shall we be like him, and see him as he is. When the warfare is ended, and we have gained the crown of immortality, the harp of God, the palm branch of victory, and wear the white robe of Christ's righteousness, we shall say, Heaven is cheap enough. (*Youth's Instructor*, Jan. 11, 1900)

"We tried to call up our greatest trials, but they looked so small compared with the far more exceeding and eternal weight of glory that surrounded us that we could not speak them out, and we all cried out, 'Alleluia, heaven is cheap enough!' and we touched our glorious harps and made heaven's arches ring." (EW 17.2)

Part 5: Key Points of Daniel and Revelation   227

Sequence of Final Events:

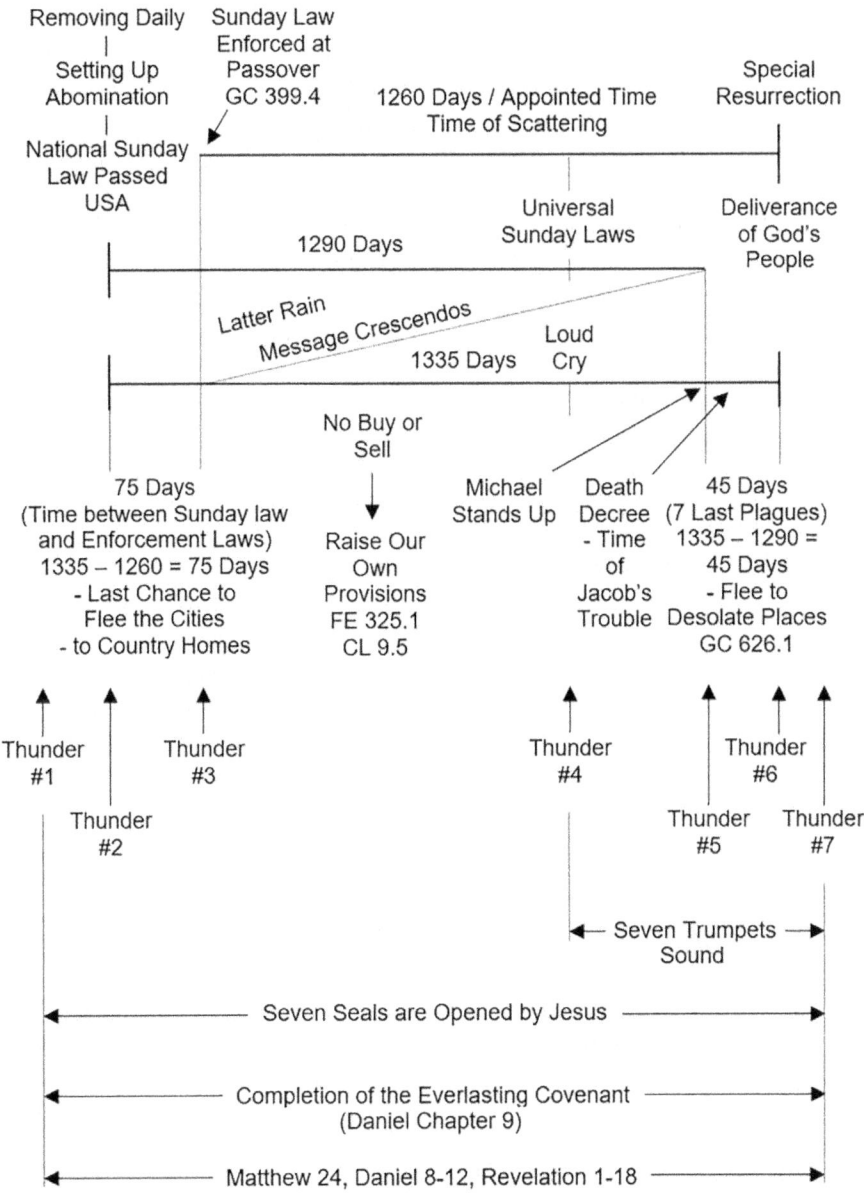

Delineation of the Seven Thunders

1. Seals begin

   The judgment of the living is underway, and the 144,000 (symbolized by the white horse) go forth, giving the warning:

   Soon, time will be no longer delayed!

2. 1290/1335 days begin

   The "Daily" is taken away by the removal of God's Sabbath, and the "abomination of desolation" begins with the passing of the Sunday law.

3. 1260 days begin

   Enforcement of Sunday laws begins and the scattering during the 1260 days of witnessing and 42 months of persecution begin. The seals continue.

4. Trumpets begin

   The martyrs under the altar (fifth seal) symbolically cry out when the Sunday laws are almost universal and God responds with the sounding of the trumpet judgments. This is also the time when the loud cry goes forth.

5. Close of probation

   Michael stands up. The seven last plagues begin. The death decree and the "time of Jacob's trouble" follow.

6. 1260/1335 days end

   The special resurrection and the deliverance of God's people take place.

7. Second coming of Jesus

   The time of the seventh seal and the seventh trumpet takes place sometime after the final time prophecies are complete and Jesus returns to take His faithful home.

Part 6: Outline of the Three Angels' Messages

Our Elijah Message

The Three Angels' Messages—a Call to the Word of God

And I saw another angel fly in the midst of heaven, ... saying with a loud voice, *Fear God*, and *give glory to him*; for *the hour of his judgment is come.* Revelation 14:6, 7.

The proclamation of the first, second, and third angels' messages has been located by the Word of Inspiration. Not a peg or pin is to be removed. No human authority has any more right to change the location of these messages than to substitute the New Testament for the Old. The Old Testament is the gospel in figures and symbols. The New Testament is the substance. One is as essential as the other. The Old Testament presents lessons from the lips of Christ, and these lessons have not lost their force in any particular.

The first and second messages [Revelation 14:6–8] were given in 1843 and 1844, and we are now under the proclamation of the third; but all three of the messages are still to be proclaimed. It is just as essential now as ever before that they shall be repeated to those who are seeking for the truth. *By pen and voice we are to sound the proclamation, showing their order and the application of the prophecies that bring us to the third angel's message.* There cannot be a third without the first and second....

The book that was sealed was not the book of Revelation, but *that portion of the prophecy of Daniel that related to the last days.* When the book was opened, the proclamation was made: "Time shall be no longer." The book of Daniel is now unsealed, and the revelation made by Christ to John is to come to all the inhabitants of the earth. *By the increase of knowledge a people is to be prepared to stand in the latter days.*

[Revelation 14:6, 7 quoted.] *This message, if heeded, will call the attention of every nation and kindred and tongue and people to a close examination of the Word, and to the true light in regard to the power that has changed the seventh-day Sabbath to a spurious sabbath....* The Sabbath memorial, declaring who the living God is, the Creator of the heavens and the earth, has been torn down, and a spurious sabbath has been given to the world in its place. Thus a breach has been made in the law of God....

In the first angel's message people are called upon to worship God, our Creator, who made the world and all things that are therein.... The message proclaimed by the angel flying in the midst of heaven is the *everlasting gospel*, the same gospel that was declared in Eden when God said to the serpent, "I will put enmity between thee and the woman, and between thy seed and her seed." (CTr 338; Ms. 32, 1896)

More Three Angels Concepts

These messages we are to give to the world in publications, in discourses, *showing in the line of prophetic history the things that have been and the things that will be.* (2SM 104.3)

The messages of Revelation 14 are those by which *the world is to be tested;* they are the everlasting gospel, and are to be sounded everywhere. (2SM 111.3)

Prophecy has been fulfilling, line upon line. The more firmly we stand under the banner of the third angel's message, *the more clearly shall we understand the prophecy of Daniel*; for the *Revelation is the supplement of Daniel.* (2SM 114.2)

The fourteenth chapter of Revelation is a chapter of the deepest interest. This scripture will *soon be understood* in all its bearings, and the messages given to John the revelator will be repeated with distinct utterance. (RH, Oct. 13, 1900)

After these seven thunders uttered their voices, the injunction comes to John, as to Daniel, in regard to the little book: "Seal up those things which the seven thunders uttered." [Rev. 10:4.] These relate to *future events* which will be *disclosed in their order*. Daniel shall stand in his lot *at the end of the days*. John sees the little book unsealed. *Then Daniel's prophecies have their proper place in the first, second, and third angels' messages to be given to the world.* The unsealing of the little book was the *message in relation to time*. (Ms. 59, 1900)

The book of Revelation must be opened to the people. Many have been taught that it is a sealed book; but it is sealed only to those who reject light and truth. The truth it contains must be proclaimed, that people may *have an opportunity to prepare* for the events which are so soon to transpire. *The third angel's message must be presented as the only hope for the salvation of a perishing world*. (Letter 87, 1896)

What are the three angels' messages that are proclaimed in Revelation 14? Below is an outline showing what we need to know as we prepare to give God's final warning to the world. We must study the chain of truth that supports each item in this outline so that we can teach all who will listen. This is our service to our God and fellow men.

Angel One—Revelation 14:6, 7

6. *And I saw another angel fly in the midst of heaven, having the everlasting gospel to preach unto them that dwell on the earth, and to every nation, and kindred, and tongue, and people,*

7. *Saying with a loud voice, Fear God, and give glory to him; for the hour of his judgment is come: and worship him that made heaven, and earth, and the sea, and the fountains of waters.*

- The everlasting gospel to be preached throughout the world includes
  - the infinite love of God for every soul—Jesus' sacrifice for us on the cross (John 3:16, 17; 1 Cor. 15:1-4; 1 John 3:4),
  - enmity between God's people and the serpent's people—"It shall bruise thy head, and thou shalt bruise his heel" (Gen. 3:15)—the first prophecy,
  - the gospel of Christ—the law exemplified in character (2SM 108.2),

- righteousness by deep trusting faith in Jesus and all He has done for each one of us (Rom. 3:22–24).

- Fear God and give glory to Him means to:
    - honor and respect God deeply (Ps. 111:10; Prov. 1:7; Ps. 74:20; 119:6, 15),
    - reflect His character (Col. 1:27; 2:2),
    - represent the character of God as it is represented in His holy law,
    - be a "repairer of the breach" and "delight thyself in the Lord" (Isa. 58:12–14),
    - give glory to God means revealing His character in our own and thereby making Him known. In whatever way we make known the Father or the Son, we glorify God (Ms. 16, 1890).

- The hour of judgment is come; we must teach the prophetic chain of truth.
    - The judgment of the dead began in 1844 with Jesus transitioning to the Most Holy Place of the heavenly sanctuary (Heb. 8:1, 2; Rev. 3:7, 8; Dan. 7:9, 10; 8:14).
    - Judgment of the living begins shortly before the Sunday Law is passed. We need to —
        - understand the basic end-time context of Daniel 8–12 and Revelation 1–18,
        - proclaim the message of Revelation 11:1–3 (see also 1 Peter 4:17; Revelation 4–6; and similar passages).

- "Worship Him." Worship our Creator whose seal is found in the Sabbath commandment, identifying—
    - His name—the LORD,
    - His title—Creator,
    - His dominion—heaven and earth,
    - Our need to worship God with the whole heart (Ps. 138:1–5).

Angel Two—Revelation 14:8

8. *And there followed another angel, saying, Babylon is fallen, is fallen, that great city, because she made all nations drink of the wine of the wrath of her fornication.*

- Babylon is fallen. We need to teach the prophetic chain of truth.
  - Babylon—Revelation 17
    - The great whore, the mother of harlots, the great city
    - Rome and her daughters
    - "The term 'Babylon' is derived from 'Babel,' and signifies confusion. In Scripture it designates various forms of false or apostate religion" (*From Here to Forever*, p. 236).
    - "In Revelation 17 Babylon is represented as a woman—a figure used in the Bible as the symbol of a church, a virtuous woman representing a pure church; a vile woman, an apostate church" (*From Here to Forever*, p. 236).
    - Made all nations drink her wine (Dan. 8:11, 12; Revelation 13, 17, and 18).
    - The wine of her fornication represents false doctrines that she has accepted as a result of her friendship with the world. It includes the teaching and, eventually, the enforcement of these doctrines that are opposed to the plain statements of the Bible.
    - The False Sabbath
    - The immortality of the soul
    - Many other errors—"teaching for doctrines the commandments of men" (Matt. 15:9)
    - Fornication = idolatry, which is the forsaking of the true God and the worshiping of idols (2 Chron. 21:11; Rev. 19:2)
    - Each item in Jesus' sanctuary ministry for us—

both in the "daily" ministry and in the annual ministry—has been obscured.

- Altar of Sacrifice
  - The sacrifice of Christ has been cast down and been replaced by the works of penance.
- Laver
  - Bible baptism has been cast down and replaced by sprinkling.
- Table of Showbread
  - The Word of God and the Sabbath are cast down as they are replaced by church traditions and Sunday worship.
- Altar of Incense
  - Christ's mediation is cast down as it is replaced by the confessional booth.
- Candlesticks
  - The light of the church, given by the Holy Spirit, is cast down as God's people were persecuted for 1260 years and will be persecuted again for 1260 days, or forty-two months.
- Ark of Covenant
  - The law of God was cast down as the second commandment regarding idols was removed, the fourth commandment, now the third, changed the seventh day Sabbath to the first day of the week, and the tenth commandment was divided into two commandments. The atonement is cast down as the final cleansing of the sanctuary is obscured and the sanctuary message is rejected.
- "Men in authority will enact laws controlling the conscience [forcing men to accept a spurious sabbath], after the example of the papacy.... Every nation will be involved. ... 'These have one mind.' There will be a universal bond of union, one great harmony, a con-

federacy of Satan's forces. 'And shall give their power and strength unto the beast.' [Revelation 18:3-7; 17:13, 14]" (3SM 392.1; LDE 136.4; Ms. 24, 1891).

- "Thus is manifested the same arbitrary, oppressive power against religious liberty, freedom to worship God according to the dictates of conscience, as was manifested by the papacy, when in the past it persecuted those who dared to refuse to conform with the religious rites and ceremonies of Romanists" (3SM 392.4; Ms. 24, 1891).

- "They have divorced themselves from God by refusing to receive His sign. They have not the spirit of God's true commandment-keeping people. And the people of the world, in giving their sanction to a false Sabbath, and in trampling under their feet the Sabbath of the Lord, have drunk of the wine of the wrath of her fornication" (Letter 98, 1900).

- "To spiritual Israel is given the message, 'Come out of her, My people, that ye be not partakers of her sins, and that ye receive not of her plagues' " (PK 715.1).

- "Come out of her, my people" is the loud cry of the third angel's message (see 2SM 118.2).

Angel Three—Revelation 14:9-12

9. *And the third angel followed them, saying with a loud voice, If any man worship the beast and his image, and receive his mark in his forehead, or in his hand,*

10. *The same shall drink of the wine of the wrath of God, which is poured out without mixture into the cup of his indignation; and he shall be tormented with fire and brimstone in the presence of the holy angels, and in the presence of the Lamb:*

11. *And the smoke of their torment ascendeth up for ever and ever: and they have no rest day nor night, who worship the beast and his image, and whosoever receiveth the mark of his name.*

12. *Here is the patience of the saints: here are they that keep the commandments of God, and the faith of Jesus.*

- Time is coming to a close. There will be time and delay no longer! (Rev. 10:6). This is the *last message of warning. You must make a choice!*

- Prepare to meet your God! (Amos 4:12).
- "The enforcement of Sundaykeeping on the part of Protestant churches is an enforcement of the worship of the papacy—of the beast" (GC 448.3).
- " 'The beast' mentioned in this message, whose worship is enforced by the two-horned beast, is the first, or leopard-like beast of Revelation 13—the papacy" (GC 445.2).
  - The "beast," a symbol of Papal Rome, is described in Daniel 7 and Revelation 13:1–10, 18, and it is synonymous with "Babylon the Great," which is described in Revelation 17.
- "The 'image to the beast' represents that form of apostate Protestantism which will be developed when the Protestant churches shall seek the aid of the civil power for the enforcement of their dogmas" (GC 445.2).
- *A mark* symbolizes a sign, a seal, or a mark of approval or disapproval (Rom. 4:11; Rev. 7:2, 3; Ezek. 9:4).
- *The forehead* symbolizes the thoughts of your mind and where your loyalty is (Deut. 5:7–21; 5:12; 6:6–8; 11:18; Rev. 7:3; 1 John 5:3; 2:4; Rom. 7:25; Ezek. 3:8, 9).
- *The hand* symbolizes the works of your hands (Eccl. 9:10; Deut. 5:12; 6:6–8; 11:18).
  - "Whoever shall trample upon God's law to obey a human enactment receives the mark of the beast, the sign of allegiance to the power he chooses to obey instead of God" (*From Here to Forever*, p. 368).
  - "It is not until the issue is thus plainly set before the people, and they are brought to choose between the commandments of God and the commandments of men, that those who continue in transgression will receive 'the mark of the beast' " (GC 449.1).

- o "The 'mark of the beast' still remains to be defined" (GC 445.2).
- "Knowing this, that the trying of your faith worketh patience. But let patience have her perfect work, that ye may be perfect and entire, wanting nothing … Take, my brethren, the prophets, who have spoken in the name of the Lord, for an example of suffering affliction, and of patience. Behold, we count them happy which endure. Ye have heard of the patience of Job, and have seen the end of the Lord; that the Lord is very pitiful, and of tender mercy" (James 1:3, 4; 5:10, 11).
- "And he gave some, apostles; and some, prophets; and some, evangelists; and some, pastors and teachers; for the *perfecting of the saints*, for the work of the ministry, for the *edifying of the body of Christ*: Till we all come in the *unity of the faith*, and the *knowledge of the Son of God*, unto a perfect man, unto the measure of the stature of the *fulness of Christ* …" (Eph. 4:11–13).
- **We have two choices:**
  - o Worship the beast and his image, which will result in:
    - persecuting of God's people for 42 months,
    - forcing a false sabbath and false doctrines on the world,
    - receiving the mark, or character, of the beast in the forehead or in the hand,
    - drinking the wine of the wrath of God in the trumpets and the plagues,
    - no rest on earth and no Sabbath in heaven,
    - eternal death.

    or

  - o Worship God, resulting in:
    - 1260 days of witnessing for our God

- by faith entering the Most Holy Place to find Jesus in His last phase of ministering for us—in which mercy and justice unite (Rev. 4 and 5)
- having the *faith of Jesus* which is perfect belief and trust in Jesus without fear, just like Jesus who had perfect belief and trust in His Father while He was on earth—no matter what the cost might be to ourselves

- keeping and preaching all the commandments of God including the Sabbath
- having the patience of the saints under persecution
- willing to die for Jesus. The martyrs—
  - rest from their labors,
  - have works that follow them,
  - are under the fifth seal (Revelation 6).
- "I know that poor Stephen must have suffered severely, but let us be thankful that the end came quietly. Of him the words apply: 'Here is the patience of the saints: here are they that keep the commandments of God, and the faith of Jesus' " (*The Retirement Years*, p. 62).
- "Stand firmly to God's truth. Exalt before the people the banner bearing the inscription, 'Here is the patience of the saints: here are they that keep the commandments of God, and the faith of Jesus.' " (2SM 226.3).
- What is the result? Eternal life!
- "When God sends to men warnings so important that they are represented as proclaimed by holy angels flying in the midst of heaven, He requires every person endowed with reasoning powers to heed the message. The fearful judgments denounced against the worship of the beast and his image (Revelation 14:9–11), should lead all to a diligent study of the prophecies to learn what the mark of the beast is, and how they are to avoid receiving it" (GC 594.2).

> *"When God sends to men warnings so important that they are represented as proclaimed by holy angels flying in the midst of heaven, He requires every person endowed with reasoning powers to heed the message."*

Another Angel—Revelation 18

1. *And after these things I saw another angel come down from heaven, having great power; and the earth was lightened with his glory.*
2. *And he cried mightily with a strong voice, saying, Babylon the great is fallen, is fallen, and is become the habitation of devils, and the hold of every foul spirit, and a cage of every unclean and hateful bird.*
3. *For all nations have drunk of the wine of the wrath of her fornication, and the kings of the earth have committed fornication with her, and the merchants of the earth are waxed rich through the abundance of her delicacies.*
4. *And I heard another voice from heaven, saying, Come out of her, my people, that ye be not partakers of her sins, and that ye receive not of her plagues.*
5. *For her sins have reached unto heaven, and God hath remembered her iniquities.*

- This angel has "great power."
- Heaven and earth are lightened with his glory.
- Message: Babylon the Great has fallen …
    - It has become the habitation of devils, foul spirits, and unclean and hateful birds.
    - All nations have drunk the wine of her fornication and false doctrines.

- - Kings have committed spiritual fornication with her via her false system of worship.
  - Merchants have become rich by allying with her, and the world must serve Babylon or be prevented from buying and selling.
  - Her sins have reached to heaven, and God has remembered her iniquities.
- Message: Come out of her! (Rev. 18:4).
  - That you receive not of her plagues.
- "Thus the substance of the second angel's message is again given to the world by that other angel who lightens the earth with his glory. *These messages all blend in one, to come before the people in the closing days of this earth's history. All the world will be tested*, and all that have been in the darkness of error in regard to the Sabbath of the fourth commandment *will understand the last message of mercy* that is to be given to men" (2SM 116.2).
- "When Jesus began his public ministry, he cleansed the temple from its sacrilegious profanation. Among the last acts of his ministry was the second cleansing of the temple. So in the last work for the warning of the world, *two distinct calls are made to the churches*. The second angel's message is, 'Babylon is fallen, is fallen, that great city, because she made all nations drink of the wine of the wrath of her fornication' (Revelation 14:8). And in the loud cry of the third angel's message a voice is heard from heaven saying, 'Come out of her, my people, that ye be not partakers of her sins, and that ye receive not of her plagues. For her sins have reached unto heaven, and God hath remembered her iniquities' (Revelation 18:4, 5)" (RH, Dec. 6, 1892).

Many saw the *perfect chain of truth* in the angels' messages, and gladly received them in their order, and followed Jesus by faith into the heavenly sanctuary. *These messages were represented to me as an anchor to the people of God.* Those who understand and receive them *will be kept* from being swept away by the many delusions of Satan. (EW 256.2)

This is a time for the Lord's servants to work with undiminished zeal to carry the third angel's message to all parts of the world. The work of this message is spreading far and near; yet we should not feel satisfied, but hasten to carry to thousands more the truth regarding the perpetuity of the law of Jehovah. From all our institutions of learning, from our publishing houses, from our sanitariums, the message is to be proclaimed. The people of God everywhere are to be aroused to co-operate in the great, grand work represented by the first, second, and third angel's messages. This *last warning* to the inhabitants of the earth is to make men see the importance God attaches to his holy law. So plainly is the truth to be presented, that no transgressor, hearing it, shall fail to discern the importance of obedience to the Sabbath commandment. (RH, March 26, 1908)

Closing Thoughts from the Pen of Inspiration

All that God has in prophetic history specified to be fulfilled in the past has been, and all that is yet to come in its order will be. Daniel, God's prophet, stands in his place. John stands in his place. In the Revelation the Lion of the tribe of Judah has opened to the students of prophecy the book of Daniel, and thus is Daniel standing in his place. *He bears his testimony, that which the Lord revealed to him in vision of the great and solemn events which we must know as we stand on the very threshold of their fulfillment.* (Ms. 32, 1896)

A transforming power attended the proclamation of the first and second angels' messages, as it attends the message of the third angel. Lasting convictions were made upon human minds. The power of the Holy Spirit was manifested. There was *diligent study of the Scriptures, point by point.* Almost entire nights were devoted to earnest searching of the Word. We searched for the truth as for hidden treasures. *The Lord revealed Himself to us. Light was shed on the prophecies, and we knew that we received divine instruction....* (2SM 109.3)

After the great disappointment there were few who set themselves to seek the Word with all their heart. But some souls would not settle down in discouragement and deny that the Lord had led them. *To these the truth was opened point by point*, and entwined with their most hallowed recollections and sympathies. *The searchers after truth felt that the identification of Christ with their nature and interest was complete.* Truth was made to shine forth, beautiful in its simplicity, dignified with a power and invested with an assurance unknown before the disappointment. We could then proclaim the message in *unity*. (2SM 109.4)

What Characterizes the Final Time of Witnessing?

The great work of the gospel is not to close with less manifestation of the power of God than marked its opening. The prophecies which were fulfilled in the outpouring of the former rain at the opening of the gospel are again to be fulfilled in the latter rain at its close. Here are "the times of refreshing" to which the apostle Peter looked forward when he said: "Repent ye therefore, and be converted, that your sins may be blotted out, when the times of refreshing shall come from the presence of the Lord; and He shall send Jesus." Acts 3:19, 20.

Servants of God, with their faces lighted up and shining with holy consecration, will hasten from place to place to proclaim the message from heaven. By thousands of voices, all over the earth, the warning will be given. Miracles will be wrought, the sick will be healed, and signs and wonders will follow the believers. Satan also works, with lying wonders, even bringing down fire from heaven in the sight of men. Revelation 13:13. Thus the inhabitants of the earth will be brought to take their stand.

The message will be carried not so much by argument as by the deep conviction of the Spirit of God. The arguments have been presented. The seed has been sown, and now it will spring up and bear fruit. The publications distributed by missionary workers have exerted their influence, yet many whose minds were impressed have been prevented from fully comprehending the truth or from yielding obedience. Now the rays of light penetrate everywhere, the truth is seen in its clearness, and the honest children of God sever the bands which have held them. Family connections, church relations, are powerless to stay them now. Truth is more precious than all besides. Notwithstanding the agencies combined against the truth, a large number take their stand upon the Lord's side. (GC 611.3–612.2)

> *The message will be carried not so much by argument as by the deep conviction of the Spirit of God.*

Part 7: The Most Important Questions

Quotations to Contemplate

The great burden of every soul should be, Is my heart renewed? Is my soul transformed? Are my sins pardoned through faith in Christ? Have I been born again? Am I complying with the invitation, "Come unto me, all ye that labor and are heavy laden, and I will give you rest. Take my yoke upon you, and learn of me; for I am meek and lowly in heart; and ye shall find rest unto your souls. For my yoke is easy, and my burden is light." Matthew 11:28-30. Do you count *all things but loss* for the excellency of the knowledge of Christ Jesus? And do you feel it your *duty* to *believe every word* that proceeds out of the mouth of God? (Ms. 32, 1896)

"God so loved the world, that he gave his only begotten Son, that whosoever believeth in him should not perish, but have everlasting life." He who repents of his sin and accepts the gift of the life of the Son of God, can not be overcome. *Laying hold by faith of the divine nature, he becomes a child of God. He prays, he **believes**. When tempted and tried, he **claims** the power that Christ died to give, and **overcomes** through his grace. This every sinner needs to understand.* He must repent of his sin, he must *believe in the power of Christ*, and accept that power to save and to keep him from sin. How thankful ought we to be for the gift of Christ's example! (RH, Jan. 28, 1909)

Profound theories and speculations of human creation may abound, but he who would come off conqueror in the end, *must be humble enough* to **depend** upon divine power. When we thus grasp the power of Infinity, and come to Christ, saying, 'In my hand no price I bring; simply to thy cross I cling,' then divine agencies can co-operate with us to sanctify and purify the life. (RH, Jan. 28, 1909)

Let no one seek to evade the cross. It is through the cross that we are enabled to overcome. *It is through affliction and trial that divine agencies can carry on a work in our lives that will result in the love and peace and kindness of Christ.* (RH, Jan. 28, 1909)

A great work is to be accomplished daily in the human heart by the study of the Word. *We need to learn the* **simplicity of true faith.** This will bring its returns. Let us seek for decided advancement in spiritual understanding. Let us make the precious Word the man of our counsel. **We need to walk carefully every moment, keeping close to the side of** Christ. The spirit and grace of Christ are needed in the life, *and* **the faith that works by love** *and purifies the soul.* (RH, Jan. 28, 1909)

Elijah was a type of the saints who will be living on the earth at the time of the second advent of Christ and who will be "changed, in a moment, in the twinkling of an eye, at the last trump," without tasting of death. 1 Corinthians 15:51, 52. It was as a representative of those who shall be thus translated that Elijah, near the close of Christ's earthly ministry, was permitted to stand with Moses by the side of the Saviour on the mount of transfiguration. In these glorified ones, the disciples saw in miniature a representation of the kingdom of the redeemed. They beheld Jesus clothed with the light of heaven; they heard the "voice out of the cloud" (Luke 9:35), acknowledging Him as the Son of God; they saw Moses, representing those who will be raised from the dead at the time of the second advent; and there also stood Elijah, representing those who at the close of *earth's* history will be changed from mortal to immortal and be translated to heaven without seeing death." (PK 227.2)

Addendum

More Thought-Provoking Ellen G. White Quotations

Additional Thoughts

These messages were given, not for those that uttered the prophecies, but for us who are living amid the scenes of their fulfillment. (Ms. 32, 1896)

When God's people are at ease and satisfied with their present enlightenment, we may be sure that He will not favor them. It is His will that they should be ever moving forward to receive the increased and ever-increasing light which is shining for them. The present attitude of the church is not pleasing to God. There has come in a self-confidence that has led them to feel no necessity for more truth and greater light. (5T 708.3)

Privileges and duties which they do not even suspect to be in the Bible will be made manifest. (MH 465.2)

Don't Reject New Light

If light come, and that light is set aside or rejected, then comes condemnation and the frown of God. (1T 116.1)

When a message is presented to God's people, they should not rise up in opposition to it; they should go to the Bible, comparing it with the law and the testimony, and if it does not bear this test, it is not true. God wants our minds to expand. (TM 119.1)

Take your Bible, and in a kindly spirit weigh every argument that he presents and show him by the Scriptures if he is in error. When you do this without unkind feelings, you will do only that which is your duty and the duty of every minister of Jesus Christ. Letter 21, 1888. (CW 50.2)

We are to be judged according to the manner in which we use the knowledge of the truth which has been presented to us. (RH, June 18, 1895)

There are many, many in our churches who know little of the real meaning of the truth for this time. (8T 252)

The Lord will hold both ministers and people responsible for the light shining upon them. He calls upon us to work diligently in gathering up the jewels of truth, and placing them in the framework of the gospel. In all their divine beauty they are to shine forth in the moral darkness of the world. (GW 289.3)

Those who turn away from the light which God has given, or who neglect to seek it when it is within their reach, are *left in darkness.* (GC 312.3)

Satan as a powerful general has taken the field, and in this last remnant of time he is working through all conceivable methods *to close the door against light that God would have come to his people.* He is sweeping the whole world into his ranks ... (RH, Dec. 24, 1889, Art. B)

Increased Light

There are wonders to be revealed. (5T 301.2)

Glorious things are to be revealed. (MH 465.2)

Whoever is with singleness of purpose seeking to do God's will, earnestly heeding the light already given, *will receive greater light;* to that soul some star of heavenly radiance will be sent to guide him into all truth. (GC 312.3)

He is watching those who are walking in the light as fast as they receive it. They are the objects of his *special care.* (RH, March 27, 1900)

Notes:

TEACH Services, Inc.
P U B L I S H I N G

We invite you to view the complete
selection of titles we publish at:
www.TEACHServices.com

We encourage you to write us
with your thoughts about this,
or any other book we publish at:
info@TEACHServices.com

TEACH Services' titles may be purchased in
bulk quantities for educational, fund-raising,
business, or promotional use.
bulksales@TEACHServices.com

Finally, if you are interested in seeing
your own book in print, please contact us at:
publishing@TEACHServices.com
We are happy to review your manuscript at no charge.

www.ingramcontent.com/pod-product-compliance
Lightning Source LLC
Chambersburg PA
CBHW071154160426